Going to See

Going
to See

30 WRITERS ON NATURE, INSPIRATION, AND THE WORLD OF BARRY LOPEZ

Edited by Kurt Caswell and James Perrin Warren

MOUNTAINEERS BOOKS

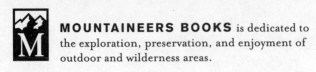

MOUNTAINEERS BOOKS is dedicated to the exploration, preservation, and enjoyment of outdoor and wilderness areas.

1001 SW Klickitat Way, Suite 201, Seattle, WA 98134
800-553-4453, www.mountaineersbooks.org

All contributions to this work are used with generous permission by the individual writers; see the Acknowledgments for additional information. For additional permissions, see page 270.

Mountaineers Books and its colophon are registered trademarks of The Mountaineers organization.

Printed in Canada
Distributed in the United Kingdom by Cordee, www.cordee.co.uk
27 26 25 24   1 2 3 4 5

Design and layout: Jen Grable

Library of Congress Cataloging-in-Publication Data is available at https://lccn.loc.gov/2023042032. The ebook record is available at https://lccn.loc.gov/2023042033.

Mountaineers Books titles may be purchased for corporate, educational, or other promotional sales, and our authors are available for a wide range of events. For information on special discounts or booking an author, contact our customer service at 800-553-4453 or mbooks@mountaineersbooks.org.

♻ Printed on 100% recycled and FSC-certified materials

ISBN (paperback): 978-1-68051-661-6
ISBN (ebook): 978-1-68051-662-3

An independent nonprofit publisher since 1960

For Barry's family, friends, and readers—today and tomorrow

CONTENTS

A Definition, Bill McKibben **9**
Introduction: Servants of Memory, James Perrin Warren **II**

MAPPING

WITNESSING

LISTENING

A DEFINITION

BILL MCKIBBEN

When I talk with young people—students, activists—about Barry Lopez, I find that many have him pigeonholed in their minds as a solitary, most at home in the remote and wild places of Earth. This is not wrong—it's clearly one side of his majestic life—but it's very much incomplete. His ability to thrive in landscapes others would find bleak, barren, and beyond human scale was complemented by an equal ability—and an equal impulse—toward a kind of constructive sociability. He was an organizer, especially among a widespread community of artists and writers that he sometimes tried to turn into an effective moral force.

Though it's not the project on which his fame mostly rests, *Home Ground: A Guide to the American Landscape*, may be one of the books nearest his heart, a kind of dictionary of geographical terminology that he compiled with his wife, Debra Gwartney. I can remember him calling me early in the project, to see if I could turn out some definitions for the book proposal—he was excited both at the scope of the plan and the opportunity it represented for the community of nature writers to come together on a shared project.

The finished work, I think, is a masterpiece that reflects its master's mind—careful, precise, attentive to language, and at the same time sprawling—an invitation to see the world both more exactly and more poetically. I had a fine time with my collection of words, some of them wonderfully obscure ("tombolo," "monadnock,") and others in which the delight came from explaining the obvious ("hill," "mountain"). The definitions are all succinct, marked by a careful economy of language—every single word tells.

So, in homage to this volume and Barry's stewardship of it, let me attempt a small definition:

> Barry Lopez: an American writer, born in 1945 at the end of the Second World War, and dead in 2020 at the confluence of the Covid-19 pandemic and the great western fires of the early greenhouse era. He wandered the wide world, describing some of the most ancient and cohesive human enterprises (Indigenous hunting, for example) and some of the most modern and disruptive (from the cargo hold of a 747, a primer on the distribution of goods on a globalized planet). His concern for human and non-human life was painfully deep—he may have been the greatest living example of Aldo Leopold's creed that "One of the penalties of an ecological education is that one lives alone in a world of wounds." Except that he insisted on not living alone, but on engaging others in the struggle for a world that worked better and protected more. He had about him some of the aspects of the old-growth forest where he lived: old snags and crags, dynamic new growth, a humming and regulating sanity.

INTRODUCTION

SERVANTS OF MEMORY

JAMES PERRIN WARREN

In October 2008, Barry Lopez—the acclaimed author of the National Book Award–winning *Arctic Dreams*—gave an inspiring and eloquent address to the winners of that year's Whiting Awards, given annually since 1985 to support emerging writers. It is a signal example of the way Barry could reach others with his words and voice, a speech that strikes his most fundamental and deeply held convictions about the role of the writer in human communities. Imagine his famously rich baritone as you read these words:

> Without making too fine a point of this—because writers with one frame of mind about storytelling might bristle in the presence of writers with another frame of mind—it seems to me that all writers work within the tradition of storytelling, and that, further, storytellers are primarily pattern makers, and also the keepers of proven patterns.

They are, in the phrase of the Uruguayan writer Eduardo Galeano, "the servants of memory." Our Achilles' heel as a species has always been that we forget. And my own belief about this is that story arose early in our history as a response to this cultural problem, to the danger of forgetting, and also to the fear that comes over us when we realize that it is because we forget that our plans to improve the present so often go awry.

It is not necessary, in fact I think it is rare, for a storyteller or a writer to be a wise person. What is essential to the work is that the writer be able to create a trustworthy pattern, and to set that pattern out in a modern idiom, a pattern of thoughts and emotions and scenes that serves the reader in her effort to remember who she is, what she means by her life, and where she is going.

I hear Barry's voice in these sentences, the current of his thinking, the force of his convictions. He appeals to the deep past, to the storytellers of prehistory, and he sees how these ancient patterns of story come down to an interaction between the writer and the reader of the present. As Galeano says, writers are the servants of memory, and Barry is reminding his audience that they face an ever-present danger in our species: the danger of forgetting. As an able servant of memory, the writer will help us find a trustworthy pattern that reminds us who we are and where we are going.

The book you now hold in your hands, *Going to See: 30 Writers on Nature, Inspiration, and the World of Barry Lopez,* collects essays by thirty writers in tribute to Barry Lopez, who passed away from metastatic prostate cancer on Christmas Day, 2020. Many of the essays here take us to the past, to specific, personal places in which Barry wrote, spoke, and acted deeply in support of the writer. Not only do we hear from Barry's wife of thirteen years, Debra Gwartney, who penned "Siri Tells a Joke," but also from close personal friends like Rick Bass and David James Duncan. We hear about a gathering like the Orion Society's Fire & Grit conference in Shepherdstown, West Virginia, which brought together over 500 participants and a score of writers associated with *Orion* magazine to mark the millennium and inspire people working for nature in community. Sometimes the writers are professional colleagues and fellow artists who worked with Barry and Debra on their book *Home Ground* or other projects, or presented with him at a conference. Other times they are younger writers who never met Barry, or perhaps met him once, only to find their writing lives changed forever.

Barry reached all these writers and offered them a gift: the knowledge that they were not alone. He let them know that they were heard and appreciated. He told them that their work was vital to the well-being of the world. Even though each writer might not see the others often, or perhaps never meet them, they formed a community. Barry gave them a way forward.

The essays gathered in *Going to See* answer, with imagination and love, Barry's call for a trustworthy pattern. They answer in memories of walks in the desert, woods, and tundra. They remember simple joys as well as griefs and regrets. They remember Barry and the patterns of his own life. They never forget the gifts of his writing. You will find moments of laughter and tears, sometimes right next to one another.

I'm writing on Christmas Day 2022, two years after Barry's passing. Memory reaches back over twenty-five years. I remember when I heard him speak, in 1997 in Missoula, Montana, at a literary conference. On the first day, Barry sat on a panel with the writers Rick Bass and Pattiann Rogers, and he spoke at length about Enlightenment epistemologies and other ways of knowing. I had never heard a writer combine such intellectual power and eloquence.

There was a moment on the last day—with a double rainbow—that has become lore. Barry stood on a platform by Clark Fork River, first evoking the memory of Wallace Stegner, then reading his own story "Lessons from the Wolverine." As he came to the moment of the two dream wolverines telling the storyteller, "Keep going," a glowing double rainbow appeared behind the audience. Barry paused, looking out to admire the wonder of arcing colors behind us. Then he kept going, like a trusted storyteller. For me, it was an extraordinary punctuation to the experience of finding a community of scholars and writers.

In October 2017, Barry visited my wife, Julianne, at our home in Fairbanks, Alaska, staying several days and attending a memorial service for his friend Bob Stephenson. I was away for three weeks, guiding trips across Canada. After his visit, Julianne told me that if I wanted to see Barry, I should go as soon as I could. So, in February 2018, I spent three days at Barry's home in Finn Rock, Oregon, deep in the Willamette National Forest, talking about the drafts of his last major work, *Horizon*. It was to be the last time I saw him face to face.

Barry was not at his best. Knee-buckling bouts of pain coursed through his pelvic bones. He was unsure about the book. He was unsure about his place in the world, even about how much time in the world remained to him. He seemed to have more questions than answers. What would be a worthy legacy to leave behind? Could he make a trustworthy pattern again? After so many years and drafts, would a final pattern emerge?

Barry had sent me a sixth draft of *Horizon,* and I had read it carefully, but more than once during the visit he said he didn't want to talk about the book. It was easier to remember stories and tell them together. The caracaras at the end of the continent. The black mamba gliding through the dry wadi. The rescue of sea lions caught in fishing nets. And always his beautiful voice, the care in his words.

From the initial diagnosis of metastatic prostate cancer to the end, we shared the pain of Barry's decline and the way his body seemed to betray him at every turn. He never gave up. Despite the uncertainties, he kept writing, searching for patterns, and finding a trustworthy pattern for *Horizon*. Astonishing, really, to think how much physical pain he endured to bring the book home.

When I returned to Finn Rock in October 2021, ten months after Barry died, I recalled those moments with Barry. Driving out from Eugene, I saw how the ridges on either side of the McKenzie River were scorched to bare ground and black stumps, the massive forest gone, as if it had vaporized in the track of the Holiday Farm Fire. I imagined the treasures of Barry's writing life, burned up in the archive building behind their home.

So much lost, but not all was lost. Debra, the archivist Ken Lopez, and I worked for nearly a week in the house and studio. Sifting through Barry's upstairs writing study, boxing up books and papers. Correspondence with dozens of friends, artists, and fellow writers. Drafts of essays and stories. Broadsides, posters, and artworks. Scores of books, with hundreds of annotations and marginalia, some recent and others reaching back decades. Talismans of every sort, from landscapes I would never see. Perhaps most touching, memorabilia from his childhood and youth. A Cub Scouts neckerchief holder. Photographs of high school girlfriends. Notebooks and essays from college classes. Deep layers of an educated person who had led a life of traveling and writing, a life of going to see.

At the end of one bright day, the three of us walked down to the edge of the McKenzie River running fast in front of the house. Debra pointed out the long, dark shadows of salmon near the shore, the fish spawning within a few feet of logging trucks whizzing by on the road to Eugene. The trucks were hauling salvage logs out of the woods after the fire, the bark singed, blackened, or burned away. And yet the river was still running, the salmon still returning.

Eventually we would ship eighty boxes of Barry's papers and other materials to The Sowell Family Collection in Literature, Community, and the Natural World housed at Texas Tech University, in Lubbock. Even though the Holiday Farm Fire had destroyed the archive building at Finn Rock, the Sowell Collection is a vital servant of memory, holding a rich and varied range of Barry's books, papers, notebooks, journals, manuscripts, correspondence, photographs, and other materials. Nine separate collections and nearly three hundred boxes. Some scholar in the future will no doubt handle Barry's neckerchief holder, along with so many other treasures.

From the time Barry looked out at the horizon from Mamaroneck Harbor, New York, where he was born, to his last journey, he had been going to see. The title of this book evokes Barry's call to travel widely, along with the complex work of reporting faithfully to readers from the writer's perspective. In "Looking for a Ship," the introduction to *Horizon*, Barry devotes a section to those twin projects, "To Go/To See." It's a meditation on his early search for patterns, both in his life and in his work, and on the responsibilities of the writer:

> Initially I thought of myself on these journeys as a reporter, travel- ing outward from a more privileged world. I believed—as well as I could grasp the idea back then—that I had an ethical obligation as a writer, in addition to an aesthetic one. It was to experience the world intensely and then to put into words as well as I could what I'd seen. . . . I saw myself, then, as a sort of courier, a kind of runner come home from another land after some exchange with it and its denizens, carrying, by way of a story, some incomplete bit of news about how different, how marvelous and incomprehensible, really, life was, out beyond the pale of the village in which I had grown up.

If that urge to go and see shapes the early work, in *Horizon* we see how Barry also returns to the significant places of his journeys, to "look again at nearly everything I had seen" and to measure, in a sense, how far both he and the world had traveled over the intervening years. The need to remember, to search for the threads of a meaningful pattern, balances the need to go outward to the horizon. At the same time, Barry is mindful of serving the reader, helping us remember who we are and where we are going.

The three sections of *Going to See* feature essays in a variety of forms and lengths, and they present several generations of writers. In "Mapping," "Witnessing," and "Listening," some writers remember Barry as a contem- porary, someone they could sit with and tell stories about distant lands and cultures. These companions often evoke their friendships as well as offer readings of works they find inspirational. The essays give us surprising insights into Barry's life and writing, and the combination of stories comes to resemble a mosaic or a kaleidoscope, offering parts that together reach toward a many-sided whole.

For me, the new generations are poignant and vital—those who remember him as a mentor, an older guide, a wise supporter, an elder and leader. Many of the writers, of all generations, were able to ask Barry for advice about their projects, their travel aims, their home places, to talk on the telephone or converse through letters and emails about where they were going. Then some see him as a ghostly spirit, known only in his words but so vividly that he is clearly alive for them and helping them in the present. In their essays, they remember when they first read him, or first heard him speak, or how they might still speak with him today.

In every generation, the writers in *Going to See* are servants of memory, fitting their own experiences into trustworthy words and patterns. And yet there is still another aspect of their tributes to Barry Lopez and the gifts he gave us. *Going to See* carries these writers and their work, along with Barry and his work, to readers who will be of one or another generation themselves. Some older readers, some younger, and some who are not yet born. We are carrying him and his writing cohort to a future day, to future generations.

In the third section of "Looking for a Ship," Barry describes the work of the Russian painter Nicholas Roerich, focusing on his Himalaya painting *Remember*. The frontispiece of *Horizon* reproduces the central image, a horseman standing in his stirrups to look back at the mountain home he is leaving. "The painting," Barry writes, "is about space as much as it is about departure, and few pieces I've ever seen say so poignantly how one's memory is activated by leave-taking." Barry calls the traveler's situation "the predicament of departure—the desire so strong to head out, yet at the same time feeling a breach opening, the breaking of a bond that can be repaired only by returning."

The towering landscape of the painting adds to that sense of space, the gap opening between the horseman and his home. The foothills recede in abstract blue ridgelines, and the great mountains, snow and rock and ice, dwarf the human beings in the foreground. What is the traveler going to see? What experience will he bring home to justify his departure? What will he remember, and how will he be a servant of memory?

For Barry, the desire to head out became more compelling with each departure, for he was always finding experiences to bring home. With each encounter of a new land and its inhabitants, he was feeling a growing sense of urgency. What is going to happen to us, and how can we learn to safeguard ourselves and this world we live in, on, through? And he was always feeling the need to bring the stories home, to tell them as an act of recollection, an act of service to the reader. Now we weave these threads into our own patterns, carrying the traveler forward.

Mapping

"To inquire into the intricacies of a distant landscape, then, is to provoke thoughts about one's own interior landscape, and the familiar landscapes of memory. The land urges us to come around to an understanding of ourselves."
—Barry Lopez, *Arctic Dreams*

AN UNBROKEN GRACE

FRED BAHNSON

When I first arrived at the home of Barry Lopez one November day in 2018, he pointed to a fresh Douglas-fir stump and said, "We had to put down that tree." The fir was one of many old-growth trees surrounding Barry's home at Finn Rock, Oregon, along the McKenzie River. The tree had become diseased, and Barry worried that it might fall on the house, so a few days before my visit, he and a neighbor got out their chainsaws and put down the tree. That's the phrase Barry used, *put down*, as one might speak with regret after euthanizing an animal.

I first discovered Barry's work thirteen years earlier, and had immediately known I'd found a writer I wanted to learn from. He wrote convincingly about the power of the natural world to heal us, about numinous encounters with wild animals, about the seemingly forgotten qualities of reverence, mutuality, and ecological humility he found in traditional cultures. In Barry's words I'd found a measure of solace for what plagued me, as well as for what plagued the world. The writer and editor John Freeman has described Barry's work as "a prosthetic of kindness," an appendage to help us face the anomie and dislocation of our modern age.

I came to Finn Rock in 2018 ostensibly to interview Barry for a magazine, but also because I was in despair over the state of the world and haunted by old childhood wounds; I sought healing. Barry and his wife, the writer Debra Gwartney, offered to host me for three days in their guest cottage. Each morning, Barry arrived at the cottage door sporting a pair of worn cowboy boots, faded jeans, an old plaid work shirt, and a 1970s-era down vest with a duct-tape patch on the right shoulder. I'd invite him in and get a fire going in the woodstove.

For the next several hours, our talk would range as far as Barry's imagination took him, which was so very far, covering the breadth of the eighty countries he'd visited in his travels, the long span of human and geological history, the importance of elders, the need for vulnerability on the part of the storyteller, the depths of evil we're capable of inflicting on one another—and which he himself had survived in his own childhood—and the difference between a boundary and a horizon. Barry's reputation as one of our preeminent nature writers had long been established; his corpus included more than a dozen books of fiction and nonfiction and the National Book Award–winning *Arctic Dreams*. Soon after my visit in 2018, Knopf would publish *Horizon,* a monumental work in the making for thirty years, in which Barry described the ecological and moral horizons we face as a species. Still, lying underneath these conversations was the knowledge of Barry's own horizon as he faced the late stages of metastatic prostate cancer.

No longer able to travel as he once did, Barry was preoccupied by what he called "a pressing question." In a cancer-survivor group, an older woman who was a therapist and former nun had asked Barry: *What is your second ministry?* Though he'd grown up Catholic, he had left the Church without rancor or regret, seeking holiness and mystery instead in the natural world. The language of *ministry* was not his. But the question nagged him nonetheless, for it reminded him of the need to face, even in his diminished state, the question he'd been asking for most of his life: *How can I be of service? And of what does that service consist?*

Barry was also preoccupied with the unseasonably dry weather. We had our recorded conversations each morning, and when Barry's energy flagged, we would step outside onto the guesthouse deck and stand under the firs, watching the river's current. The McKenzie River Valley is a temperate rainforest, but that year brought drought. During one of our breaks, I remarked at the quality of light filtering down to the forest understory. Barry was silent for a moment. "I must tell you," he said, "it's very strange in November to have this much clear weather. The reservoirs are empty. I've never thought about this, because you think you live in an unchanging environment, but this might shortly become a place in which it's not good to live."

How could this lovely river valley not be a good place to live? "Because of the fires," Barry said. There was no question of moving, however. As he told me, "The cells of my body have been shaped by what's right here in front of us."

The cells of Barry's body had been shaped and nourished by the forests and waters, the salmon and beaver of the McKenzie, but they also were under attack. By December 2020, the prostate cancer advanced too far, and he decided to enter hospice care.

On Christmas Day, surrounded by his family, Barry Lopez slipped quietly from the world.

In the weeks since Barry's passing, I've been returning again to his pressing question, the question of service, what he called in *Arctic Dreams* "the desire for a safe and honorable passage through the world." When we spoke in early December, a few weeks before he died, it was clear this was still a live question, especially when he described a decisive moment more than fifty years earlier when he'd nearly become a monk.

It was fall 1966. Barry had recently graduated from Notre Dame and landed a job as a sales representative with the educational-publishing imprint Signet Mentor. He could hawk textbooks to college professors by day and write by night, a perfect job for an aspiring writer, except for one nagging thought: *Did he have a monastic vocation?* He was captivated by Thomas Merton, the famous writer-monk whom Barry had begun reading at Notre Dame, and who lived as a hermit in the woods at the Abbey of Gethsemani, a Trappist monastery near Bardstown, Kentucky.

"I was enamored—*intensely* enamored—of that life at Gethsemani," Barry told me. His bookseller job required him to attend a conference nearby in Ohio, so he decided he would first visit the abbey to find out just how enamored he was. Should he become a monk, or stay in the world and become a writer?

Barry remembered attending mass with the monks and seeing their immaculate white robes, knowing they would later trade those robes for work jackets and muddy boots before heading out into the fields. The Trappists lived a life of medieval austerity. They rarely spoke except through sign language, slept and ate little, and spent most of their time either in prayer or performing arduous chores. As the philosopher William James wrote, every individual soul works best under a certain steam pressure. Trappist life was attractive, but Barry worried that it would be a comfortable nest, and he was too young to settle into a nest.

The decisive moment came during a walk around the monastery grounds. Barry recalled walking past a door in one of the outer walls. As he approached the door, he noticed a smaller opening at head height, a kind of window-within-a-door, which allowed him to peer into the inner cloister and its gardens. He saw two monks walking along a road toward a dairy barn in the distance. They were signing to each other, obviously engaged in earnest, albeit silent, conversation.

Barry thought: *Everything I want is right here. Spiritual context, physical labor, friendship—so it can't be right."*

He moved to Oregon, deciding to become a writer. In 1970, he bought the house along the McKenzie River that would be home for the next fifty years.

As I reread Barry's work, it seems to me that the monastic impulse never abated. It simply expanded to include the whole world. His seeker's vision that would have been confined by a monastery's walls reached out to every horizon it could behold, from Skraeling Island in the Canadian Arctic to Australia's Nullarbor Plain, guided all the while by a belief, as Barry wrote in *Horizon*, "that the physical land . . . is sentient and responsive, as informed by its own memory as it is by the weather, and offering within the obvious, the tenuous."

This search for what one of Barry's fictional characters called "the foundations beneath the ephemera" is one of the lasting qualities of his work, and it's everywhere. One of the chapter titles in *Arctic Dreams* is "The Intent of Monks." Standing on a cliff looking out to sea, Barry watches a narwhal "as still as a cenobite in prayer." In *Horizon*, he describes the polar expanse of Antarctica as "the geography for an anchorite." It is a mystical vision, one that also finds powerful expression in his short stories.

I'm thinking of "Pearyland," in which a wildlife biologist named Bowman recounts his discovery of a place in the High Arctic where animal spirits wait to receive their bodies. Or "The Letters of Heaven," in which a young boy in Peru discovers the secret love letters of two seventeenth-century saints, Martín de Porres and Isabel Flores de Oliva—also known as Rose—whose passion for each other spilled over into selfless compassion for the needy, which "they gave away in all the dark corners of Lima." In "The Construction of the Rachel," a recently divorced man goes to live at a Benedictine monastery in California's Santa Lucia Mountains where he spends months building a model ship, only to discover that when he sets it afloat in the ocean, the model becomes a full-sized nineteenth-century sailing vessel. He and the monks climb aboard and set sail for the Isles of the Blessed.

John Freeman, the founder of Literary Hub and publisher of many of Barry's essays, described Barry's fiction like this: "The voice is patient, wandering, thoughtful and exposed—that's what is so unusual about it in American fiction by a white writer, the way the voice in Lopez's fiction is trying to situate itself with care and respect to older and more complex ways of knowing."

I'm haunted by one story in particular. In "Teal Creek," the fictional narrator recounts his strange fascination with James Teal, who came to settle in the Magdalena Mountains of southern New Mexico. Teal was tall and lean and walked with a slight limp, which might have been the result of a war wound. He was seldom seen by the townsfolk, building a cabin on Teal Creek far up in the range. An anchorite. Several times over the years, propelled by his desire to meet Teal, the narrator hikes up the creek, but each time turns back. On one approach, he feels a certain dread as he nears Teal's cabin. "It occurred to me that maybe Teal was dealing with menace," the narrator says, "that out here he went chin to chin with an evil I could not imagine." Years pass. On his next attempt to meet James Teal, the narrator hikes up in a downpour and finds him out past the green rows of a new garden. Teal is standing on a treeless bench of land, and we're given this extraordinary description:

> [Teal] was bent far over before the flat gray sky in what appeared to be an attitude of prayer or adoration, his arms at his sides. The rain had plastered his shirt to his back and his short black hair glistened. He did not move at all while I stood there, fifteen or twenty minutes. And in that time I saw what it was I had wanted to see all those years in James Teal. The complete stillness, a silence such as I had never heard out of another living thing, an unbroken grace. He was wound up in the world, neat and firm as a camas bulb in the ground and spread out over it like three days of weather.

A person wound up in the world, firm as a camas bulb—that was also Barry. He assumed a prayerful, listening posture in whatever place he landed, whether it was researching human origins in the Turkwel River basin in East Africa or uncovering human indifference at a former child penal colony in Tasmania. While traveling in Alaska's Brooks Range, he stopped to bow before the nest of a horned lark. "In such a simple bow from the waist," Barry wrote, "you are able to stake your life, again, in what you dream."

That gesture of adoration—the deeply human urge to genuflect before the world's mystery—threads through Barry's life and work. In the final chapter of *Horizon*, he describes a moment driving to Port Famine at the tip of South America. As he passes a lone man walking toward him on an empty road, a rainbow appears in the distance. Of that moment he writes, "We go on professing confidently what we know, armed with a secular faith in all that is reasonable, even though we sense that mystery is the real condition in which we live, not certainty." A spiritual vision, yes, but one inspired more by place than by any religious tradition. During my visit in 2018, as we sat beside the woodstove in his guest cabin, I asked Barry what it is looking back at us through the eyes of a wolf, say, or from a particular landscape. Some would call that God or some other word for the divine. How would he name it?

"I would say it's an encounter between the two sides of a lopsided divorce," Barry said. "It's a breach, you know. If you can imagine a divorce in which only one member of the dyad—modern humanity—made the decision to create a breach and then enforced it, you can begin to understand what the growing malaise in human culture is about. It occurs to humanity that it has lost its spouse."

When Barry was traveling widely across the Arctic in the 1970s and '80s, he spent a lot of time among Inuit communities, and in each village he would ask people there what adjective they would use to describe White North American culture. The word he heard repeatedly was *lonely*. "They see us as deeply lonely people," Barry told me, "and one of the reasons we're lonely is that we've cut ourselves off from the nonhuman world and have called this 'progress.'" Such divine encounters in nature are moments of reconnection, part of the human search for reciprocated love.

Like his fictional anchorite James Teal, Barry Lopez also confronted menace, going chin to chin with the evil of childhood sexual abuse, as detailed in his essay "Sliver of Sky," which appeared in the January 2013 issue of *Harper's Magazine*. "The *Harper's* piece," as he referred to that essay in our conversations, chronicles the serial rape Barry suffered at the hands of a fraudulent medical doctor from the time he was seven years old until he was eleven.

The one thing that calmed Barry during those years of abuse was contact with the natural world. But even the healing power of nature was not enough to quell the lasting trauma, and for years Barry struggled to deal with it on his own. "I'd spent enough time dealing with this—memories, disruption, some chaotic corner of darkness that was always apparent—and I thought, 'I need to be done with this,'" he told me. He started therapy in 1996, and it lasted four years. The metaphor he used for the process was an image of him and his therapist sitting opposite each other at a clean, wooden table. Onto that table, he laid out all the components of his trauma. For the child, those traumatic events were defining, but during those four years Barry rearranged the components to create a new story, until the trauma was no longer the organizing principle of his life. When he was done, he knew he needed to write an essay, as he told me, "with as much objectivity as I wrote the polar-bear chapter in *Arctic Dreams*." The desire to write about those dark years was subliminally motivated by something a friend had said to him years before: "'Your work is so comforting for people who have been wounded,'" Barry recalls the friend telling him, "'But we all wonder, do you really know what it is to be wounded?' And I thought, yeah, actually I do, but I'm not ready to say anything about it."

Barry didn't write the *Harper's* essay because it was cathartic or because he thought his personal suffering was a story worth telling. "What I went through is irrelevant for me as a writer," Barry told me. "People die every day in miserable ways, so another person living through difficulty is not even news. What is news is if one person can get on the other side of that suffering and say, 'This is how it worked,' and if you write well, what you're offering the reader is a narrative they can subscribe to and change the parts according to the incidents in their own lives."

That was one of Barry's gifts, the way in which he decentered himself in service of the story. The writer's job, he believed, is to give language to pain or injury or injustice. "The one skill a writer must have is the ability to make meaningful patterns, in the same way a dancer or choreographer or a composer makes patterns," he told me. Those patterns "prompt an emotional or intellectual response. You achieve a level of clarity as a reader that you hadn't been able to achieve before."

During those three days at Finn Rock, we came back many times to the cultural and spiritual role of story, especially Barry's love for "the way story reconstitutes, reorients, and elevates human beings." He saw storytelling as a kind of stewardship. "My particular reason for writing is to provide illumination for a nation that is chronically, pathologically distracted," he told me. He wasn't interested in writing those everyday stories that enter-tain or make us laugh or create conviviality—what he called *maintenance* sto-ries. Three-meals-a-day stories. They might fill the belly, but they don't nourish. "The stories I'm trying to write, and which I want to promote, are stories that contribute to the stability of my own culture," Barry told me, "stories that elevate, that keep things from flying apart." As he said in an interview in *The Believer*, "In the process of telling a story, and also of listening to a story, the teller remembers what he or she represents in a community, and the listener remembers what they want their life to mean."

In *Horizon*, Barry suggested that the culture hero—Prometheus or Siddhartha Gautama or Odysseus—is no longer relevant in an age when humanity is exceeding ecological limits. The scale of the problems we face in the Anthropocene, the era in which humans have altered the very bone structure of the planet, are simply beyond the lone hero's ability to fix. I asked him what stories should replace the lone-hero story.

"They haven't been written yet," Barry said. "We need new narratives, at the center of which is a concern for the fate of all people. The story can't be about the heroism of one person; it has to be about the heroism of communities."

It's a profound idea—that our world is changing too quickly for the lone-hero story to be of much use any longer—and yet how to tell a story that puts community at the center? "A story is merely a pattern that signifies," Barry told me. "The blueprint for our story is before us all the time." Like a murmuration of starlings, for example. Barry recalled driving beneath the ample skies of California's Central Valley and being witness to starlings by the hundreds "carving up open space into the most complex geometrical volumes, and you have to ask yourself, how do they do that?" Each bird looks to the four or five birds immediately around it to coordinate its movements, he explained: "To behold starlings is to take in something beautiful, a coordinated effort to do something in which there's no leader, no hero."

Starlings show us a way around the dilemma of scale, a model for human cooperation and deference toward others. A murmuration shuns the idea of genius residing in one individual, and recognizes that it's actually possessed by the community. Human genius "might rise up and become reified in a single person in a group," Barry said, "but it doesn't belong solely to that person."

Even as he prized the wisdom of community, one of the paradoxes of Barry's life was the way in which a particular genius rose up and became reified in his own life—a genius he put to work not only in his writing, but in his role as mentor, teacher, and supporter of other writers and artists.

During my visit in 2018, after the long days of recorded conversations, we walked at dusk amid the ancient forests of Douglas-fir or examined salmon redds along the banks of the McKenzie. We were mostly silent, talked-out from the interviews, allowing our thoughts to drift in the gloaming. On one of those walks, Barry asked about my own life, the things that mattered to me, the books I wanted to write. I told him how his work had given me a level of clarity about a difficult three-year period in my own childhood. When I was ten years old, my parents moved our family to Nigeria so they could volunteer as medical missionaries, and I was sent to a mission boarding school. I never experienced sexual abuse, as Barry had, but the absence of parental love during such a formative time in a child's life took its toll. I knew I wanted to write about those years. I also worried that my experience was too specific to me. Barry helped me to see that if I could write that story, it could be of service to others who were struggling to find a way through their own pain.

As we walked through the woods, he was quiet for a moment, considering. He recalled a line from the Gospel of Thomas, and when he spoke, I felt it coming from the depths of his own struggle, his words and the words of the ancient text offered up as both gift and challenge: "If you bring forth what is within you, what you bring forth will save you. If you do not bring forth what is within you, what you do not bring forth will destroy you."

We writers are given our yearning, and our wounds, for a reason, I understood Barry to mean. Our task is to write a story that will be of service, to write from a place of moral responsibility. We must attend to that yearning, or it will destroy us.

In *Horizon*, Barry gave us language that limns our uncertain future as we face the effects of climate change, what he called "this throttled earth." The beauty and clarity of language in that book work in counterpoint to the multiple threats—droughts, melting ice caps, increased wildfires—it describes. The language elevates rather than suppresses our desire to face the dark horizon, to try to ameliorate our situation. In the final months of Barry's life, that future arrived at his door.

On the evening of September 7, 2020, a fire started roughly ten miles upriver from Barry and Debra's home. High winds had snapped a tension wire and ignited dry grass. With winds gusting up to forty miles per hour, the fire was off and running. "It was a climate fire," Barry told me. "It came from the east, and the east winds down the canyon caught us by surprise. Normally weather comes from the west." They awoke at 1 a.m.

on September 8 with firefighters banging on their door. Barry walked outside in his bedroom slippers and down vest. "The ridges all around us, horizon to horizon, were aflame. The roar of the fire was unmistakable," he told me.

Barry and Debra drove into Eugene, where they sheltered in a hotel. A few days later, they got word that their house was still standing, but as Barry told me, "We took no relief, because those were words from people who didn't know the difference between a house and a home." When they returned, they found that the house stood, but the forest was decimated. Worst of all, the shed where Barry had stored his archives—the first eighty volumes of his journal, which he'd written in nearly every day over the past fifty-four years, artwork from his books, gifts from friends and readers, boxes of correspondence—all of it was gone, ash. The only thing left was a set of steel steps anchored to a concrete pad. His life's work, along with the forests of his beloved McKenzie River Valley, had become throttled earth.

"When the archive burned," Barry told me, "fifty-four years of life burned with it. I felt like I'd been erased."

He and Debra had become climate refugees. Three months later, Barry started hospice care.

In our last conversation, Barry told me how two weeks after the fire, he walked the land with an old friend, a nurseryman from California. A bracken fern, already two inches tall, pushed up through the black debris. They collected mother stock from Douglas-fir, wild ginger, inside-out flower, pig-a-back plant, redwood sorrel. The friend planted the propagules, and by December had two greenhouse benches full of mother stock reclaimed from the ashes. Barry was looking ahead to summer. "We'll gather some people together and plant. We'll plant trees and shrubs and grasses and forbs," he said. He wanted to restore the place that had shaped the cells of his body, even as those cells were dying.

After he told me the story about his visit to Gethsemani, when he'd considered becoming a monk, he paused for a long moment, inhaled deeply, and said: "The point of a life—at some moment in the evolution of that life—has got to deal with the question of service. I have become a kind of vessel for a set of ideas about how to conduct your life." Barry's path led away from the nest, out to the remote corners of our world, and into the dark corners of the human psyche. His service lay in his ability to find stories that might heal, that might show us a way out of our predicament.

"You have to find a metaphor," he said, "and when you feel the surge of life, you're in the right place."

CONVERGENCE

J. DREW LANHAM

Dear Barry,

I know we never met, but I wanted to make contact in spite of you being on the other side. I suppose I come honestly by the belief that such a thing is possible. My Grandmother Mamath used to speak nightly to the ghosts of those gone on before. I peeked once from under the quilted protection of my bedcovers to see the physical manifestation of a ghost she spoke to, a tall, dark stick figure with arms outstretched to the upper corners of the door frame. It's not that I didn't believe her before that incident, but it was certainly added proof.

My name is Drew Lanham. I'm a college professor, an ecologist, and an ornithologist—a bird-obsessed man. My dear friend, the writer John Lane, whom you know well, used to talk frequently about you, and so I feel like I at least have that one degree of separation that allows me to speak with familiarity. He truly loved you. And through his admiration and all that you wrote, I've developed some pretty strong feelings, too. I guess you could call John our medium. Maybe you can consider that part of your legacy. I see myself in ways as a part of John's legacy, and so I suppose that connects us too. Thank you.

It's been quite the journey to get to this place of trusting heart to head. Though I grew up wanting to be the naturalist wanderer writer that you were, others had designs on me being something else, their expectations a stalling headwind. But heart has the edge now and here I am, writing to you from a place of desired kinship, a metaphysical chance for us to explore the strata and streams running through the existential chasm between us to some shared alluvial convergence. I write with no expectation of you other than to let the words be lightweight seeds carried on some wind to the hopefully fertile ground where you now reside. I'll have no more control over that landing than the cattail does, though knowing the seeds have at least been dispersed will be satisfaction in its own right.

I've been thinking a great deal at this stage of my hybridized academic/artist career (thirty-plus years of professoring and almost twenty of that creating as a writer) about how best to go forward in the messy muddle of all this current age presents. Yes, I depend on nature and wildness for sustenance, as I know you did, but some days I'm consumed by waves of sadness over it all. It's a despairing that sometimes obscures the view of the bird or horizon that so many times has proven salve to the wounds we humans create. The wood thrush's song bends a little less melodic when one considers the chances of its woodlot being razed over in favor of concrete and cookie-cutter housing. Swallow-tailed kite soaring, mesmerizing as it is, on occasion gets grounded by our discord. Name the biased *ism* and we are mired in it up to our necks, evincing inextricable levels of toxic behavior toward one another and nature. I know that you saw and wrote to some of this mucked-up mess, but still you wrote to wild wonder that helped me—and all of us—to see more clearly through the haze.

You said that witness was your objective. To discern in wandering discovery what the differences were among landscapes and the way people go about their lives in them, from the Arctic to the Australian Outback and so many places in between, only a minute fraction of which I've visited, though I've traveled more than most and experienced sunsets, sunrises, storms rolling, and tidal surges that have moved me to my marrow. What your words tell me, magnificent as they are, I know to be just a fragment of what you actually felt. One might painstakingly count every starling in a murmuration but miss the whole message in the blind censusing. I know that you understood that and, though often questioning the particulars of why or how nature is as it is, never failed to let wonder be your fail-safe guide. You've had Arctic dreams. Mine are subarctic tundra. You've waxed rhapsodically to the howl of wolves. I've had chills run the length of my spine at a suburban coyote's moonlit yips. You found greatest comfort in all the globe-trotting, in your Cascades Range corner. I, in all my continental crisscrossing, rest easiest in my South Carolina rolling Piedmont.

The point here isn't comparison, my would-have-been friend, but merely a point of reference to paths traveled. I eschew the straight and narrow unless it's a slot canyon or straits, defined geographically. I have no doubt of your curvilinear choices likewise. You've led. I have happily followed. What a time we might have had together.

Wondering what a few days shared in either of our home places would've yielded? A hearty bird list, I'm sure. But I think we'd have spent more time watching and wondering over a singular bird than focusing on picking up a listed stack of many. Would you have shown me where the varied thrush sings in your lush Oregon place? I would gladly trade that ethereal deep-forest song to show you the soaring glides of cloud-dancing swallow-tailed kites over a Combahee River rice marsh. You would've told your stories of Native people living free in the wild, and I would have shared mine of bondaged Black ancestors moving mountains of pluff mud to marshal the tide. We could have claimed a catty-cornered continental exchange of ecology and culture. You spoke to diversity and noticing difference as seminal spokes in life's hub. Another node of intersection in our paths—not just applied to birds and beasts, but to us too.

Our worlds share so many similarities that I miss you in the odd space of never having sat side-by-side on some wild-seeking expedition, or shoulder-to-shoulder at some hole-in-the-wall pub, pontificating over the state of the world, as cool suds slake thirsts post-hike.

I don't think I've mentioned this yet, Barry, but I came to writing late, as a sort of post-tenured nature writer whose form follows the function of well-known wordsmiths, many dead, most White, and few personally known by anything other than reputation and their books. I also happen to be a Black man. So that sets me up a little differently, I think. A difference between us, to be sure, but one that necessarily needs seeing. Birdwise I'm a raven sitting among the great egrets. But here I am, hoping to connect. Honored to write about a man I know well but never knew. Lopez, Leopold, Carson, Thoreau, Whitman—all these dead white people who wrote about wildness. And then there's me (and a few others). I'm not sure who they lean on for mentorship or muse's inspiration, but here I am, fully and proudly ensconced in my Blackness but with thinking torqued by you and others gone on before me. But then I also have bits of Frederick Douglass, George Washington Carver, Langston Hughes, and James Baldwin within me.

I enter your realm with this open-palmed admission in an Anthropocene time defined not just by what humans have wrought (and wrecked), but also by identity. I even venture to call this age the "I-dentocene," as we seem more preoccupied with identifying ourselves and letting the world know who we are, via social media post and emoticon, than by identifying with nature in ways that broaden our connections with others. My work lies in the spaces between how we identify ourselves—the binary racial chasm between White and Black, for example—and how those differences alter our perceptions of nature. Those are the prisms that can make trees the sacred sylvan beings that some hug, and yet be damned as the same ones others once hung from. I write to connect past to present and to connect who we are to what nature means to us.

You wrote, Barry, to connect bits and pieces artfully to foster some greater appreciation of the whole. Your life was a global one, your efforts deeply divining and as expansive as any plain you ever trod. Your legacy lies even larger.

And so, like you, I write about wildness. I like to say that I conjugate *wild* in all of its tenses—*wild, wildness,* and *wilderness*—to bring a wider perspective to all of the possibilities of what those four root letters mean. I know that

that's been your work, and still is. Your words live on in me and countless others. There's nothing conditional about that.

Barry, my friend, you know of the finite nature of our existence here. Perhaps somehow, from some wild bluff above endless days that shift into endless aurora-painted nights, you sit and look out over the expanse of all the wild there ever was and that remains. The wolves howl without fear of humans, and the caribou hooves click to keep time with the whimbrel's call. And from the tussock of grass, you watch as the light bends gently to make every stone in the braided riverbed glow as if it were a star in the heavens above. The way forward looks clear. I pray to all the gods there ever were or might be, those beings with fins or fur, fangs or feathers, for easy steps through the next realm and that our improbable but possible meeting—better late than never—is made fast on the other side of whatever is.

FIREBUILDER

RICK BASS

Who knows how we come to anything? He wasn't the first writer I read, once I decided to become a writer myself, but he certainly was formative. Helpful. I had picked up his work on a suggestion. An insistence; a celebration. The book I picked up, *Desert Notes*, was a marvel in its thinness and in what it contained. My first introduction to his work—the first page—was a description of someone driving a van through the desert, not on any road or trail, just kind of magic-carpeting along, and stepping out of the van while it was idling forward, and running around to the other side then and climbing into the passenger side, and continuing on. He did not present it as metaphor, but as truth. The truth of a landscape without boundaries and an imagination likewise. This was valuable to me. I had always suspected—believed—that was the way the world was, but it was extraordinarily valuable to me to have that belief validated. Encouraged.

He did this thing a lot, where he helped us see anew—usually deeper, but sometimes broader—things we'd been looking past, or looking at incorrectly: with a flawed set of assumptions, or with faulty logic. He helped us look at landscape differently. A classic example is in his celebration of the photographer Michio Hoshino, who was revolutionary at the time for photographing the grizzly bears of Denali and other wildlife not with nature-porn close-up head-and-shoulders portraits, but with images where enormous herds and individual animals were tiny against the landscape they inhabited.

Barry questioned pretty much everything. I think that might have become exhausting at times.

Something else he taught me, or rather, served as exemplar: he made it easier for me to make hard and stubborn, even obstinate, choices, with regard to what some might call art, and the artist's relationship to the rest of the world. He helped remind me—with the unquestioning insistence of his intensity—that art was *different*. Different from everything. And a way through. A way through everything.

He did not die a rich man. This is nobody's business, certainly not the future's. I bring it up only to verify to the reader, and to other writers and artists who will follow, that his decisions—as they always do in a life of meaning, which is to say, engagement—were not based on finances but rather on artistic and personal integrity.

He was a man who in some ways was very aware of limits—unusual for either an artist or philosopher—yet certainly had access to imagination and, one of imagination's unavoidable fruits, hope. I believe that being mortal, he had doubt. I think one of the primary doubts was his view of contemporary humanity's ability to grow and change. Of humanity's ability to not be seduced. And yet to not despair.

I think it was his doubt that made him fierce. It was his ferocity that brought the fire.

Of course, he lived in the rainforests of western Oregon. Sea fog, mist, and the broad red backs of salmon. And yet of course the fire eventually found him. Each seeks its own. Each seeks our own. Our kin, our kind, our community.

Because he understood science as perhaps only a poet can, he was unafraid to move in directions that seemed opposite to science. Spirituality and storytelling were his foundation. The facts mattered to him as much as they would to a journalist, and yet at the end of the day I think he was most ardenthearted about magic. That he had seen and felt enough of it to be comfortable trusting its presence. Whether Crazy Horse actually flew up onto his horse like a bird, never touching it; whether Moses parted the Red Sea—one must consider that the things we call miracles might once have been almost commonplace. That somehow we lost the ability to summon or even receive them.

They still happen, now and again: but on a scale that feels muted. And we tend to call them coincidence. We tweeze them apart and try to use our always incomplete, always inadequate science to explain the coincidence.

You might think at this point that as a writer I am going to tell you a story about a coincidence, or magic. As if to prove a point. And I will tell you the first time I met Barry was at Edward Abbey's memorial, outside of Moab. And when Barry walked up to make his remarks, out in the orange cliffs, beneath an April-blue sky, a raven followed him above, like a pet, then flared away. And that before Barry could speak, the wind picked up the American flag and hurled it to the ground.

But there are a lot of ravens around Moab, and it is true also that in the canyonlands there can be sudden gusts of wind. And it is possible too, I suppose, that we are each alone and all we have in the world and forever is each other.

He was a leader—along with Richard Nelson, and others—in helping white-folk appreciate certain Indigenous teachings not just as an abstract way of listening, but of a sometimes-deeper learning that comes from curiosity. In an era when there was not much listening going on to First Nations and Indigenous people, it was instructive to see him and a few others asking questions, and listening, rather than presuming or not thinking about such things at all.

And he knew from the beginning, as Robin Wall Kimmerer and others remind us, to be unafraid of creating our own rituals and ceremonies; that gratitude is or once was and can be again an underpinning of our species, and our route, our path, to connecting back to the tree of life from which we fell, like an apple. Or from which we were cast.

He still visits me in dreams. Not a lot. But checks in, now and again. I fill Debra in on what he was up to. To say that she misses him—that she and her daughters, Amanda, Stephanie, Mary, and Mollie, miss him—is the wildest of understatements. What he gave was huge; how then could what he took with him, or rather what went away, not also be immense? Grief upon grief upon grief becomes—what? Water? Enough water to extinguish all fires, if for but a while?

She kayaks. She paddles a lime-green kayak on a blue lake beneath a blue sky. She still lives in Oregon, on the rainy coast. The fires from the Southwest have found even this place. She was born into a time of rot and lives now, as do we all, in a time of burning.

In one dream, I was at a campfire in the woods and he came from out of the forest with an envelope he said he wanted me to have. He said I would need it. The envelope was unsealed, and when I looked in it there was some paper money—ones and a five, adding up to about ten dollars. Maybe a little more. I thanked him, but thought, How far is *this* going to take me, and how am I going to make this last?

Another one: There was a war going on, as there have been in so many of my dreams these last few years—in the bombed-out Gaza Strip, in Afghanistan, in Ukraine. And in this one I had of him, he was young, thirty-five (I don't know how I knew this exact number), and was running toward, rather than away from, the active war; toward the smoke and rubble and collapse. He was looking back over his shoulder at me with a look of wild exhilaration and fearlessness—something more than fearlessness;

the delight of meeting a destiny—and he was a journalist, with camera and notepad and flak jacket, and the look on his face said clearly that he was doing what he loved, and he was good at it. It was the happiest I'd ever seen him.

Still another—he was driving at night, trying to get somewhere. A big old low-to-the-ground four-door gas-hog sedan. Belly-scraping, really. Big old goggle headlights. Fins. A Detroit relic. Not a Cadillac Eldorado, I don't think. Some kind of Oldsmobile. And it was snowing—a blizzard, a whiteout. He was in a hurry to get somewhere and had been driving a long time; I was riding with him, and we went off the road just as he was coming into sight of the place he was trying to reach. Down in a ditch. Out onto a sagebrush prairie—night-blizzard, us snowblind from the roost-ertails of snow thrown up by the car, just the shushing sound of snow all around us as we ploughed through it, an occasional feathery scratching of sagebrush against the sides and belly of the car. It looked like the end of things—there was so much snow—but I reached over and took the steering wheel and aimed the car back up toward where I thought the road was, and accelerated, gave it all the power it had rather than braking, and the car muscled up out of the snowy prairie and miraculously found the road again, in all that blizzard, and all was well, we continued on into the falling snow—following that one road that led straight and deeper into the storm.

I ragged him a little (well, probably more than a little) about his inveterate habit—a commitment, really, the way a monk or nun might commit—of writing a response to every letter he ever received. And I don't mean with a postcard, nor by the brain-scrambling wires-crossing miasma of email. He'd type out a thoughtful and generous response on the butter-colored parchment of his notepaper, sign the letter with his calligraphic flourish, then fold the letter neatly and, from a special map drawer where he kept an extraordinary volume of specialty stamps—butterflies, Arctic explorers, constellations, flora and fauna of New Zealand, what-have-you—the map drawer housed in the sun room of his and Debra's beautiful home just above the sun-bright riffling waters of the broad McKenzie, in the dappled sun and shadow of cedars—the light falling upon his hands, his face, as he opened one or another of the long, flat drawers and pondered his selection, in conjunction with the recipient and the missive's content—he would choose the just-right stamp, or stamps.

It had to it, this act, all the elements of art. Art gives. Art is selectivity. Art is creative. It was unhurried—no, more than unhurried; slow.

A story he told more than once—not so much agreeing or disagreeing (and he would do that so often; take into private counsel some thought or idea to examine, and worry over, as they say in the South, the way a dog worries a bone)—was of how he came to be a writer.

In grade school, he'd read a book (I can't remember whether novel, biography, or natural history) by some local/regional writer—I've forgotten the name, if ever I knew it—and wrote a letter to the writer. Sixty-plus years later, Barry still marveled that the writer took the time to take the child's letter seriously and write back to the child without condescension, but instead, direct intellectual engagement, and gratitude.

To hear Barry describe it was to imagine that for the child, the boy, it was the first time he'd ever felt heard; that, as he had always desired, holding out hope in the darkness that the one ray of light he saw could be something good, someone good, someone decent, someone kind.

As if his prayers had made a thing into reality. Had then summoned the thing—kindness, and intelligence. Meaningful connection.

Still, I pushed the opposite thought: You don't have to answer every letter you get, from so many thousands of strangers. *You've more than paid back your debt, your gift. Enough's enough—it takes you away from the here-and-now. You have a duty to the moment, too*, I wanted to say—not just the past, and not even always to the future. But who was I to counsel an elder? By this point he had married my dear friend, the writer and fantastic mother of four incredible young women, Debra Gwartney. Her daughters—in time, they became his, too, in the way of such meldings, and he spoke of them as daughters—and then, from the oldest, Amanda, and then from Mollie, a profusion of sweet and indefatigable grandchildren.

He encouraged me to write what I wanted to write—a slim fine-arts book about a mythical logger. A book about a caribou hunt. An extended essay about this, that, or another, when no market for such exists, or existed. To spend a month writing an introduction to a photo book, or a week or longer on a band's album liner notes. A week on an op-ed, or an essay for an obscure publication in some foreign country where my people—all five, six, seven, ten, or however many of them there are—do not live. And with my back turned on the hours with them. This awful fire; this awful light.

I do not answer the letters of strangers. By ragging him about his pro-lific letter-writing, I think I was able to pretend I was in control of my own relationship with time. With the burning.

He could be daunting. As W.S. Merwin wrote of John Berryman in his poem, "Berryman":

> his lips and the bones of his long fingers trembled
> with the vehemence of his views about poetry

He was a smart son-of-a-gun. It couldn't have been easy, holding so much in his mind—in his body. Edward Hoagland writes that Turgenev's brain was the heaviest ever measured—approximately four pounds. And I have heard it said also that of the brain's mass—so many coils and loops and folds, going who-knows-where—that we generally only use about 1 percent of it. So then where does the other 99 percent go?

I don't know how much he used. But he could be daunting. He seemed smarter. And maybe he was. But mostly I think he just went deeper. "Just." The hunter-gatherer, always giving readers more, when they asked for it. Needed it, or even just wanted it. It seemed to me to be a terrible pressure, terrible burden, in some ways little dissimilar from our own these days, of placing a four-year-old on a balance beam, or a football into a seven-year-old's hands. He gave. That old fellow he wrote the letter to as a child—it's hard to say what might have happened, if he hadn't. Maybe all of this, nonetheless—unstoppable, roaring like a long fire. Or maybe none of it. It doesn't matter, does it? He was not wrong to write the letters; he wanted to write them, he needed to write them, and so he did. He gave. He gave, and gave.

One of the great tenets of Christianity is, I think, the necessity of waiting. The Sun Dance and prophecies of seven-generations-out address better times ahead. Christianity certainly is founded on the faith of a savior's return. But I hope you are gathering that Barry was not much of a waiter. To the best of my knowledge, he worked every day, and as he grew more ill—and he was sick a long time; Debra and the girls caretaking of him, across those years—he worked harder.

It's understandable; there can be a terrible urgency for any writer with things still unsaid. I've always marveled at my old heroes for this—the way they push harder, near the end, in the way of the female shark injured in the trawl-net who, upon being extricated and tossed onto the deck, gives sudden birth to all her live babies, which skitter across the deck and over the edge, back into the sea, even as she herself will never return. The way pine trees, under stress of drought or beetle infestation or fire-scarring, or the gash of a bulldozer, will generate an extraordinary volume of cones in that same year, a last-gasp pulse of life in the dying.

This would be the opportunity for a writer to talk about Barry's last book. But I don't want to talk about *Embrace Fearlessly the Burning World*, or any of his books. What I wanted for him—when he and Debra knew, really knew, the transition was near—was for him to slow down and live. I wanted him to choose. I wanted him to feel at peace with what he had given to strangers, and pull in tight. I want that for all of my heroes—they who have sacrificed so much time away from the world, for so many years, decades. Desk-anchored, while this bright world does not slip away but rather the five senses with which they engage it. I wanted him to step away from the desk for him, but also for Debra and the girls.

Even as I, entering the first of the gray territory, where vision begins to fail and one must look more closely, and with that light fading, find myself anticipating each next day's work. As might a prisoner, the night-before, fall asleep considering his next-day's workout in the gym. Might awaken, similarly; and hastening to it, then, for two-a-days, even before breakfast. As if to a wedding.

What I was thinking, when he'd write those deeply engaged letters to strangers—to utter strangers, I'm tempted to say, even though one thing the pandemic has helped teach or remind us is that we are a global community, all eating the same food, drinking the same water, breathing the same air—that the fires burn and the seas rise whether we are Hindu or Christian, Democrat or Libertarian.

What I was thinking was of how he and Debra and I would go on walks through the old forest that had not yet burned, the ancient light that left the sun so long ago falling softly now down through the fronds of the overstory like a kind of unheard music, unheard song. On those walks through the old forest behind his and Debra's house, through ferns ankle-high and higher, across spongy green moss and the orange, vibrant, wet duff of the forest floor—through vertical columns of old-growth sunlight sliding off the feathers of cedars, with the creek trickling beside the trail, sounding not as small creeks usually gurgle but instead somehow like chimes—he would point to one giant fallen tree or another and tell how that was a place where he and Debra and Owen and Ezzie—Amanda's son and daughter—would picnic. Point to a bend in the creek and tell of how he and Harry—Mollie's young son—liked to sit in the tiny plunge pool on the hottest days, and tell stories that it seemed even the trees were listening to.

You can't put one second back. And yet you can pass forward a pebble of green sea-glass, a curl of turquoise polished by who-knows-what relentless journey. You can pass forward an image: Barry sitting in a chair next to Debra at Stephanie's wedding, on a hot August day, in the shade. Out in the country. The scent of horses.

He and Debra holding hands at the candlelit dinner table for a meal my daughter Lowry, the writer Erin Halcomb, and I prepared for them, when he was sick, a long time ago; but not yet too sick. Elk backstrap, chocolate ginger cake, dry-rubbed king salmon. Cornbread pudding. A bottle of really good Bordeaux.

You can pass forward an idea. One that is the opposite of greed, or rage, or fear. You can pass beauty forward; kindness, too. Though it is not unnoticed by me that while his and Debra's home was spared somehow, in the center of the great burning, the library where all the maps and letters were kept—tens of thousands?—is now not even ash.

And yet, what we carry from the fire remains real. It all remains present. It is just different; changed.

He was a devotee of sports, particularly that most old-fashioned and non-violent of games, baseball—what used to be called, in an earlier era, America's pastime. Picnics on the lawn, straw hampers, a blanket spread for all to sit on. He could be boyish. I think that as with so many boys, the numismatics of the endeavor intrigued him. A safe harbor, a ferocity of control in the precision, down to the thousandth of a percentage point. Al Kaline's batting average. Willie Stargell's. Pete Rose stealing 198 bases. Juan Marichal's 2,303 strikeouts and 2.89 earned runs allowed in 3,507 innings. And so on.

Something changed in him, I think, at the Fire & Grit conference hosted in Washington, D.C., by *Orion* magazine in 1999. We'd been on the Hill to lobby Bruce Babbit for national monuments, including one in the Yaak Valley. It didn't happen; I forget the reasons why, now: there are always reasons. A quarter century has gone by, the reasons are gone, the need is still there, and now they have come up with new reasons, all of which have as their common denominator the one word, *cowardice*. Mike Dombeck was chief of the US Forest Service, beginning his drive to protect all of his agency's roadless lands: a major policy victory, and one of the last I can recall.

We were seated in some conference room at the Department of the Interior and had been granted oh, I don't know, maybe twenty minutes with the secretary. Hardly the week-long camping trips of Muir and Roosevelt. Bill Kittredge was with us to lobby for Steens Mountain in Oregon, which passed; Terry Tempest Williams for Red Rocks Wilderness, which didn't, though later President Clinton, in a somewhat defiant gesture toward Senator Orrin Hatch, passed Grand Staircase-Escalante National Monument.

The Yaak, alas, with all its timber, is not yet protected. (The annular growth rings in the old-growth forests there—centuries-old giants—might be a quarter-of-an-inch thicker, while the mountains above them, also still growing, are *perhaps* a quarter-inch taller, in places . . .)

Barry wasn't there to lobby for a place, but instead an idea. Straight out of the gate—before any of us had begun to describe our native landscapes and the passions we held for them, Barry leaned across the table, both elbows on the table—flat, low, as if to minimize wind shear; as if preparing to lunge—and asked, *Secretary Babbit, when you close your eyes and sleep, what are your dreams?*

I do not remember the secretary's answer. Barry was never one to talk about the weather.

I do not know what he dreamed about. We were friends, but not that kind of friend where you share your dreams. Your waking ones, sure—aspirations. But not the ones when you sleep. When fears come skulking in.

I don't remember all the specifics, at the Fire & Grit conference, only that we were reading on a hill—some park. I read a story about wilderness, and grizzly bears, and bear spray. About what it's like to be sprayed by it—self-inflicted. The mood was light, humorous. Another era. I won't say it was better or worse. It was just a long time ago.

Then he read. He read a story about a boy hiding in a closet. A story about a boy hiding in a closet knowing the man was coming to molest him again. The boy seeing a tiny speck of light outside, from the darkness within, and then the man's shadow. The terror.

It was dark, there in D.C., even in summer. The evening had gone on long. Lightning began to flicker to the north—heat lightning at first, but then real forks of it, seeking and searching: the sky on fire. It's so hard to write about fire. The lightning splitting the darkness. The way the light scorches whatever it falls upon. The way we can be frightened of it, with an awe that—in that quick blink—is not at all dissimilar from joy. Then the dark again.

He had never before told anyone that I know of. People were only just beginning to speak of such things. I'd never read or heard anything of his remotely like it. The piece—"Sliver of Sky"—was in the first person, but at the time I believed it was fiction, and went to find him. To congratulate him, for fuck's sake. I didn't know. I thought we were there for art, and that it was a short story. I thought we were there for activism. I didn't yet quite understand there can be no difference, no matter how much one wants to believe otherwise. That the dark calls for that scorch of light.

Something changed in him, I think, after writing that story, and reading it aloud to his friends, family, and fans in D.C. that night. When I went up to him and said, "What the hell?" It was so unlike anything he'd written to that point; so unadorned by intelligence or any aspect of his intellect that I felt sometimes was employed by him almost as a shield.

He looked at me as if he had no answer, and was somehow—almost—frightened of the place he had gotten to. The place where he was. But determined. And I still thought it was a short story, and an amazing one, for the empathy he had with the character of that boy.

"I have to go off and be by myself," he said, and drifted into the night. There were not cell phones then. I do not know if he called Debra. I do not know where he walked. I never asked.

What I think changed for him was his willingness to trust—to ask for help, if but in the form of support, understanding, respect, empathy. Fifty or sixty years later, to ask, or communicate, once again, as he had to that long-ago forgotten writer who'd answered his letter.

How can a river summon fire? How can a salmon become a raven, or a cedar tree, or a grizzly? The system is closed—the energy flows where it will flow, assuming, in its passage, different forms: earth, sky, water, fire. A salmon is a salmon for a while, and then it is a raven, and then it is a river, and then it is a cedar tree, or a grizzly. There is no waste, just as there is no gain. And yet how we grieve and mourn the passage of things, just as we celebrate and exult in the arrival of things. These are not new lessons. But there is great service, I think, in finding new ways to tell the old stories. This is what life itself—evolution or, as Darwin once wrote, "descent, with modifications"—proceeds, or does not proceed.

Proceeds.

There's this thing all writers know, where the words, working their way across the page, access something deeper, or higher—a different plane, where understanding, first emotionally, but from that, intellectually—comes surging in. *Metaphor:* we're not just talking about wolves any more. And then—stay in the burning, ride it out—transcendence, or sublimation. The solid becomes a gas, the ether becomes a solid. The metaphor burns away, leaving only the thing, pure and irreducible. And we can carry it with us. We do not have to leave it behind, or be left by it. We are taught otherwise, but that is not my experience. A letter, or a book—a story or a poem—no matter; I am not speaking of symbol or metaphor, but the physical thing, held in your hands, and connecting you to the physical thing—the grove of aspen, the gray wolf on the hill, across the ravine, looking over at you—you are connected, and finally escaping the abstract cage of your emotions and beliefs, foursquare now in the land of the specific—that which many would assert is the proof of a God or greater being, proof that the abstract rattlings in the mind are not simply lost, disconnected madness or unbearable loneliness. The book or poem or letter is like the mycorrhizae in ancient forests beneath the surface connecting all trees and preparing the way for the aging and strengthening of that forest.

The forest has been made real for us. We are allowed a glimpse, touch, taste, scent, sound, of the green burning, whether we can see the flames yet or not—for what else is rot but slow burning? The letters, poems, stories, give us entry into the fire. And once it is in us, I believe it can never be extinguished.

We speak of our footprints—of being mindful. Of trying to travel lightly and minimize our impact. But even the lightest and best of our kind leave enormous prints; we all leave prints, and it seems to me our feet are burning, and that we ignite the ground now wherever we pass.

I do not mean metaphorically but instead actually. The ground beneath our feet is buckling in the heat and the heat is coming up through our shoes. Places where we step are igniting. Places here in the Yaak where I have hiked: Gold Hill, Lick Mountain, Davis Mountain, Caribou Mountain. Thrice when I have been camping a helicopter has flown to a lake where I camped, a different lake each time, and dipped water to go fight a fire just on the other side of the mountain. All trees burn, even when they are being kept in captivity— even as they are in the mill, awaiting their next journey on the way back to sky and soil. John Brown's little lumber mill in the Yaak. The Stimson mill in Libby. This year, almost, the IFG mill in Moyie Springs. The West is burning and the world is burning and there is no longer any metaphor and perhaps there never was. Perhaps metaphor was simply a device by which we avoided looking at things the way they really were, and chose instead to compare them, slantwise. To contrast them rather than to really see.

He tapped deep. He was practiced at the art of the descent into the steepest ravines and finding his way back up and out. He read a lot, and felt a lot—quivered, incandescent—and, like a boy memorizing the statistics of various players, not just batting averages or strikeouts, but on-base percentages versus the shift, percentages when facing left-handed pitchers versus right-handed, and so on—he connected various conduits and cables of knowledge, of light, and sometimes—with a bit of obstinance, I want to believe, which could also I suppose be called faith—dug his own trenches through the jungle and unspooled, with great effort and exertion.

He wasn't always fully present, I noticed sometimes, but when he was, it was an incandescence. I don't know where he went, exactly, whenever he'd step away.

As Mary Oliver writes, "Said Mrs. Blake of the poet: / I miss my husband's company— / he is so often / in paradise."

We got him when we got him. The rest of the time, he was somewhere else. It is not fair to say he was never here. It is not fair at all. He was just not always here. Nor are any of us. Nor are all and each of us. We cannot see what he left behind, but it is as real as a stone or piece of colored beach glass. Some days—as the years blow past—we might even think we have misplaced it. But then—on a walk through an old forest at twilight, the light leaving the forest so suddenly it seems taken, yet with other things seeming to glow for a moment—the carpet of butter-yellow arnica blossoms, like an expanse of miniature sunflowers or, later in the year, the entire forest floor stippled with yellow aspen coins, or the orange-gold needles of larch carpeting everything, so that every shape, every inanimate object draped with that gold, seems, in that twilight, to have been briefly animated, and awakening finally, if briefly, stunned with the wholly unexpected gift of life and surging quickly—before the dark—toward joy.

There are moments when it comes back to us, the gift—the beach glass in the palm of a hand; the elk ivory in a medicine bundle; the stone on the windowsill . . . he was here. He is here. We were here. We are here. A nation, sometimes above ground, other times, below, our tendrils and roots reaching blindly in the dark for one another, our hours and centuries punctuated by bursts of extraordinary light. Or by the phenomenon we call light.

NOW THAT IT'S COME TO THIS

JOHN FREEMAN

Once, before I knew him well, I asked Barry Lopez the earliest thing he could remember. Without missing a beat, the most widely traveled and sophisticated spiritual seeker in North American letters in a century—a writer of mystical sensitivity and grace, who'd been up to his armpits in snow, tracking wolves in Alaska, and who charted the migration of snow geese across Canada, who listened to Indigenous peoples across the globe, learning from their knowledge systems, especially in the Arctic—spoke at length about water.

His life began, Lopez said, with water.

He talked about being transfixed by the luminescence of a thin column of water as it poured from a spigot at the house in Reseda, California, where he grew up. This would have been the late 1940s, and Lopez, just three or four years old at the time, already sensed beauty's power to hold . . . to protect even. He turned toward it, he recalled, mesmerized, the way we all respond to something vital in nature.

Such a long time this memory traveled in Lopez's life, from that back porch in Reseda, along his trips through the Arctic, the Sahara, and through more than eighty countries, nourishing in him uncommon reservoirs. You knew it upon meeting him, that his spirit had been written in water. Although he voyaged widely, he lived most of his life in a small cabin on the McKenzie River in Oregon, sticking his hands into its currents daily. He grew strong from what they told him. He shared the depths the river gave with virtually anyone who asked. Were I to name them, these wells he'd scoop his cup into, I'd call them patience, curiosity, humility, and generosity. If I were telling stories about him, I might also mention his rich springs of determination, stubbornness, and loyalty. Maybe if the stories were going late into the night, I'd want to add that deep beneath all of them was a profound aquifer of faith. He didn't just believe, but did so deeply that the questions of faith became a daily practice of sacrifice. A stringency with himself I never once saw him impose on others.

He was hard on himself because he'd been taught to be, as a good Catholic. He was hard on himself because he knew if he paid any attention to what was said about him, he'd lose the equilibrium he so carefully built and maintained throughout his life. Long before he became sick, he knew he was on a journey to an endless sea, and in the years when I became his friend—rather than fight that pull—he dedicated himself to traveling there with dignity, with the least amount of harm, leaving behind the greatest amount of clarity over the danger of our situation as humans on the planet. In this regard, Lopez was a fundamentally collaborative writer. He knew he didn't have answers, only questions, and wanted to hear those of others. Even when he knew his cancer was probably fatal, Lopez fed and was fed by friendships with a vast tributary of other seekers: musicians, photographers, artists, bookmakers, botanists, field biologists, poets, priests, and war reporters.

He finally ended this trip on Christmas Day 2020, surrounded by his dear wife, Debra Gwartney, his family, and a few treasured objects, gifts given to him on his travels. He was not a taker. We'd spoken on the telephone a little more than a day before, and in the weeks preceding. An astonishing gift of time from someone who had run out of it. He didn't see it that way, though. A month before he died, he wanted to tell me the hilarious story of how the doctors in Oregon had restarted his heart. "I remember thinking, 'You're doing it wrong,'" he'd told me, bursting into a laugh. He'd thought the current in an EKG had been reversed, and instead of taking a reading, it was shooting electricity into him. Then he wanted to send love. Make that last deadline. To see pictures of our dogs. He also wanted me to work more with photographers, one of the last things he said: *Without them, we cannot see.* Then he talked to me about hominids. He wasn't born this way. This preternaturally calm, poised, generous. Like all of us, Lopez came into the world gut-slick, fur-matted, more mammal than person. But it was like he *remembered.* And he used this recollection of creatureliness, wrote it into books where he threw his point of view— miraculously—into the lives of animals. In one early book, a compilation of Native American trickster tales about coyote, there he was, so deep inside he disappeared, deep within the body of coyote himself. Later, in his breakthrough study, *Of Wolves and Men,* he did it again, penning sections, fables really, from the wolf's perspective. In *Arctic Dreams,* he did it with caribou; the beasts looked back at the figure of a human traveler, coming across the tundra. What did it want?

He had these encounters all the time. When I visited him at his home in Finn Rock, I spent the night in his green-roofed guest cabin, which was more luxuriously outfitted than the main house. A fabulous central stove heated the whole place, with double-paned windows so sealed the river was but a rumor. The morning after my arrival, he turned up in his cap and jeans with strong coffee and pointed up the hill to where he'd had an encounter recently with five or six Roosevelt bull elk, standing behind a large cow. She'd made eye contact with Barry, standing there in his slippers on the soft woodchip path to his studio. "Her inquiry," he would later write, "which fills this opening in the forest where we have encountered each other, is very much larger, I think, than, Who are you? It's closer to, What are you planning to do, now that it's come to this? One of the calves turns into her mother's flank as if to begin nursing. The lead cow continues to stand like someone straining to hear a faint sound. And then she moves and the others follow, all drifting like smoke into the trees."

This tuned-in inner ear was mistaken for wisdom, rather than coping mechanism. Maybe they're the same thing. Nevertheless, he was asked about it in interviews, asked to explain this facility to enter the lives of animals. Where'd it come from? From Port Chester, New York, to his parents' early split, the move west, to the miracle of California and the outdoors: Barry told his early life progression of spaces and domestic arrangements to interviewers over and over—dozens of times—hundreds?—always skipping over the entrusted family friend who scooped out his childhood innocence—*for years*— making him do unthinkable things. A man who reminded him of the vulnerability of animals.

I met Barry in 2011, shortly before he broke that cycle of silence. In fact, he'd already begun, in 2008 writing an essay called "Madre de Dios," which began as a piece on Catholicism and the Virgin Mary, and wound up describing how she'd come to him as a vision when he was eight years old, trapped in the bedroom of a dangerous man who did terrible things. "You will not die here," Lopez wrote she said to him. She had been right. Lopez did what he could with that survival, and when the pressure of maintaining it was too much, he went into therapy and wrote "Sliver of Sky," one of the most shattering tales of surviving sexual abuse. He received letters about it for the rest of his life. He answered every one of them individually. As we talked in that last month of his life, only one thing gave him anguish: not his impending departure, not the loss of his precious cedars around the house and archive claimed in the Holiday Farm Fire—a fire from which he and Debra had escaped, awakened by brave firefighters—not these awful blows. Fundamental blows. What he couldn't stand was that he could no longer write back to the people who were still writing to him about "Sliver of Sky."

Our first meeting, I realize, must have happened in the thick of this time—when he realized he'd have to pause the monumental book he'd begun, and work on himself. We met that first time in 2011 for an onstage interview, maybe his two hundredth—but our first—at Portland, Oregon's fall literary festival, then called Wordstock. He turned up in what I came to think of as Lopez regalia: cowboy boots, weathered jeans, old-fashioned belt, turquoise ornaments, sporting an aloofness that was frankly terrifying. It was like something wild and animal had been led into a conference hall and, though biding its time, was eager to leave. I asked or nearly asked him all the questions I later knew annoyed him: to explain where his love of nature came from. To perform his alarm about the climate. I even asked him to comment on American nature writing, the implication being it was a genre of which he partook.

Here our paucity of genres in the United States lets us down. Is there a writer who has sampled so many storytelling cultures, allowed himself to be made and remade by so many? After all, in his twenties, Lopez had assembled that book of Native American trickster stories. His first work of fiction—*Desert Notes*—is like a book on the American desert written by Castañeda or Cortázar. *Of Wolves and Men,* his classic 1978 book on our relationship to *Canis lupus,* juxtaposes Native American folklore about the wolf and the tales of field biologists. *Arctic Dreams,* his 1986 National Book Award winner, is saturated in the ways of knowing that region of the world—reminding us that imagination enters when there is a gap between knowing and not knowing.

This gap exists constantly in Lopez's work; it's where wonder emerges. It's where hope exists. He never attempted to fully close it, this gap. I also believe it's where faith exists, faith being a fiction conjured by the heart and mind to make us feel safe in that knowing of not knowing. For some reason, that day onstage, I asked Barry the question that emerged out of all the work he had published to date: *Did he believe in God?* Very little I ever saw Barry do was rushed, inelegant, unduly rapid. He was a rare thing—a graceful man. He was not tall; he was slightly round, bowlegged, bum-kneed, but he had an ex-athlete's grace to him, a pace that suggested a deep deliberation of movement. But when I asked that question, his head whipped around and he stared at me—like that elk through the trees. Not, "Who are you?" It was closer to, "What are you planning to do, now that it's come to this?"

I did, we did, what made sense. We became friends—slowly, gently. It took years before I would have used that term. I realize in the scale of a life such as his, I was far from alone. I was just a new friend, a much younger friend—also, an editor. He did not treat me like a mentor, exchanging time and wisdom for attention, or respect. It wasn't an exchange, full stop. It was like we'd met, as fellow travelers, and recognized one another instantly. The head whip.

I want to say I remember how it happened, but I don't. I want to say I have all the emails, the postcards, the letters, but I don't. We wrote letters initially, trading news, weather, gossip, philosophy. He had beautiful handwriting, long, looping prewar penmanship, and a master letter writer's lack of pretension. He instantly achieved the letter writer's easeful interiority, too. He wasn't speaking to you from a perch, but a porch somewhere deep inside his mind. Like he was his own message in a bottle.

They came irregularly. Months, half a year apart. I look back on these years in his publication cycle—no book, a few stories, the odd essay—and realize he must have been working on "Sliver of Sky," and it occurs to me what a profound capacity for intimacy he was showing when he must have been at his most frightened, or exposed. Sometimes he typed the letters, and they had the peculiar juxtaposition of his vulnerability and charm with the staunch forward, stamped march of the keystrokes.

Then in 2013, I was standing, uneasily, in a blazer, at the National Arts Club in New York, where Barry's book editor, Robin Desser—one of the great forces in American cultural life—was receiving the Maxwell Perkins Award for her tremendous work over the years as an editor. Barry spotted me, and before I could come over and think about what to say about "Sliver of Sky," he was up and out of his chair and we hugged, and I realized how deep our connection had already gone. He was a great hugger. An embracer. There was force and surrender in equal measures.

We stood for an hour, during cocktails, against a wall, talking, comparing notes as two self-identified Westerners in what felt like a very East Coast literary night. Those were poses—he'd gone to an Upper East Side prep school; I'd spent time in places like this—but they felt important to both of us. It was a distrust of institutions, partly. Also of the indoors. As much love as he felt for Robin, Barry didn't want to be in such places. He hated them; he felt they turned you into a reputation and a name, and time there led to vanity and bad manners. He told me once, much later, about going to a similar such dinner on a similar such night when no one stood up when he approached a table of luminaries—all but the notable crank, novelist William Gaddis, who stood and shook his hand and commended Barry on *Arctic Dreams,* calling it "a great book," a comment that mattered to Barry.

He told me that night in 2013 he had prostate cancer. It was already stage four. For the rest of our meetings, we'd have this talk—how he was doing, what the treatments were like. It was not the main conversation, or even the secondary conversation, but it became, to some small degree, how we planned meetings. And I call them this because one scaffolding protecting us was to call what we were doing interviews. That this was all part of an endless interview.

The interview went on so long, though, the magazine that originally commissioned it went under. The deadline for its inclusion in a book blew away like tumbleweed. And still we kept on talking. We kept visiting the landscapes and places that mattered to him: New York City and the Hudson; Oregon and the McKenzie; West Texas and its dry grandeur; California and its light bouncing off the Bay.

At some point, we simply stopped recording what we said and got together. We sat down and had meals. He told me things I won't repeat here. I felt myself change under the protection of his fond regard and discretion, permitted a seriousness I did not feel I had earned. Do I need to say how hard it is to find unguarded friendships with men as a man? How frequently what begins safely can become a kind of replication pattern—a mirror to the past? What if you get lost in that maze? Given his past, Barry never in my presence gestured toward these patterns. There were bigger concerns. Driving in 2015 across the plains in Texas, filling me in on his latest treatment, he paused—and then, immediately, caught himself—and redirected to appreciate that he could have such phenomenally expensive drugs while so many could have none.

Give it time, and water builds our world, patiently, sometimes ferociously—without it, there's no life, and in its reflection, sometimes, we see ourselves. Lopez's patience, his deliberation, and his ability to see his life like a landscape allowed him to become a conduit in others' search. In this, he became a crucial land bridge between the early North American explorers who, filled with wonder and notions of Christian dominion, wreaked terrible destruction, and the precarious future their encounters seeded. Lopez put the moral responsibilities of this original meeting in human scale, replaying it, trying to fathom whether we were doomed to replay our patterns—or if we could find other, more subtle patterns.

The emotional power of Barry's short stories emerged from the tension this awareness of the past's eternal dangers produced. In *Winter Count*, and *Light Action in the Caribbean*, Lopez set his heroes—and they're often men—into landscapes charged with beauty, wracked with exploitation. His vision of the short story was huge, nonfictional, stuffed with the past. There's a reason his heroes were often historians, researchers, specialists in archive work. He wanted to make fiction that touched the world of ten thousand things but made room for the past and its reckoning.

Lopez's equal sensitivity to the vast lacunae that exist in human knowledge and his grasp for what has been assembled made him an extraordinary guide, a lamplight in a world made by destruction; in this spirit he wrote his great book-length essay, *The Rediscovery of North America*, gave birth to dozens of fictional characters existing on this precipice—a moral one, he would argue. Between states of being.

In a world seemingly defined through forms of chaos and exploitation we cannot stop, or sometimes even fathom, Barry was a poet of questions. They are what would save us, he often said in passing. I often wonder if that was why we conducted so much of our friendship in dialogue. What aren't we asking? he often wanted to know, breaking into a kind of reverie. How does this journey through life change a person? What are the pleasures of collaborating with people in search of such engagement? What exactly causes our despair? Is there a way we could conceive of knowledge that didn't include extraction and violence? Was friendship one form of knowledge?

These were the questions driving Lopez's last book, *Horizon*, which wrestled again and again with the frames we've put around the grand questions humans often pose of ourselves. Who are we? Why are we here? What is good? What is justice? Gestated, he told me, for twenty-five years, written over the last five of his life, *Horizon* narrated with restorative complexity a traveler's life in search of better ways to understand the umbrella such questions make.

What a lot of ground it covered. A partial list of coordinates from which Lopez's dispatches emerged includes the Bering Strait, West Antarctica, Cape Foulweather, Botany Bay, Afghanistan, Kenya, Tasmania, the Falkland Islands, South Georgia, Idaho, Auschwitz, the Canadian Arctic, the Grand Canyon, New York City, and—vicariously—the Mariana Trench, some seven miles beneath the surface of the ocean.

Threading these journeys together were stories of fellow seekers, not just the archaeologists and paleobotanists and biologists and field guides over whose shoulders Lopez gently peers, but the lives of explorers themselves. Figures like Columbus, or Captain James Cook, whose legacy and achievements Lopez measures with monumental clarity, as well as lesser-known figures, like Ranald MacDonald, a mestizo explorer who managed to gain entry to Japan when it was a closed society.

Each long chapter pried open vast, almost Bierstadtian—minus the assumption of dominion—space. Acres of storytelling made three-dimensional by Lopez's evocations of history, Native culture, personal anecdote, and exquisite sensory detail. If anything else, the book revealed Lopez the seer coming home. What a palette! Prune, oxidized copper, the white of church linen, beryl green . . . Not to mention Lopez's enormous, sensuous, and often antique vocabulary: who in their recent Scrabble game has deployed *xeric, rill, talus, tombolo*? Buoying us across oceans of time and spaces we took too much for granted, Lopez ended his life in books as a navigator, out on the water itself. Our navigator in a time looking for one.

It wasn't his last work, though, not even close. The last time we saw each other in person was in Berkeley, over tacos. He was coming to grips with the fact that his days of traveling might be over. Even if he wanted to dream of one last cross-country road journey. Maybe with a sparrow. The bird had been another friend's idea. Barry would drive from Florida to Oregon. He would do it alone. It wouldn't be an expedition, just a coda—a return to the small scale of his Jeep-bound travel that had provoked *Desert Notes*.

He liked symmetries, returns. He never got that coveted orbit, back to *Desert Notes,* but he did achieve another. In the last year of his life, he spent his time writing about other people's work. He wrote five forewords for five different books by other people, some he didn't even know, a final dip into his well of generosity. It was a late burst, this series of essays, which fanned out to contemplate respect for the knowledge of Indigenous people, landscape, the power of photography, and yes, for water. In the final piece published in his lifetime, just days before he died, he mused on the connection between love and water. How the latter often brought animals together, and how if you were quiet and respectful, you might get to observe them from an unharmful distance, a microcosm of the "incomprehensible privilege" of being alive. He saw it early in that shimmering, cord, and never stopped; he found a million ways to express his love to the world. Some of it is in books. The rest of that great aquifer is all of ours now.

ELEVATION

PICO IYER

January 2006, the Key West Literary Seminar. I find myself onstage with Barry Lopez, a longtime hero whom I've never met until this week. Our moderator, Michael Shapiro, offers a rich and eloquent introduction about the differences between us and then asks me how travel might be akin to love.

I offer a very quick answer, throwing off ideas like fireworks, about attention and transformation and surrender, and mentioning all the zany signs I've seen around Key West. Not least a store that says, "Sorry, We're Open!"

The audience bursts into happy laughter and then Barry begins to speak: patiently, very slowly, in precise and intricate sentences. He speaks of "profound and common compassion for the predicament and challenge of being fully human." He speaks of a "tremendous longing" among us all "to be touched and to be known." He speaks of vulnerability and trust.

Instantly, I'm brought to attention and humbled. This is a rare chance, his gentle and thoughtful words might be reminding me, to share something sustaining that will leave all of us with something true before we disperse. We're beings of weight, of responsibility; let's use this invitation to speak with intimacy, so that maybe this entire community can be brought closer to its better self.

It was just the voice of conscience and rigor I'd met for decades already on the page. Reading Barry, I'd always imagined someone who was part priest and part explorer. The light within was what guided him, and the light without was what he wished to bring us to. Grace and discovery were the engines, and better action the destination. In his collection of stories *Light Action in the Caribbean*, I'd read of a wounded character on retreat in a monastery, fashioning a thing of beauty, a small three-masted boat; at some level, that was how I always saw this uncommonly searching and self-questioning soul, working tirelessly to turn his spiritual reflections into art.

Barry was accompanied, that week in Key West, by one of his radiant daughters, Stephanie, so I could also see the warm companion and counselor in him. But what moved me most was to realize that the man and the writer were of a piece, inseparable; both were committed to the undistracted penetration that makes for a kinder world. Waking us up was a large part of what he was doing.

That would always be an invigorating goal, but as the world rushes toward ever more diversion, forgetfulness, and carelessness, Barry's special gifts—of deliberation, of meticulous care, and of sobriety—come to seem more and more bracing. In my mind he was traveling widely, to forgotten places across the globe, with a searchlight, like some archaeologist of the inner landscape, hoping to remind us of what we could be. Working, in effect, to bring us back to our senses.

Nine years on, Barry and I met again on that same stage in Key West, and this time I was ready. I hadn't enjoyed—and surely won't enjoy—many chances, ever, to engage in a real talk in public that has the closeness of a private conversation; it's not often one can share what one cares about most and know that someone else will listen, understand, and respond in kind.

In a crowded greenroom at the beginning of the week, Barry had taken me aside to tell me, quietly, that he was very sick. But that was not, he added, something we needed to worry about. He had deposited in his New York editor's office a large book, with instructions that she not read it for now. I couldn't find the words to tell him that I had sent a link of our first talk onstage to that same editor, the only such gift I'd inflicted on her in our thirty-four years of friendship.

Today, a writer who was in the hall that day in 2015 sends me the news that Barry is gone, along with a link to an interview that reminds us both that Barry will never really be gone. In it he describes being invited to deliver a lecture at an Athenaeum in New England and asking his host what Emerson had sought when he had done the same.

"Elevation," came the answer. That part, I felt, Barry had mastered long since.

We'd met only three times in all when we converged in Key West that final time. But after I'd gone onstage to say a few words, and returned to my seat, Barry smiled, patted me warmly on the arm, and said, "I'm so proud to be your friend." As ever, he was giving me a model for what I would wish to write to him.

THE BLACKPOLL'S SURGE OF SONG

GRETEL EHRLICH

The winters in the 1980s were cold and hard, and the end-of-the-road mountain ranch where my then husband and I lived was almost impossible to access between December and April. When Barry called and said he wanted to visit that February day, we were snowed in. Almost. Our only transportation was a team of horses and our hay wagon, so we harnessed up and started down the road, a tipsy-turvy ribbon pocked with hardpacked snowdrifts and deep, snow-filled troughs between. The horses—two big Belgians—managed. Barry would be our only winter visitor for eleven years.

The "we" I refer to is Press, my ex. He and Barry had worked together at the Triangle X Ranch in Moran, Wyoming, owned by the Turner Family. (My father had also worked there as a young man with the previous generation of Turners—Louise and her father, the Captain.) Barry and Press quickly found friendship while wrangling horses on the big, grassy pastures overlooking the Snake River and the Tetons. Both had curious, well-educated intellects; both were fervently dedicated to understanding the intricacies of the natural world and preserving wild lands and animals.

I don't remember exactly how that day went, once we had put the horses away. I made dinner and a pie in the wood cookstove, and we talked about birds, coyotes, grasses, horses, arrowheads, and the Ordovician rimrock towering above our ranch that held sponges from what had once been a shallow sea. I was just finishing writing *The Solace of Open Spaces*, and Barry had *Desert Notes*, *Of Wolves and Men*, *River Notes*, and *Winter Count* under his belt. But I doubt that we talked about writing. Our mutual curiosity took us outside: We tromped through snow and wondered which tribes of Native Americans had used the place as an "arrowhead factory" and in which season. We tried to re-imagine how we might have lived in this place as subsistence hunters. We tracked wildlife—elk and deer—and before dusk, which came early, at 4:30 p.m., we checked water gaps where the horses and cattle drank, then hurried inside and built fires in the woodstoves as the temperature dropped to twenty below.

Right away I saw how patient Barry was. He was an ardent observer, but quiet about it. Step by step, he overlooked nothing. We showed him the brachiopods and Ordovician sponges, Lakota arrowhead chips—handfuls of them—and native grass species we'd restored to the ranch by planning grazing with cattle and horses. We laid out taped-together topographical maps of the Bighorn Mountains and its foothills, draws and drainages, the remnants of hanging glaciers, waterfalls, and the Medicine Wheel up top, where I'd tended sheepherders' camps in the 1970s. We ID'ed birds and animal tracks. Looked at the stars that night, the fast-moving drawing sticks of meteors blazing by.

Later I saw that curiosity and precision in his prose, too. One inquiry after another, the riprap of questions layered up until he stopped in his tracks and dove down to the beginning again. Deeply attentive, he was devoted to detail, as if turning every found object over and over in his hand, never dropping it back to the ground.

The next time I saw Barry, we were on our way to accept awards at the American Academy of Arts and Letters on the old Audubon farm north of Harlem, New York. My publisher hadn't bothered sending a car for me, so I shared a ride with Barry. On arrival at the all-day gala, we were met by paparazzi, but they looked baffled when we got out of our limos. They didn't know who was who—this was before the endless parade of self-promotion on Instagram—and we went on our way unbothered, happy that we could continue to wander the world anonymously.

Those first two visits turned into a loose thread of connections. At a fun-filled gathering of nature writers in Jackson Hole, Wyoming, we teased Barry about taking too many "earnest pills." He smiled. It was a loving, respectful tease, but perhaps he was too serious-minded to laugh. Or maybe he was just fatigued: he'd begun traveling incessantly. I'm not sure how he planned his peregrinations and managed to hook up with various scientists going somewhere interesting, or what exactly propelled him from one place to another, but from his early essays, I sensed an acceleration taking place. At first, he stayed local, looking at geese and horses and mountains. But when he went to the Brooks Range in Alaska, an explicit and lifelong inquiry arose. The extraordinary beauty, harshness, and remoteness of those places caused him to ponder the outer and the inner landscape. In his essay "Landscape and Narrative," he writes, "what makes the landscape comprehensible are the relationships . . . One learns a landscape finally not by knowing the name or identity of everything in it, but by perceiving the relationships in it—like that between the sparrow and the twig."

He went on to consider the way mind is shaped by the land and its interconnections as it constantly unfolded before one's feet. He considered "the line of a falling leaf" and "a blackpoll's burst of song," as well as the feeling of granite and humidity, and how each affects the other; how every element shapes the mind—what might be called one's internal weather. He writes: "The interior landscape responds to the character and subtlety of an exterior landscape; the shape of the individual mind is affected by land as it is by genes."

In magnificent early works, especially *Crossing Open Ground*, *Desert Notes*, and *Of Wolves and Men*, Barry dove deeply into the uses and influences of

Indigenous cosmology, especially the Navajo sense of "sacred order," ritual, and ceremony, storytelling, and the innate harmony within the natural world. Moral imperatives were implicit; storytelling was a social obligation. He reiterated all the way through his last work, *Embrace Fearlessly the Burning World*, the importance of prayer-like attention and free-form ceremony in life and in writing.

Barry's style expanded from concise but eclectic stories and observations to much longer disquisitions, often returning to the various fonts that most deeply inspired him: Alaska, the Antarctic, Nunavut, home. Often, he stepped outside his ongoing narrative to explain: a point of view, an instruction, a request for the reader to ask the same questions he was asking himself: *Where am I? What is this place? Who am I in it?* "This is what I am doing," Barry seemed to be saying; "This is why it's important." Perhaps it was the Catholic education that began in early school all the way through college that propelled him to teach in this way. In *Crossing Open Ground*, the essays about his travels in Alaska—the Brooks Range, Yukon-Charley, and the eastern Arctic coast—are particularly dense and rich in the ways he reminds us to let sights and sounds and stories heal and illuminate our troubled lives.

In the mid-1980s, Barry began his long sojourns to the Arctic. He took the writer N. Scott Momaday's words to heart: He gave himself up to a particular landscape; he looked at it from many angles, he wondered about it, and dwelled upon it. In the preface to *Arctic Dreams*, Barry thought about the polar explorer Edward Israel, who was on the ill-fated 1881 Greely Expedition to Ellesmere Island. After seeing Israel's gravestone, he wrote: "Perhaps he merely hungered after the unusual. We can only imagine that he desired something, the fulfillment of some personal and private dream, to which he pinned his life." Thus, the full title of the work, *Arctic Dreams: Imagination and Desire in a Northern Landscape*.

Further along in the preface, Barry described his own mind: "full of curiosity and analysis, disassembles a landscape and then reassembles the pieces—the nod of a flower, the color of the night sky, the murmur of an animal—trying to fathom its geography." Then adds: the "difficulty in evaluating, or even discerning, a particular landscape is related to the distance a culture has traveled from its own ancestral landscape." Barry continued to undertake these discoveries with ferocity, exhaustively so. "Get on with the story, Barry," I'd say to him whenever we happened to meet, and we'd both laugh.

My own Arctic travels began in 1991, five years after *Arctic Dreams* had been published. At the end of a month's stay at a seal biologist's camp in Nunavut, I was urged by the marine ecologist Brendan Kelly to go to Greenland. "If you want to see a true, intact Arctic culture, you have to go to northern Greenland. In the midst of modernity, their language and traditional lifeways are still there," Brendan told me. So, I went to Greenland. Barry had written majestically about the entire history of the Arctic, but Nunavut and the European expeditions of "discovery" whose arrogance caused the explorers' deaths didn't interest me. I wanted simply to travel with subsistence Inuit hunters who had taken what they wanted of the modern world, and had chosen to live and travel in ways not much different from their lifeways a thousand years ago. I went to Greenland alone, and they kindly let me travel with them.

All that Barry had so eloquently spoken about was implicit there. Intentional living and moral imperatives kept the Inuit's small societies humming. As the sea ice kept failing, as early as 1993, 1994, and 1995, I went to the two northernmost villages and traveled with one extended family for twenty spring and summer seasons. While Barry covered the entire North American part of the polar north, I homed in on a single Greenlandic coast with a family of four men and their wives, resulting in my book *This Cold Heaven: Seven Seasons in Greenland*. Later, as the sea ice disintegrated and with it the extraordinary Arctic cultures and icescapes we had both encountered, Barry and I compared notes sitting by a roaring fire in the lobby of the Four Seasons Resort in Jackson Hole on a thirty-degree-below-zero winter evening. In that luxurious place we acknowledged two realities: that climate is culture, that extinction is real.

Somewhere Barry commented that his aim was to "think wisely about what we're doing on this planet." Perhaps that's what kept pushing him in his intense searches, from the Arctic to the Antarctic, Africa, Tasmania, Australia, Chile, Tierra del Fuego, and Finn Rock where, sadly and ironically, climate-driven Oregon fires burned his own home. His later books take us back to some of those places but with such new research and insights, they seem completely new. He gazed at the planet and its inhabitants from every angle, as well as at his own experience of being alive in so many places, and ultimately, with a bad diagnosis, knowing he would soon die. The compelling question for him was: What will it take for our civilization to survive? Or, as he puts it in his foreword to the anthology *Hearth: A Global Conversation on Community, Identity, and Place:* "What is the modern pivot for these values of love, comity, and courage needed to face the outer dark?"

Barry's essays are like hailstones crashing to Earth, melting in a little cup of soil, providing water and a safe place for a seed to germinate and flower. He asked and asked and asked: *How should we behave here?* He fussed and needled himself and others to get to where he wanted to go, and once there, fussed some more, turning things over and over in his hands, always perfecting his mind. How did he do it? How did he keep his dedication and precision so sharp?

A conference in Seattle in 2014 would be my final time seeing Barry. The organizers had asked Neal Conan—war correspondent, news analyst, and host of NPR's *Talk of the Nation*—to interview Barry and me together. They didn't realize that Neal was my husband. (Always a professional, Neal never revealed to me what his questions might be.) I recall reading from my recent *Harper's Magazine* essay about the consequences of failing sea ice. Barry kept steering the conversation in a different direction. He talked of Native American ceremony, community, and compassion. He was dying and he knew it. Unbeknownst to us, my husband, Neal, was dying too, though from a different form of cancer, and would pass away seven months after Barry.

That night, in a large hall, Barry leapfrogged over my pessimism. I couldn't help my dark view: I'd experienced firsthand, on a dogsled, the end of ice and understood exactly how the Arctic's albedo tempers the climate of the rest of the world, leading to drought, famine, and thirst when it becomes compromised. Barry had other ideas of how to see things. He looked beyond the radical actions that must take place to save our civilization and returned to square one: facing one's own death. Sometime that evening, in a quiet voice, he asked an approximation of the question posed in his final book: "Is it still possible to face the gathering darkness and say to the physical Earth, and to all its creatures, including ourselves, fiercely and without embarrassment, I love you, and to embrace fearlessly the burning world?"

THE OCEANIC *I AM*

On Literary & Geographical Influence, Salmon as Isumataq,
Barry as Blesser, Ocean as Destiny & Death's Inability to Kill a Battlefield I Am

DAVID JAMES DUNCAN

I.

The ways in which writers influence other writers is a mysterious business.
Among the writers I know best, influence has varied from outright imitation in their early years, to impulses so subtle, variegated, or quicksilver as
to be impossible to accurately describe. When writers are contemporaries,
and come to know and read one another, influence can also become a
two-way street with no speed limit, traffic signals, or center line. Other
writers I've known make a habit of being so outraged by the work of certain
other writers that they compose books bent on destroying the offender's
reputation, in one case I know of with such vehemence as to contribute to
the loss of a worthy author's life.

Such confustications and vendettas lead me to thank heaven for writers
whose works influence us in a beneficent manner, sometimes nudging us
toward writing in ways we may never have imagined without our inspirer.

Barry Lopez has done this for droves of us, and so the question naturally arises: *How was one man able to inspire so many?*

I trust Barry's own answer to this question. "As I see it," he wrote in the afterword to his 2014 short-story collection, *Outside,*

> the same handful of questions I possessed about the meaning of human life when I was a young writer have remained with me. These concerns, about personal identity, for example, or the ethereal dimensions of reality, are now, I hope, simply more nuanced, more informed.
>
> When I write a story, I am not trying to make a point or demonstrate any particular proficiency as a writer. I am trying to make the patterns of American cultural life more apparent . . . patterns that I hope will serve the reader's own search for meaning. In the creation of the story, it is the reader's welfare, not the life of the writer, that is finally central.

Barry's insistence on the centrality of the reader's welfare has been a steady guiding light. So has a truth he brought south from elders in the Arctic: that of the *isumataq,* the Inuktitut word for one whose stories simply create an atmosphere in which wisdom reveals itself. The writer who uses their story, memoir, poem to dump their notion of wisdom upon us has forgotten that wisdom lives, hidden, inside the reader, from whence only they can free it. An isumataq knows otherwise. No writer has ever bequeathed me a more invaluable aspiration.

Once Barry and I met, performed a few readings together, and became friends, we did not so much influence as reinforce each other when we discovered mutual passions, a big one being our home waters and their denizens, which was ever the McKenzie and its salmon for Barry, and perhaps ten rivers—coastal, mountain, and desert—in my more polyamorous relationship with Pacific-bound flows.

A surprise to me in undertaking this essay was discovering in the *Oxford English Dictionary* how strongly the definitions of *influence* relate to Barry's and my river love. The noun *influence* (to paraphrase) is defined as *the inflow of a divine or secret truth*; as *the force flowing in thus*; or as *an action exerted imperceptibly, or by indirect means, by one person or thing upon another, so as to cause changes in conduct, in what unfolds, or in overall conditions.* And influence, the verb, means *to cause to flow in; infuse, instill.* While researching an upcoming novel, I invited scores of wisdom texts, including major works by several thirteenth- and fourteenth-century Beguine women mystics, to flow into me and instill what they would. But I did not expect *OED* definitions of *influence* to sound so riverine and mystical as to remind me of this passage from the Beguine, Marguerite Porete's, Catholic Church–condemned classic, *The Mirror of Simple Souls*:

> God has transformed the soul of Himself for the soul's sake into His goodness.
> And if she is thus encumbered in all aspects, she loses her name, for she rises in sovereignty. She loses her name in the One in whom she is melted and dissolved, through Himself and in Himself, becoming like a body of water that once began in the sea and now returns toward the sea, bearing some name such as Aisne or Seine, losing her course and her name as she enters the Unbounded Sea.

Toward the end of Barry's life, Porete's words brought home not only how carried away we often were by our home waters, but how being carried away may offer an ultimate end to river-lovers unimaginably greater than our mere human mortality.

Barry had this to say about his beloved McKenzie River:

> To stick your hands into the river is to feel the cords
> that bind the earth together in one piece.

And he said this of our wonder species, salmon: "The world of variables salmon are alert to, to which they respond, is astonishingly complex. The closer we look the more we see the individual animal is a reflection of the organization of energy around it. To try to understand the animal apart from its background—except as an imaginative exercise—is to risk the collapse of both." I would add that wild salmon are isumataqs: To witness closely their migration and total self-sacrifice to create tiny silver offspring is to experience salvific wisdom alive in running water. Barry felt this so strongly that he couldn't sleep during the McKenzie's modest fall salmon run if he didn't first check on the adult chinook that reproduced in the side channel closest to his home.

Because our friendship was often conducted in *Salmon Speak*, he also knew that, on my Rocky Mountain streams, I was losing sleep over the spring and summer chinook that had ceased coming home to their birth houses because their migratory passage has been chopped into eight fatally overheated reservoirs by gigantic dams. Because those Rocky Mountain salmon are indispensable to the diet of orcas, impending extinction is also speeding toward the southern Puget Sound killer-whale pods a thousand and more miles away. If you have not made a study of the grief-shattered orca mother, Tahlequah, who with the help of her loving pod carried her dead and disintegrating calf a thousand miles around the Salish Sea for seventeen days, you have missed a tragedy more poignant than any by Shakespeare or the ancient Greeks.

This might be the place to admit that educating your wild heart teaches, in the words of Saint Benedict, that *Amor ipse intellectus est*: "Love itself is knowledge." But it's also the place to admit that love for salmon and orcas in our current world teaches, as the poet Stanley Kunitz wrote, that *in a murderous time / the heart breaks and breaks / and lives by breaking.*

II.

While I loved nearly everything Barry wrote, I'm going to confine my exploration of his literary influence to two short stories. I found the first, "The Interior of North Dakota," in a 1992 issue of *The Paris Review*. The story is modest in length, perhaps three thousand words. It situates the narrator in a landscape in which communion with the land becomes so powerful as to be life-endangering, not just due to the possible harms of the wild, but out of possible extremities of joy—for me, a stunningly influential idea. Wrote Lopez, in the piece:

> One morning, feeling somewhat apprehensive . . . , I walked east along the Heart (River). . . . I then headed south toward the Bergdorf Hills. I'd not gone very far before I felt I could go no farther. The character of the land had changed distinctly in less than a mile. It had risen up gleaming, like a painting stripped of grime, the prairie color richer, the air more prismatic. The smell of sun-warmed grasses and brush had become dense and fresh. I was still eager to go on, but in the face of this intensification I felt like an interloper . . . I withdrew because it was so obvious to me that I was unprepared. I was also afraid. The vividness of the land was intimidating, almost overwhelming. It had in every detail the penetrating aura, the immediacy, the insistence of a creature viewed through ground glass. . . .

This passage landed in my wheelhouse for several reasons. The uncanniest is the resemblance between the trajectory of Barry's central character and that of my own life. During my forty years in Oregon, desert river canyons, high mountain wilderness, and coastal headlands like Cape Foulweather all struck me as places of "unreasonable extent"—of both magic and terror—and I was drawn to them early. At age eight, I fell for northeast Oregon's Wallowa Lake and pined to know the mountains that towered over it. At nine, I fell for desert canyons the first time I fished the Deschutes River with my father. At eighteen, I was moved to erase the dark influences of my Vietnam War–era public high school by immersing myself in a wild landscape: the day after I graduated, I hiked to a lake in the Cascades where I camped for ten days, fasted for seven, pored over three volumes of wisdom literature throughout the fast—and, by damn, along with thirty pounds of body weight the negative high school influences *were* erased. At nineteen, I fulfilled my early Wallowa yearning by landing a job that allowed me to spend a hundred days, most of them alone, at a small cabin on Aneroid

Lake, 7,500 feet up in the Wallowa Mountains miles from any roads, again carrying wisdom literature with me, opening up more landscapes and inscapes. These experiences made some characters in Barry's early stories not just characters, but familiars I invited deep into my psyche. And this influence continues.

In my novel, *Sun House*, what distinguishes one of my narrator's places of pilgrimage is high elevation. All those years ago, high in the Wallowas, I grew to love the way the lack of oxygen forced slower, more deliberate movement, and the way straining upward created thirst, forcing me to my hands and knees to sip some of the purest water on Earth because it had become an indigen—Latin root of *indigeny*, meaning simply "a need." I came to cherish the indigenous summer aridity, relentless clarity of air, much deeper blue of the sky. I loved the overabundant light in the great batholith's vertiginous landscape of white marble and off-white granite; the scarcely believable intensity with which wildflowers, aquatic insects, and other life-forms proliferate in the brief high-elevation summer; the intricacy of tiny streams on ground so high that their branching rills, right at my feet, looked like river deltas viewed from a jet. And somehow I knew, like Barry's nameless narrator in "The Interior of North Dakota," that I was striking not gold but some more invaluable magic.

III.

Shortly after Barry departed this life, I was flooded with memories of the time we'd spent together at the Orion Society's Millennial gathering near Shepherdstown, West Virginia. The event featured three solid days of testimony by scores of writers, scientists, and poets, most of them expressing grief for the irreversible abuse being suffered by the planet and accelerating loss of species. It was all so overwhelming that it felt appropriate to spend our fourth and final evening on the Antietam National Battlefield where, on a pleasant September day in 1862, young men in a single country that had divided like a cell donned Union blue and Confederate gray uniforms, obeyed orders to attack one another, and inflicted 22,717 casualties in 12 hours, leaving 3,654 dead, 1,771 missing or captured, thousands of parents grief smashed, young wives widowed, children orphaned, and horses and mules and God knows who and what else slaughtered.

As Barry and I strolled the battlefield together, bewildered that a place so lovely had ever staged such carnage, we said next to nothing, the number 22,717 being the only comment needed. Then Antietam offered us a surprise. As we approached a long row of carefully preserved cannons, a robin shot between our shoulders and disappeared down a cannon barrel. We exchanged a stunned look, turned to the cannon, and stood motionless and silent so as not to disturb whatever was happening. When the robin, a female, flew back out into sunlight and away, how strange it was to watch Barry place his face squarely in a cannon barrel, peer into its depths, turn to me with a half-exultant, half-crushed smile, and, with a little sweep of the hand, invite me to look.

As my eyes adjusted to the dark, I spied the cause of Barry's expression: an iron-cooled mud bowl of a nest in which five pale-blue eggs emitted an almost bioluminescent glow. We stepped a few yards away, waited for the mother bird to return to her repurposed cannon, and commended her on her life-giving new breed of cannonball.

For the four prior days of the Millennial gathering, my feelings of grief and gratitude had been taking polite turns. Beginning with those miniature pale-blue cannonballs, grief and gratitude fused and a great pressure began to build like a thunderhead inside me.

As dusk descended upon Antietam, the hundreds of Orion attendees gathered on a small hillside facing a lit stage. As grace would have it, the Jesuit-trained non-Jesuit, Barry; the Mormon-raised non-Mormon, Terry Tempest Williams; and the Adventist-raised Adventist apostate, me, found ourselves huddled together on the grass as the air cooled. Though a program of music and poetry commenced, we three couldn't take our eyes off the hundreds of fireflies rising from the broad field like (pick your poison) the departing souls of thousands of vanquished soldiers, or of thousands of vanquished species. The grief/gratitude thunderhead continued to build.

When an Orion Society emcee invited the celebrants to observe a half hour of silence, I realized I was in trouble. In certain conditions, thirty minutes of silence can be almost unbearable—say, when robin-egg cannonballs, an interior thunderhead, and the silence of so many burgeoning wounded hearts converge.

A few minutes into the silence, Barry surprised me by taking my hand and holding it. Not till he did so, and I felt his steadiness, did I realize I'd been trembling. Seeing what he'd done, Terry placed both our hands on her knee, then laid her hand over ours. I was already pretty far gone when the solace of touch from two humans I adore threw me into the deep end. No words avail to describe where I landed, but I must say nevertheless: *a still, small voice released two tiny syllables.* A crush of feeling usurped me, the thunderhead released its load, and I began to weep a small ocean, as if to house beloved orcas and salmon, or the world's sorely needed isumataqs. Silence flooded the night, but for two still, small syllables. I welcomed the overwhelm they delivered.

IV.

Long before I met Barry, I was deeply influenced by his short story "The Location of the River" in his 1981 collection, *Winter Count*. I was twenty-nine at the time. The story is narrated by an unnamed twentieth-century scholar enamored of the work of a mid-nineteenth-century historian/anthropologist, Benjamin Foster, who spent much of his life researching Indian tribes still living in the lands they'd inhabited for centuries. I found Barry's story most harrowing when, after grounding itself in a specific Great Plains geography, events befall both the nineteenth-century historian and the twentieth-century narrator that a good Desert Father would term *apophatic*. A few passages from Barry's story set up its *apophasis*—its "unsaying":

> According to a journal kept by Benjamin Foster, a historian returning along the Platte River from the deserts of the Great Basin at the time, the spring of 1844 came early to western Nebraska. . . . This

unseasonable good weather induced him to stay a few weeks with a
band of Pawnee camped just south of the Niobrara River. One morning he volunteered to go out with two men to look for stray horses.
They found the horses grazing near an island of oak and ash trees
on the prairie, along the edge of the river. . . .

On the way back, writes Foster . . . (one of) the Pawnee told him
that the previous summer the upper Niobrara had disappeared.

At first Foster took this for a figurative statement about a severe
drought, but the other Pawnee told him, no, the Niobrara had not
run dry. . . . It disappeared. That Foster took this information seriously, that he did not treat it with skepticism or derision, was characteristic of him.

In the story, the narrator wonders whether the Pawnee were literally
correct—"that sometime during the summer of 1843 the upper reaches of
the Niobrara River, above the present town of Marshland and westward
into Wyoming, did vanish for four or five months"—or whether the people
Foster camped with were not actually Pawnee, but instead the imposters
whom Foster detailed in other writings, playing out "a rite of imitation
in which a band of people from one tribe, Arikara, for example, would
imitate a band from some other tribe for long periods of time, fifteen
years or more."

The Niobrara's disappearance stopped me in my tracks when I first read
the story forty years ago. In my novel, *Sun House*, Barry's Arikara tricksters
have resurfaced as secretive high-elevation pilgrims known as the Lûmi,
whose cosmology came to me in a lucid dream. The Lûmi are contemporary to our time; they live in select North American mountain ranges five
months of the year, and then dissolve, incognito, into the low-elevation
populace during the months of snow.

Elevation creates things, and uncreates other things, including, as in
"The Location of the River," "the crushing loads of crap we think we know."
In the piece, Barry's twentieth-century narrator learns that Foster spent
three decades with six or seven tribes, staying with each for years before

moving on, taking richly detailed field notes that he'd deposit "periodically at various American and British trading posts for safekeeping, intending one day to collect them all." However, this never came to pass:

> This is what [Foster] was doing in 1844 when he was waylaid by the Pawnee and good weather. He had eleven pack mules with him at the time, all of them burdened with manuscripts. . . . He was en route to Kansas City, where the great trading family of Chouteau had offered him money for publication. . . . It is one of the great tragedies of American history that he did not arrive and that his manuscripts were ruined. .
>
> In late June 1844, after Foster had begun to despair of ever understanding either the fact or the meaning of the disappearance of the river, after a time of ritual cleansing and dreaming, perhaps agoraphobic or maddened by the interweaving of literalisms and metaphors and forms of proof, Foster began throwing his manuscripts into the river.

Eventually, after Foster, wading into the Niobrara naked each afternoon, had jettisoned all of his writings into its waters, "he went away to the north, 'like a surprised grouse whirring off across the prairie,'" per a Pawnee named Wolf Finger who had borne witness to the events.

The apophatic impact of this ending is total. But Barry, with ferocity, doubles down on it. More than a hundred years after Foster unsays himself and his work, his narrator ends "The Location of the River" with this harrowing experience:

> What was left of these documents came into my hands through my father, a tax assessor. He found them in a barn near Lusk, Wyoming, in 1901. . . .
>
> In an attempt to understand what little Foster had written down about the disappearance of the Niobrara . . . I visited that part of the state in 1963. I stayed in a small hotel, the Plainview, in the

town of Box Butte. I had with me all of Foster's water-stained notes, which I had spread around the room and was examining again for perhaps the hundredth time. During the night a tremendous rainstorm broke over the prairie. The Niobrara threatened to flood and I was awakened by the motel operator. I drove across the river—in the cone of my headlights I could see the fast brown water surging against the bridge supports—and spent the rest of the night in my car on high ground, at some distance from the town, in some hills the name of which I do not remember. In the morning I became confused on farm roads and was unable to find my way back to the river. In desperation I stopped at a place I recognized having been at the day before and proceeded from there on foot toward the river, until I became lost in the fields themselves. I met a man on a tractor who told me the river had never come over in that direction. Ever. And to get away.

I have not been back in that country since.

It is necessary to define words, but also at times to undefine them. One of my aims as a writer is apophatic, from the Greek *apophasis*. An apophasis is *an unsaying:* a negation of an accepted definition or truth. In what Barry's twentieth-century narrator calls "one of the great tragedies of American history," Benjamin Foster chucks his painstakingly researched manuscripts into the Niobrara, unsaying even brilliant anthropological knowledge of the Plains tribes. Why? Perhaps because anthropology, a supposed "Enlightenment" discipline of eighteenth-century Europe claimed that reason, by following defined principles, had the power to comprehend human behavior and advance knowledge, yet this vaunted discipline was brought to the Plains by the same America that by 1844 was annihilating the tribes with viciously deliberate incomprehension while stealing and killing everything these tribes had and were.

Each story in *Winter Count* is headed by an illustration. The illustration for "The Location of the River" is a torn fragment of paper hovering beneath a cloud, containing nothing but this handwritten unsaying penned by Foster himself:

that I got everything wrong

A resounding *apophasis*. To what end? The anonymous author of the spiritual classic *The Cloud of Unknowing* deploys apophasis to say this: "No one can truly think of God. It is therefore my wish to leave everything that I can think and choose for my love the thing that I cannot think. God can be loved but not thought. He can be taken and held by love, but not by thought." I feel Barry doing for the Niobrara and its Indigenous people what *The Cloud* author is doing for God: No one can truly think a river or a people. It is therefore my wish to leave everything that I can think and choose for my love the thing that I cannot think. A river and a people can be loved but not thought. They can be taken and held by love, but not by thought.

In this early story, as so often throughout his life, Barry is attempting to reframe the way our country and world are perceived. *Winter Count*, in the words of the author William Kittredge, "is luminously inhabited by mystery, radiant with possibilities which transcend the defeats we find for ourselves." One of these "defeats" is that rivers *do* disappear, not by mystery but by brutal industrial scheming impervious to thought. Consider the 450 miles of salmon-murdering, salmon-tribe-and-orca-starving slackwaters that were once the free-flowing Snake. Consider the iconic Big Blackfoot of *A River Runs Through It* fame, damned by the Mining Law of 1872 to be savaged by a massive cyanide-heap leach goldmine if it weren't for a ragtag army with no weapons or power but our adamant protest and truthful words. Consider Idaho's wild and scenic Clearwater River, and *again* the Snake, and *again* the Blackfoot, damned in 2010 by ExxonMobil and our fine politicians to serve as the main tentacle connecting the monstrous Alberta tar sands to the eastern Pacific Rim's industrial countries, forcing thousands of people into desperate action and Rick Bass and me to co-write, in seven torrid weeks, a book titled *The Heart of the Monster* after the Nez Perce creation myth (with permission). Our literary Paul Revere ride helped awaken thousands of brave protestors to the fact that the American people's love for wilderness, clean water, and truly wild and scenic rivers cannot coexist with ExxonMobil's greed for tar-sands fuel without Earth's climate going wildly and scenically berserk.

Barry was one of the first of his generation to call for a complete *apophasis* of what we might call the Unrestricted Free Market Exploitation View of the living world. He sounded the same call in his lecture and book, *The Rediscovery of North America*. Please don't laud such men or women as prophets. It only distracts them from being the self-effaced thing itself. Bless their dire unsayings.

V.

The last four days I shared with Barry were at a gathering of writers under the auspices of The Sowell Family Collection in Literature, Community, and the Natural World at Texas Tech University, where our literary papers are housed, and where I experienced Barry as a different man since I'd last seen him.

Still, Barry possessed his lifelong cogency, and his famed determination to get to the bottom of mysteries he hadn't fully grasped. After dinner with a large group of us, it was the cogent Barry who cornered me, laid a firm hand on my shoulder, and announced, "It's time you told me what you were feeling all those years ago at Antietam! You've never said. *Your tears were running down my hands!* What was shaking you so?"

His forcefulness stunned me, but also lifted me. It felt like an honor to have presented such a mind with a mystery it yearned to solve. My memory isn't keen enough to recall just what I said to Barry, but I do know it was an outpouring. And here is what his life, work, and friendship move me to say about that outpouring today:

Barry, we both know you've met people who experience states of consciousness that go places where language cannot follow. And you know I've said that the only mode of expression I have in such places is what we might call *Beyond-Language*. You yourself use Beyond-Language beautifully, as in your essay "Madre de Dios" about your two clear experiences of the Mother of God and in your short story "The Letters of Heaven," which wed eros and sanctity more perfectly than I'd ever seen it done. I'm sure you're familiar with Lao Tzu's lines: *Before heaven and earth came to be, there was something nebulous, silent, isolated, unchanging and alone, eternal, the Mother of All Things. I do not know her name.* This is Beyond-Language. And I have only this language, unknowing, and love with which to tell you this.

As you and Terry and I huddled together in that silence over Antietam, veils somehow lifted, and I felt the Mother of All convey, *IAM*. The walls of my being then expanded out and out toward your beloved "horizon," and it felt as though we three were standing on the wave-crushed south jetty at Astoria, watching the Columbia, the West's Great River, pour miles wide into the Pacific as we were losing our course and our names as we rose in sovereignty, melting into She into whom we are dissolving, now bearing the name *McKenzie*, now *Willamette*, now *Columbia* as we flow toward and into the oceanic Mother whose name we do not know.

EVERY TIME I'M ON THE ROAD

STEPHEN GRAHAM JONES

Every time I'm on the road, Barry Lopez is with me. Because, once, around 2008 or so, he really was. We were in the boarding area of an airport and happened to run into each other. By then, I'd already been hanging out with him for years, so it was cool to see him in whatever the random place was that day.

I wasn't at all new to traveling, then, but neither was I—nor am I now— remotely as well-traveled as Barry. Dude's been everywhere, twice. More than that, he's considered every place he's been. He's noticed things others walk right past, and he's written about them in meaningful ways. For Barry, the world was full of meaning to unpack. But it was also all right just to be in it, to experience it. Not everything has to be a critical engagement.

I was carrying a shoulder bag—one in a long, long line of shoulder bags. This one, though, seemed like a factory second, as it had this weird loop-thing on its back that was maybe an umbrella holder? I decided that the bag had been made for people from the city, who probably always went out into the world with an umbrella. I'd tried to make the weird slide-through loop work to hold an umbrella, and failed, but, too, I'd never actually used an umbrella, right? I imagined that, probably, you didn't close an umbrella all the way when it was wet. If you left its canopy slightly open, then this loop could hold the umbrella while it dried.

City people, right? They're forever a mystery to me.

Anyway, so I'm standing there jawing with Barry about this and that, and I'm eating a bagel or something, and Barry starts digging in his leather duffel bag for . . . I don't remember. Some thing.

Around us, travelers were whisking by, their roller bags humming behind them. I was leaning on mine, handle up, my shoulder bag hooked across my chest. Barry had a roller bag too, which I initially thought odd, as he seemed more like a hardy duffel kind of traveler—wheels on a bag aren't much good in the places he was always going. However, bouncing from city to city for talk after talk, he'd probably decided that wheels were handy, at least for places where there were sidewalks.

I mention all this about bags because that's what this is about.

After Barry was done rooting through his duffel, he held it out over his roller bag with the handle up, and then . . . slid the duffel right onto the roller bag's handle, using a slide-through pocket on the back of the duffel to hang it!

Somehow, in all my travels, all my years, I'd never seen this done. It was, seriously, one of the more amazing moments of my life.

"Wait, what just happened?" I asked Barry.

"Excuse me?" he said, looking around for whatever I was talking about.

It was him I was talking about, though.

"Can I?" I asked.

Hesitantly, maybe not sure exactly what he was getting into here, Barry stepped aside, presented his boring-to-him bag to me.

I slid that duffel up the handle and then let it back down to rest on the flat top of the roller suitcase.

"Seriously?" I said.

Barry, then, realizing what was happening, nodded, grinned, and explained to me how most travel bags have a loop like this. At which point the truly impossible happened: he guided my shoulder bag around to show me how it would fit on my drag-bag.

My heart was beating so hard.

It is again, writing this.

But?

This is what Barry Lopez did, for all of us. This is what he's still doing—he's teaching, he's explaining the world, he's making it fuller, he's showing us the majesty, the mystery, and it's not all about grand vistas and surprising animals. There's majesty and mystery in the smallest, most common-place stuff.

I'm writing this from a hotel room far from home, now.

Coming down the jet bridge a few hours ago, I guided my drag-bag to the side, out of the way of the other passengers, so I could slide my shoulder bag down over the handle, and just glide—practically float—along my journey.

When I stepped aside, too, Barry Lopez was waiting there for me.

He was showing me something I'd never seen.

Thank you, Barry.

Now, let's go see the rest of the world.

THE MAPPIST

ROBERT MACFARLANE

There's a German word, *Totenpass*, which translates into English as "a passport for the dead" or, more figuratively, "a map for the afterlife." It refers to the funerary practice—found across ancient Semitic, Orphic, and Egyptian religions—of burying a set of navigational instructions along with the deceased. These *Totenpässe* include directions for avoiding hazards in the realm of the dead, landmarks to help identify the correct route, and answers to give the judges of the underworld when they question the traveller as to past journeys and future intent. Some of these Totenpässe were pressed onto sheets of thinly beaten gold and placed in the palms of the dead. Others were housed in small boxes made of leather and wood, and left close to the body in the grave. Others were rolled up and slid into amulets, to be strung on chain or cord and worn around the necks of the dead. The texts inscribed on these *Totenpässe* speak—often with surprising authority—about the greatest *terra incognita* of all, that of the afterlife. Richard Janko, a leading scholar of what he calls these "golden tablets of memory," gives a paraphrase of the kinds of textual route-map they carry:

As you enter the underworld you will find on the right a spring, and by it stands a ghostly cypress tree. Chill water flows from the pool of Memory, over which will stand guardians, who will ask you with keen mind what your quest is in the gloom. Tell them the whole truth straight out . . .

In the months since Barry Lopez's death, I've begun to think that his extraordinary body of work reverses the principle of the Totenpass. Barry has crossed over, but he has left behind him maps to guide us, the living. His books are those maps, offering instruction and orientation as we walk tentatively forward into a future that shimmers with heat-haze, that is gouged by floods and rockslides and injustices, the skies of which are burned red and black by wildfire. His writing offers us answers to catechisms we do not yet know we will be asked. His prose tells us the whole truth straight out; it shows us what our quest must be in the gloom.

Barry's short story "The Mappist," collected in his book *Light Action in the Caribbean*, is his best-known piece of fiction; it's much anthologised, and the subject of a thousand high school and college term papers. Its narrator, Phillip Trevino, is obsessed with the work of an enigmatic cartographer-writer called Corlis Benefideo, who produces extraordinary "deep maps" of the American landscape, believing, wrote Barry in the story, that "in order to effect any political or social change, you had to know exactly what you were talking about. You had to know what the country itself—the ground, the real thing, not some political abstraction—was all about."

Trevino eventually tracks Benefideo down to a modest house in a small town in the Upper Midwest. There Benefideo—now nearing the end of his life—shows Trevino his impossible master project: a series of 1,651 maps of North Dakota, each representing a different aspect of the state's human and other-than-human complexities: a map of the ephemeral streams in the state's northeast quadrant, for instance; a map of eighteenth- and nineteenth-century foot-trails in the western reaches; a map showing the summer distribution of Swainson's hawks, partnered with a map showing "the overlapping summer distribution" of the hawk's "main prey species, the Richardson's ground squirrel." "This information is what we need, you know," Benefideo tells Trevino, "[t]his shows history and how people fit the places they occupy. It's about what gets erased and what comes to replace it. The maps reveal the foundations beneath the ephemera." At the end of their evening together, as Trevino is readying to drive off, Benefideo tells him: "The world is a miracle, unfolding in the pitch dark. We're lighting candles. Those maps—they are my candles. And I can't extinguish them for anyone."

Like Phillip Trevino chasing after Corlis Benefideo, I'd been obsessed with Barry's work for decades. I had read *Arctic Dreams* in my early twenties while travelling in the Pacific Northwest, and it had changed the course of my life. Simply put, it made me a writer. In the years that followed, I read everything by Barry I could find. He became my North Star: a remote, astonishing, boreal presence who helped guide me in the choices I made, both in place and on the page. Later, much later, Barry opened a correspondence with me. I still remember returning home one day and pushing open the front door to see, lying there on the mat, an envelope addressed to me in clear cursive black script, postmarked Oregon and stamped on the outside with Barry's name and address. I was stopped in my tracks—as astonished as if I'd found a rattlesnake or a heart-sized nugget of gold waiting on the threshold.

In June 2019, I finally had the chance to meet the person who had opened a life's path for me, as for so many others. I was passing through Portland, Oregon, and Barry—though then ill with advanced cancer, and in chronic pain—made the long car-journey to town from his home on the McKenzie River. We met in the lobby of my hotel. My body prickled all over with anxiety about disappointing Barry in some way I could neither foresee nor forestall. When I arrived, he rose with some difficulty, greeted me with great warmth, invited me to sit next to him, and then pointed to a big book on the coffee table in front of us. It was a world atlas. He opened it. "I brought this," he said, turning to the Europe section. "I thought you might show me some of your journeys and point out the landscapes you've described for me in your books." Set instantly at my ease, I leaned forward, and for a while we passed the atlas back and forth, tracing paths and telling stories of journeys taken and places known. It was, I reflected later, a beautiful thing for Barry to have done: geography as generosity.

Like his alter ego Corlis Benefideo, Barry lit his candles slowly. He knew the centrality of fieldwork to his method as a writer-mappist—what Benefideo calls "inspection and interviews. Close personal observation and talking with long-term residents." Though people tend to know Barry best, and sometimes only, for *Arctic Dreams*, I take his vast and diverse body of work to be a single, immense atlas—its many overlapping plates together comprising a palimpsest of the Anthropocene, documenting its wonders and horrors, seeking to fathom "what the country itself . . . was all about." In his memoir *Berlin Childhood Around 1900*, Walter Benjamin reflected on the possibility of representing one's life cartographically. Barry's oeuvre comes as close as any I know to realizing this ambition, culminating as it does in the vast prose-map of *Horizon*, which tells the stories of Barry's life through six main landscapes: from Cape Foulweather on the Oregon coast to the Queen Maud Mountains of Antarctica, by way of Ellesmere Island in the Canadian Arctic, the Turkana Uplands of East Africa, the Galápagos Islands, and Port Arthur in Tasmania. In *Horizon*, place becomes the means of telling time; the book also moves over its course from Barry as an "unsuspecting boy, a child beside himself with his desire to know the world, to swim out farther than he can see," to Barry in the closing years of his life, become an "elder" who carries a huge weight of wisdom, and is committed to leaving it behind him in the forms in which it might do the most good.

In the winter weeks running up to Barry's death—when it became clear that he would surely cross the river before the year's end—I felt a pressure building behind my eyes, in my throat. It was the pressure of words unvoiced. I wanted to tell Barry what he'd meant to me. I wanted to speak to him from a continent and an ocean away. I wanted somehow to keep him company as he readied for his last journey. But I also recognised that I was a peripheral figure in his life—and I felt a burning shame at the possibility that I might ask or claim too much of him and his family at that most private of times. Then I had an idea. I consulted with Jim Warren, a dear friend to both me and Barry, and one of the truest people I know. I told Jim I wanted to record poems for Barry, to speak them aloud and send the voice-files through, so that Barry could listen to them only if and when he wanted. Jim encouraged me to do so.

It was only later that I realised, though without surprise, that all of the poems I chose to read aloud for Barry inhabited that borderland between matter, metaphor, and metaphysics, a terrain Barry had mapped with grace and attention for more than half a century. I read Joy Harjo's "Eagle Poem" and Emily Dickinson's "'Hope' is the thing with feathers." I read Edward Thomas's poem "Roads," about how paths run through our hearts as surely as they run through places, and I read all of Walt Whitman's "Song of the Open Road," with its dream of departure into an unknown future teeming with possibilities: "Afoot and light-hearted," it begins, "I take to the open road / . . . the world before me / The long brown path before me leading wherever I choose." I read Gerard Manley Hopkins's "As Kingfishers Catch Fire," and Seamus Heaney's late poem "Postscript," in which a flock of swans "catch the heart off guard and blow it open." Later, Barry's friend Scott Korb wrote to tell me that Barry had played my recording of the Heaney poem, with his "arms crossed over his chest, arms closed, in prayer, at peace, fully with us." It moved me greatly to think of that poem, lifted out of my mouth as sound, paused, held, and carried across the world, to be unfrozen into that moment, that place, that gathering of people.

A few days before Barry died, I also sent through a long voice-message. I wanted to tell him how profoundly his work and life had shaped my own. I wanted to tell him how often over the years I'd glimpsed him far ahead of me on the path, and how he'd always paused long enough to show me where the slender trail led on over boulder fields, through willow thickets. I haven't been able to listen back to that message, and I doubt I ever will.

I was, of course, only one among hundreds of people who were at that time trying to voice what Barry and his writing meant to them. His family set up an online page where memories and messages could be left, some of which they would read out to Barry. Quickly, a clear-running stream of tributes began to flow. I was struck by how often people reached for metaphors of cartography, navigation, and orientation, and I thought again of Corlis Benefideo making his maps and lighting his candles. "You've always gone ahead," began one of these messages to Barry as he lay dying, "moving towards the big things and leaving us a map to follow you, pointing to what you've found along the way. [. . .] Fare well." "I want you to know that you have been one of my navigators," read another, "your words and wisdom helping me to see and care about this Earth we all share." Another: "You have been a polestar for me in this life, and your spirit and wisdom will continue to guide me through the rest of my days." Another: "As always, dearest friend, you're tracking a path for the rest of us." One signed off: "See you on the trail."

The one that jolted my heart hardest was, I realised, a kind of Totenpass—a map for the mappist:

> The *Tibetan Book of the Dead* advises looking for the following signposts along the journey to keep the passage straightforward. First you will see something that looks like a mirage. Watch for it. Then you will see smokiness. Then fireflies in the sky. Then a clear candle flame. Then clear moonlit sky followed by red sunlit sky. Then pitch darkness followed by clear bright open space. Go that way in peace knowing all of our love is with you.

On the winter night I heard that Barry had died, I walked out of my house. I needed to put miles in my legs, and to think alone. The wind was strong and cold, and it burned my cheeks. Dense cloud scudded across the night sky above my suburb. In one hand I held tight a stone that Barry had given me when we'd met in Portland, a smooth-sided ventifact he'd collected high on the Antarctic icecap decades earlier. I followed a narrow path out past the edge of the city, beyond the last of the streetlamps, into unlit fields where I could see more clearly in the pitch darkness. At last, up near an old hangar of beech trees that top a shallow chalk hill, there was a brief break in the clouds and there it was—Polaris, the North Star, glimpsed for a few seconds before it disappeared again.

(STILL) LOVING THE BURNING WORLD

DEBORAH A. MIRANDA
Ohlone/Costanoan Esselen Nation, Chumash

In the spring of 2007, Barry Lopez sat at our dining table savoring my wife, Margo's, venison stew from a deep ceramic bowl and chatting with her about writing, research, travel, and his deep concerns about the planet's well-being. Meanwhile, I sat tongue-tied as evening twilight fell over our log cabin wedged in the saddle between Big House and Little House mountains in Virginia.

I'd met Barry Lopez that semester at Washington and Lee University. I was teaching a creative writing course while my colleague Jim Warren and Barry co-taught an environmental studies class during our short spring term. At dinner that night, Margo and Barry immediately bonded over their stewardship of what each thought of as their "place" in the world: for Margo, this sixty-eight acres of mostly vertical oak and cedar-rich land with its wandering, unnamed creek; for Barry, the McKenzie River and the timberlands surrounding his nearby home.

Unlike Margo, I had not read every word of Barry's work—in fact, at that point, I had read just one essay: "Landscape and Narrative," first published in 1984, and collected in *Crossing Open Ground*. The essay raised both resonance and questions with me, particularly the concept Barry describes as two landscapes: exterior, the intricate and perfectly balanced network of relationships that create the physical environment/world; and interior, what he calls our own "speculations, intuitions, and formal ideas," which are also a set of relationships. I loved Barry's ideas about storytelling as the bridge between those two landscapes (now separated, he noted, and resulting in both environmental and personal havoc). These ideas almost felt like the traditional ways of thinking about storytelling and human/ nonhuman relationships in Indigenous communities. Almost, but not quite.

I must admit, I was wary of this White man sitting at my table. Perhaps growing up Indian, being an Indian writer and scholar in the academy, and the brutal facts of colonization in general had left me jaded when it came to listening to White men talk of their relationship with the landscape. The phenomenon (though not rare) of Pretendians, White Shamans, and Wannabes, whose wallets and egos fatten on Indigenous concepts gleaned from dubious or glossed-over sources, has damaged not just Indigenous cultures but those who entrust their well-being to false spirituality. And so, I listened carefully to Barry that night, a little shy, a little reticent, not wanting to misplace my trust. Looking back now, I feel sad that it had to be that way; but I don't blame myself. This is the world I was born into: where appropriation and exploitation of Indigenous spirituality and culture are not always blatant or easily pegged. Too often, such theft takes place wearing pleasant disguises.

Then Margo shared the story of how she and I had met: " . . . a little town in Oregon called McKenzie Bridge, at a place right on the McKenzie River," she said with a smile, and in a rush of memory, I felt myself standing on the wet, mossy banks of that river—coincidentally, very near Barry's home.

Margo and I had both come to Oregon separately to attend a weeklong summer writing workshop. For seven days, I was immersed in the cold buffeting of air hovering above whitewater rapids, the river's endless song as it wove itself through my hair, skimmed my skin, flowed deep into my lungs, saturating my blood so that, when I wrote, it seemed that the river itself poured out of my fingers, into my pen, and onto the page. The river was not just a cleansing, awakening force, but a demanding one. It required a response, an engagement, with a kind of sacred power that rose out of the riverbed and charged me with telling a story I had not yet heard from anyone else: the story of what happened to my father's tribes during the series of invasions by Spain, Mexico, and the United States. This place, made of rain, stone, deer, moss, air, cedar, trout, earth, maidenhair fern, osprey, and yellow swallowtail butterflies emerging from cocoons into June sun, brought that story out of me as a poem that would alter the course of my life.

In "Landscape and Narrative," Barry writes that the power of storytelling helps connect interior/exterior landscapes, "reorder[ing] a state of psychological confusion through contact with the pervasive truth of those relationships we call 'the land.'" Although this language felt a bit jargony, stilted, academic, I couldn't help feeling the truth of where Barry directs these words. Because the exterior landscape is a self-sustaining web of relationships that depend upon, and support, the whole, Barry writes, it is a model for human cultures, a map into what is possible: in other words, a teacher, a guide, who shows us how to bring our interior landscape into the same intricate network of balance as the exterior one.

I must confess that I loved this concept; it resonated with the way that storytelling works within the Indigenous communities that I knew. "The interior landscape responds to the character and subtlety of an exterior landscape; the shape of the individual mind is affected by land as it is by genes," he went on. *The character and the subtlety of an exterior landscape.* What a strange way to speak of the beloved homeland. I felt that something key had been left out—a crucial part of this idea of landscape. Barry's language is accurate, yet complicated; rational and powerful, yet—paradoxically—

keeps its distance, avoiding expressing the risky vulnerability that such an intimate bond brings.

As I read Barry's essay, I realized that it just misses recognizing the absolute reality of *Mother*. The "exterior landscape" he speaks of *is* our Mother, and within Her, every place and being is our relative. If we act as if we are separate, or superior, without need of that teaching or relationship, then we become what the Laguna Pueblo writer Leslie Marmon Silko calls "destroyers." The opposite of this would be creators. Caretakers. Nurturers. *Storytellers*.

And now here was the storyteller Barry Lopez right in front of me, speaking tenderly of the river he loved, glowing with adoration for her cold waters, her many moods. I took a chance and spoke of my own experience with that river. I told Barry, "The things I wrote on the McKenzie could never have been written before I met that river, and there are probably things I will never write until I go back there. She brings our stories out of us, like a good teacher."

Barry looked at me for a long moment. Then he said simply, "Yes."

I knew, then, that the two of us had much more to say to each other. But we could only dip our toes in the water that night before it was time to say goodbye. When we met again, far down the road, it was on the page, as with my earlier encounter. By then, much that Barry told us he feared for our world had come to pass. Curiously, it was an essay published near the end of his life that showed me how far we both had come.

In August 2020, I read Barry's deeply moving essay "Love in a Time of Terror: On Natural Landscapes, Metaphorical Living, and Warlpiri Identity," and could not get the images of that Australian Outback out of my mind, or the love story of two Warlpiri people, Warri and Yatungka. They had married even though such a union broke the social taboo of being born into the same moiety. Cast out of their community, even when forgiven, the couple refused to "come in" to the White settlements despite the brutal combination of colonization and drought that had driven most other Aboriginals to leave their traditional homelands. Just as Warri and Yatungka wanted to honor their love for one another, so they also desired to honor their obligations to care for the land through ritual observances that could not take place anywhere else. Love, they understood, must be honored. Barry tells us that he carried this story with him as he walked into the stark devastation of drought, through a landscape so barren that it recalled other places equally bereft: a war zone in Kabul, a patch of tundra littered with whale skeletons in Nunavut, Birkenau's dark barracks. It was in that moment, he writes, that "another thought burst in: that most of the trouble that afflicts human beings in their lives can be traced to the failure to love."

The failure to love.

Love: he doesn't mean lust or possession or obsessive attraction (he quickly notes that "to suddenly love without really knowing is to opt for romance, not commitment and obligation").

I thought back to that first Lopez essay I'd ever read—the one in which he concludes that we must use storytelling to build (or rebuild) a bridge between interior landscape and exterior landscape in order to achieve what he calls our "mental health." But in "Love in a Time of Terror" he goes much further, into a state of true vulnerability. Here, he can ask a terrifying question, one that shows a true evolution in his language and thinking from 1984 to 2021: "in this moment, is it still possible to face the gathering darkness and say to the physical Earth, and to all its creatures, including ourselves, fiercely and without embarrassment, I love you, and to embrace fearlessly the burning world?" I would have known from this essay alone that Barry's search (and research) had expanded to include Indigenous leaders, storytellers, and communities who provided him with direction, and encouraged his observations and interactions with both unfamiliar human relatives and non-human relatives. Barry Lopez, as a man, had worked his way through the complexity of language and analysis to the difficult simplicity of love.

This is something I have learned the hard way, too. To say, "I love you, fiercely and without embarrassment," to Earth requires an opening up of that hard outer shell of cerebral theoretics about storytelling and relationships, revealing all the ways loving this world makes us vulnerable to shame, pain, grief, and regret—and empowers us with hope.

The poem, "How to Love the Burning World," became my response to Barry's essay.

In the poem, I try to describe what this relationship with the burning world feels like to me, a woman of Ohlone/Esselen-Costanoan, and Chumash ancestry, whose homelands in what we currently call California have for centuries now been occupied by settlers who do not want to share Carmel or Santa Barbara with Indians. I respond to Barry's piercing question with another question: How can we *not* love the burning world, hold her in our arms even as she burns, even as we burn with her? We are not separate from this world in flames. Her fate is our fate. She is our Mother. We love Her even as our skin blisters and our hair catches fire, even as we simultaneously despair, and yet find possibility in the very openness created by such love.

Perhaps this particular essay strikes me so powerfully in part because I know we Indigenous peoples have been loving the burning world for a long time. Colonization is a holocaust that sweeps across every continent, burns up homelands, creatures, and beings that are essential to the thrivance of each other. Even now, Indigenous arts and literatures are typically described as acts of resistance, whereas we see them as acts of love, a kind of love medicine. Indigenous people love this world *even when it is on fire*, even when it seems like we will lose everything, precisely because we know the value of such love and its crucial role in sustaining and nurturing our Mother and all our relatives, as well as ourselves.

It's why we can keep on writing even as the world we revere seems beyond recovery.

In North American Indigenous terms, we say that the people and the land are one. This is a truth we didn't need Western science to know, but even Western science admits it: our bodies are made of the same elements as

Earth's body—oxygen, carbon, hydrogen, nitrogen, calcium, and phosphorus. All of this comes from the body of our Mother, and inevitably returns to Her. There is no distance between us. We may imagine that we've built a separate camp, burned our bridges back to that relationship, but the terrible (and wonderful) truth is that we can't ever actually be separated. We can deny relationship, but that doesn't make it any less the reality of our existence. By embracing the burning world, however, we admit our vulnerability. We admit our connection, our obligation. We will not leave Her side. We are burning because She is burning.

"It is more important now to be in love than to be in power," Barry writes.

I think it has always been so. To *be*. In love.

This kind of love is a long-haul love. A hard-working love. High-maintenance love. Quotidian love, requiring rituals of daily attentiveness and adaptation. A love that isn't performative. A love that knows, and still embraces, scars and wounds—and thus contains the medicine to treat them. (Transformative love.)

I think that with this quote Barry intimates that stepping into that embrace means that the dominant patriarchal, capitalist culture must acknowledge and own all its human mistakes—colonization, capitalism, abuses of power—which led to this burning. Wouldn't that mean learning self-love despite those mistakes? Within that healing embrace, might we all—White and Indigenous—find the courage and strength and strategies by which to salvage or even nurture not just this landscape, but the very *concept* of relationship? To fall in love with our Mother again and realize that we have always been one with her?

Earth is burning because we are burning. Somewhere in our journey, humans turned away from understanding that the sun is a miracle, water is a miracle, and beings made of these miracles *are miraculous.*

Barry knew that this is not the kind of knowledge that dominant cultures steeped in the fantasies of colonization, industry, and greed want to pursue. He also knew his own role in such a culture. Near the end of his life, when asked in an interview for his own obituary about his motivation to write, he affirmed, "I am a traditional storyteller," adding, "This activity is not about yourself. [As a storyteller] It's about culture, and your job is to help."

Even before the publication of "Love in a Time of Terror," I had long since ceased to be concerned that Barry was one of those who appropriated Indigenous knowledge for their own benefit; but as I consider Barry's work in light of his recent death, this essay brings into beautiful clarity his long vocation of educating, supporting, and "helping" others negotiate personal and global chaos via the very human vehicle of story. His words reflect the accumulation of not just knowledge and research, but lived experience and passion for seeking out truths—skillfully translated into language that can accomplish that task. I think that "Love in a Time of Terror" might be the greatest gift Barry could have left us.

Barry's earlier work on interior and exterior landscapes clarifies the stakes: the work of building connection with all our relations is more urgent than ever. In 1984, Barry speaks of ordering our interior landscape according to the exterior landscape—"To succeed in this means to achieve a balanced state of mental health." But, by 2021, he has come to a still more central truth: a new definition of what it means to succeed. He writes, "It is more important to live for the possibilities that lie ahead than to die in despair over what has been lost." He understands that such love has the potential to prevent us from succumbing to despair even as the beloved Mother burns.

We know now that terrible changes to our world are inevitable. Frequently, despair seems the only path open to us. Yet Barry's words remind us that there are also possible transformations for our times which are not apocalyptic. Transformations that lead to beginnings, rather than endings. He urges us not to overlook the rich, creative power inherent in claiming relationship as our inheritance, and as our responsibility.

I'm thinking of Barry Lopez on this blessedly cool afternoon at the end of September almost two years since his death in Eugene, Oregon. Margo and I have driven across the country from Virginia to our new home in a cohousing community being built (both physically and culturally) on the banks of the Willamette River in Eugene. We've come full circle, returned to the land where we met and became friends, then lovers, now an old married couple ready to cast our lot with the places and people we love. Although the sky is a soft blue just now, smoky haze lies over Creswell Butte to the west of our temporary rental; the 113,809-acre Cedar Creek Fire, sparked by lightning, still burns, and only by the wind's grace (which often shifts hourly) are we spared the ash and smoke that plagued us in previous weeks.

Despair is always close by. Barry knew that. He wanted to help us see an alternative.

How to Love the Burning World

. . . is it still possible to face the gathering darkness and say to the physical Earth, and to all its creatures, including ourselves, fiercely and without embarrassment, I love you, and to embrace fearlessly the burning world?

—Barry Lopez

Tell yourself it's like sitting at the bedside
of your mother; scorched with cancer,
her hand already almost ash in yours,
her words already smoke so thick
it obscures your vision of a future
without her. You want to look away.
You want to find a cave, drink yourself
into oblivion, sleep while ugliness smolders.
Admit it. You want someone else to tend
the deathwatch. Instead, moisten her tongue
with a sponge; bathe dry skin
with lavender cream; braid her hair
with tender, trembling fingers. Take care
not to pull on knots. Stay in the room:
let the last thing she hears

be your voice, thanking her
for every single time she didn't
kill you, for the eons she waited
before you realized her brilliance,
her wisdom, all the days she bit
her tongue, let you think you had
the last bloody word.

You aren't required to love the flames.

But love the burning world.
You owe her that. Fear is no dishonor.
Her fever so hot even metaphors
melt at a touch. Memorize her.
Praise each scar on her body,
beauty ablaze. Pray for a clean
ending, a phoenix purification.
Pray for mercy. Pray for the only thing
that can save us now:
every lesson she ever taught us
about the sweet, bitter grace
of transformation.

SIGNAL FLASHES ON THE LLANO ESTACADO

KATE HARRIS

The cheapest red-eye ticket I could get from the Yukon to Lubbock, Texas, involved so many stopovers I could've reached the Norwegian archipelago of Svalbard in the same amount of time. After twenty hours in transit, I knew I had arrived on the Llano Estacado by the wilting heat, even in April, the father in the terminal calling to a son nicknamed Bubba, and the extravagant lack of topography. This was tumbleweed country, some of the flattest terrain on Earth, spanning northwestern Texas and eastern New Mexico. Although its name means "palisaded plains" in Spanish, the Navajo called it "The Horizontal Yellow" and the Comanche "The Place Where No One Is." And while the Llano Estacado looks level, the plateau slopes down ten feet a mile to the southeast, toward Lubbock, as if everything will roll there eventually. It was 2012. I had just finished a long bike ride on the Silk Road. As I struggled to write a book about that trip, I found myself wondering if

Barry Lopez's early drafts were even fractionally as flawed as mine; if so, there was hope. I'd flown to Lubbock because his papers are housed in the Sowell Collection at Texas Tech University. Better yet, Lopez himself would be on campus, as part of a free conference. Not wanting to miss his opening talk, I took a taxi straight there from the airport.

I figured I wouldn't be alone in making a pilgrimage to Lubbock, clutching a dog-eared copy of *Arctic Dreams*. But as I ate free pastries from the coffee table in the conference room, it became clear that most of the people there already knew each other. I recognized two other writers I revered, David Quammen and Gretel Ehrlich, whose papers were also housed in the Sowell Collection. Suddenly aware of my rumpled clothing, the bags under my eyes, and my conspicuous solitude in the back of the room, I worried I'd made a mistake in coming. Then Dr. Diane Warner, the director of the Sowell Collection at the time, came over to introduce herself. She made me feel so welcome I didn't notice a slim man with a neat white beard enter the room. "Hey, Barry," Diane waved him over. "Let me introduce you to our Canadian visitor."

To put our encounter in context, I was a writer who hadn't yet written anything, or at least hadn't published anything of note. Still, Barry made me feel like the opposite of a nobody. I remember his kindness, his genuine curiosity—about where I was from, what I was working on, my impressions of places we'd both traveled. I remember the wide silver band on his wrist, studded with turquoise, in part because he mentioned it in the talk he gave that morning. He told us he only wore the bracelet when he traveled, because the weight of it reminded him to behave. It was honestly hard to imagine Barry Lopez ever *not* behaving. He had the center of gravity of a sage, possibly a saint. This impression was reinforced by a story someone shared at the conference later that day, about hearing Barry speak a few years earlier in Montana. That event had taken place in a large, open tent during a heavy rainstorm. "To banish the numinous, to banish the spiritual," Barry had said over thunder and lightning, "is a mark of madness." The audience gasped, because just at that moment a double rainbow shimmered over the mountains beyond him.

I had a similar experience when I first read *Arctic Dreams*. I brought the book as topical bedtime reading at an intensive summer course on sea ice on Svalbard. For two weeks, the other graduate students and I studied the frozen ocean from every possible angle—its physics, meteorology, chemistry, ecology—except for actually seeing the thing itself. I suppose this syllabus of abstraction made sense, given the most pertinent fact about sea ice, then and still, is its absence on a warming world. Still, it was disappointing to travel that far north to mostly sit in a windowless lecture hall. To say something was missing for me on Svalbard, and in science more generally, was an understatement. Through *Arctic Dreams*, Barry Lopez showed me the full spectrum. I hadn't known it was possible to refract places or experiences through so many wavelengths at once: not just science but history, philosophy, poetry, and intimate, firsthand encounter. Soon I was smuggling his book into class in my three-ring binder. I sat in the very back so nobody could see that my "lecture notes" didn't just pertain to empirical matters at these latitudes, but also the sorts of mysteries "we can do no better than name narwhal." When I glanced up at thermodynamic equations on a blackboard, the swerve from awe to analysis gave me vertigo. The professors said, "Frazil, shuga, nilas," but I heard, "Mystery, mystery, mystery." I became a writer to apprentice myself to it more directly.

Of course, not even rainbows are "all rainbows." They depend on rain and clouds to scatter light. They are often associated with storms. Barry doesn't shirk from darkness and dispersal; indeed, his whole oeuvre is an unflinching etiology of the sort of cultural and planetary disintegration for which there is no easy cure. When he wonders, in *Arctic Dreams*, what it might mean "to live at moral peace with the universe," the inquiry isn't dewy-eyed but deadly serious. Yet the literary critic Michiko Kakutani accused that passage, in an otherwise rave review in the *New York Times*, of being "tinged with a sort of *Whole Earth Catalogue* sentimentality." Given that ironic remove is the accepted register of modernity, such a critique is not surprising. We live in a culture that exalts wit over wisdom, surface over soul, snark over sincerity, but is this really serving us or the planet well? I was grateful someone was still asking what intimacy looks like, what justice looks like, as Barry would do in his talk that day in Lubbock. I was grateful someone was preoccupied with "the relations between things," as he put it, instead of what divides them. However craven our culture, however frayed our attention spans, there remains a need, an existential longing, for authentic storytelling: tales "about *us*," as Barry explained—meaning the larger experience of being alive on Earth—not "about *you*," the storyteller. Barry took life seriously ("How else," he once wrote, "could you take it?"), but he was hardly humorless, on the page or in person. In fact, David Quammen, in his own talk that day, fondly referred to his longtime friend as a "puckish cut-up"—which cracked everyone up, Barry especially.

One of the joys of being in that room was witnessing such teasing banter between friends who, by my reckoning, happened to be some of the most brilliant writers alive. It was like seeing a scatter of stars resolve into a constellation. One night, Gretel Ehrlich got up on stage and gave a talk on the "rod-and-cone-shaking beauty of ice" that stunned everyone with the wonder and grief of its subject matter, and with the grace of expression that made those extremes bearable. "Both view and viewer," she told us, "are sacred." Nobody had any questions after. Nobody wanted to break the spell. It was the talk the other students and I had needed to hear on Svalbard. As Ehrlich headed offstage, visibly drained after giving herself over so completely to the reading, I saw Barry walk over and wordlessly give her a hug. Another day, after one of his own readings, someone asked a question that prompted a characteristically wise and lyrical answer. I regret that I didn't write his response down, but what I do recall is the hush in the room that followed, the sort of silence that builds after a gong is struck. That's when David Quammen, sitting in the audience, pertly raised his hand. "Hey, Barry," he called out. "Can you do that thing with the double rainbow again?"

When the conference wrapped up, I had planned to spend a couple days studying Lopez's early drafts in the Sowell Collection, hoping to glean how he travelled from ambition to reality, rough draft to resplendent book. But when Barry invited me to join him and some friends, Bill and Andy, on a day trip to a Paleoindian archeological site, I didn't hesitate to change plans. Our destination was Blackwater Draw in New Mexico, host to the oldest known human artifacts on the Llano Estacado. The fluted Clovis points and bone and stone tools found there date back at least 13,000 years, which, when the site was discovered by Western archeologists in 1929, was 10,000 years earlier than they thought people had reached North America, despite Indigenous testimony otherwise. As Bill drove us there with the air conditioning on, under clouds like ice floes, Andy told Barry about the ancient flint quarries at Palo Duro Canyon near Amarillo, Texas. "Lots of chips down off those cliffs," he said, meaning flakes of stone. "Any salsa?" Barry joked.

There are no fossils for most of what matters about life. What makes a person laugh. What makes them weep. What moves them to sing or dance or praise. Here is what we know about Paleoindians at Blackwater Draw, according to the information-center displays: that they pounded yucca species into sandals; that they invented thin, needly spears to penetrate the tight-pronged ribs of mammoths; that both these technologies, the shoes and the spears, enabled prehistoric hunters to kill on an unprecedented scale. When the megafauna was gone, possibly as a result of the human genius for survival, hunters deliberately herded buffalo into the grassy arroyo that Barry, Andy, Bill, and I walked up now, until we came to a dead end. This was where the herds realized they were trapped. Hunters could sit back and wait as the buffalo trampled each other to death in their frenzy to escape. The last kill here was 8,500 years ago.

Barry trailed the rest of us as we climbed up out of the draw, back to the present day, to the high point—a vantage he would describe, in his final masterpiece, *Horizon*, as "the sill of the sky, separating what the eye could see from what the mind might imagine." From there, I could almost feel the land's tilt. A slight lean toward Lubbock. We were on our way back to the parking lot when Barry, who was still behind us, announced that he found an arrowhead. We all whirled around to see it, then Bill and Andy groaned. In Barry's hand was a dusty shard of broken mirror. "It's the imp in me," Barry said with a grin. "Very puckish," I affirmed. He wiped off the mirror and flicked it back and forth, catching the sun, skipping light across the Llano. I wish I'd kept that shard, slipped it into a pocket as a souvenir. My own reminder to behave. But Barry threw it in the trash at the information center, where the person at the front desk told us about how the neighboring ranchers shot bullets down the shared fenceline, how they "didn't give a good goddamn about Paleoindian history."

On the way back to Lubbock, we drove past massive feedlots in which cattle hid in the shade of open-walled sheds, and where center-pivot irrigation systems spun out green circles. Barry asked Andy if the unirrigated edges of those fields, where the water didn't reach, had a name. Andy told him they were called "corners." Barry said they reminded him of the stranded bits of earth between highway ramps, which were called— he thought; he couldn't remember exactly—"gores." He was right about the term, as I later confirmed by Googling it. From the old English for *gãra*, "triangular piece of land," which is in turn related to *gãr*, "spear." I saw them from the air on my flight home, grass needling up between curved concrete ribs, the world reasserting itself in the gaps between our ambitions for it.

Barry told me to keep in touch after Lubbock, and I took him seriously. Once or twice a year, a typewritten letter would show up in my mailbox like a signal flash on the Llano Estacado—a reminder that I wasn't alone in this apprenticeship to what can't be said, that in striving to say it anyway I was bending my days into something worthy. I never did get to see his early drafts in Lubbock, but his letters hinted at the rigor of his methods, the way, after taking nearly twenty years to complete the first draft of *Horizon*, he wrote five or six more over as many years before considering the book finished. Even for Barry, writing was mostly a matter of rewriting and not giving up. "The continuous discovery of deeper meaning as you go along fuels your belief in the project and the sense that yes, you are on the right road," he explained in one of his letters to me. He shared his plans to travel less, both for health reasons and because he'd been meaning for a long time to "go deep" right out his backdoor, just as soon as he got back from Jordan, or the West Bank and Israel, or Germany, or Western

Australia, or the Horn of Africa to visit refugee camps. He didn't often offer direct advice, but when he did, it was galvanizing. "You didn't say much in your letter about your own travels," he once wrote, "but I must assume you're getting about. Do it, Kate. You will never regret taking on the world the way you have. And are."

Not long after Barry passed away, I drove into town from my cabin in the woods to interview someone for a book project. Because my driveway is mostly potholes, as is the gravel road beyond it, making for noisy driving, it wasn't until I hit pavement that I heard the voice. Someone was speaking in the car, quietly yet unmistakably. The sound wasn't coming from the radio or my phone, because both were off. I couldn't figure it out: a gravelly baritone; a warm, thoughtful murmuring. I pulled over and unzipped my backpack, and Barry spoke up louder.

It was another flash of the mirror. I must have accidentally hit my voice recorder's "on" button when I'd tossed my backpack in the car, because it was playing my last voice-to-voice conversation with him, a phone interview I'd conducted in 2019 for a magazine profile. At one point, I'd asked Barry what gave him heart, what kept him going despite everything—the absence of sea ice, the abundance of neighbors shooting bullets down shared fence lines, not to mention his own health struggles. He told me he took solace in the fact that we have "never truly tested the human imagination." Against a darkening sky, in this gathering storm, there is a wider range of possible futures than we can easily make out. It takes a visionary like Barry Lopez to gesture toward them. A rainbow, after all, is not an arc from one point to another but a circle with a completeness we can't see. The rest is hidden by the horizon.

Witnessing

"I believe in all human societies there is a
desire to love and be loved, to experience
the full fierceness of human emotion, and to
make a measure of the sacred part of one's life."
—Barry Lopez, "A Voice," *About This Life*

STILL ON THE TRAIL

JOHN LANE

In the spring of 1979, a small literary conference called The Power of Animals was held in Port Townsend, Washington. The writers present that weekend included Gary Snyder, Howard Norman, Melinda Mueller, Susan Griffin, Paul Shepard—and Barry Lopez. I had been working all year at Copper Canyon Press; the press editor and conference's organizer, Sam Hamill, had asked me to assist with logistics. I was twenty-four that spring, and Barry would have been thirty-four. Barry had just published *Of Wolves and Men*, and he was hard at work on *Arctic Dreams*. That weekend, he inscribed my hardback copy of *Of Wolves and Men*: "For John, in memory of a few fine days in Port Townsend, in the respect for the words and sacred dances that bind us together."

My journal from that weekend is mostly pages of notes taken like a college student. When I heard Barry talk publicly for the first time, he was precise in his foraging among ideas and stories, each word and act considered. I noticed that in my notes, I mostly made side comments about a crocodile study I would end up helping with a month later in Belize. "Why my interest in reptiles?" I had written in the margin next to this quote from Barry: "Animals can become what we are. Men are interested in prey/predator relationships because of the cultural bearing." Later that weekend, I was in line to get food at lunch; Barry was in front of me, picking items out of the salad bar. I asked what he thought of the sessions so far. He turned in that solemn way I have seen so many times since and said, "I've been thinking beaver, and I feel everyone else is thinking caribou."

Could he have been commenting at the beginning of our friendship on the sorts of animals that call to him, therefore prompting me to think in such metaphors as well? Caribou are numerous, big herd animals of the Arctic, charismatic ungulates like moose and elk. But beaver—they are constructors of dams and houses and ponds, openers of waterways. Nomads versus engineers? Herds versus family dwellers? *What had he meant?* Later that spring, Barry wrote me a letter. There was plenty about animals, but nothing about caribou or beaver: "I spent the last few weeks in Alaska, most of it on the upper Yukon," he said, "looking for peregrine eyries, fishing for grayling and following animals about. I am always overwhelmed with a sense of fortune in doing such things."

In January of 2021, I took a four-mile hike with my wife along the mostly undeveloped southeast coast of Kauai. The hike started at one of the most opulent beach hotels I've ever visited—the Grand Hyatt—built around a huge, open courtyard with full-sized trees and scarlet macaws tethered on isolated perches. Once a day, at four, the macaws are gathered by their caretakers so children can get their photos taken with them. The birds are always a draw, as fascinating for the kids as for their parents taking the pictures.

Outside the Grand Hyatt, my wife and I hiked past a series of lava-rock waterfall swimming pools cascading down to the beach, with misting stations, artificial tide pools, private cabanas, mechanical blowholes, and plastic waterslides. At the bottom of those fake falls, we hopped on the Mahaulepu Heritage Trail, which follows along lava shelves up Shipwreck Beach, then enters a mile or so of sandstone cliffs that were dunes 300,000 years ago and have been carved into hoodoos by wind and water. The cliffs are dramatic in color—beige and red where iron shows through.

Halfway along on the walk, we skirted the edge of a golf course for a quarter mile. The incongruity of natural and manmade beauty increased even more when the trail passed through a native Hawaiian sacred place called Hoʻoūluiʻa, an ancient fishing *heiau* (temple), a field of black lava boulders shaped into a terrace. A sign there suggested we not stray from the narrow footpath bordering those sacred grounds. Another sign, a little farther along, spelled out the outline of ceremonies and rituals once performed there. Early Hawaiians are believed to have left offerings of fish at Hoʻoūluiʻa in hopes of securing good catches. Along the cliffs, the ocean can smash hard and go airborne. My wife thought it was raining, and I swear I smelled fish as I walked the sacred ground.

As we passed through this heiau, the hike changed. I thought of Barry, who'd been dead a little over a year. I thought of how his last major book, *Horizon*, begins in Hawaii and how he would like the thought of me here. The aging narrator, Barry's nonfictional persona, had spent his life with a "fierce desire to go and see." At the book's beginning, the narrator is resting with his family beside a fancy pool on Oahu like the one we'd passed at the Hyatt, a place unlike most of the difficult and remote landscapes conjured throughout the considerable bulk of *Horizon*. What the narrator sees around him is the full bloom of the twenty-first-century tourist in Hawaii, yet he does much more than reflect on resort comforts and capitalist industrial tourism. He also recalls snorkeling with his wife and his grandson earlier on the trip and watching as foreign visitors waded into the surf. Natural beauty is everywhere, "a dense, perfume-like scent—tropical flowers blooming in a nearby hedge. Is it bougainvillea?" Every moment is sacred—even at the opulent tourist pool.

What will happen to us, asks the narrator as he stays at the posh resort. He wishes "each stranger he sees in the chairs and lounges around [him], every one of them, an untroubled life . . . to survive what is coming."

Our hike that morning was the most strenuous exercise for me in three months. I had come to share something entirely unexpected with my old friend Barry. I too had been diagnosed with prostate cancer. As we hiked in Hawaii, it had only been a month since my radical prostatectomy. I was still weak, and I had to stop often to pee. I didn't let on, but I was wiped out the first mile and fell behind my wife. I had trouble picturing myself as a grand adventurer in the mold of Barry Lopez. My wife looked back with concern as she waited for me. I'm sure she was worried that all our shared adventures were in our past, and that our future was sedentary.

I received my own diagnosis in July 2021, seven months after Barry died, so I never had to tell him. We'd talked once or twice about my own fluctuating PSA (prostate specific antigens), and he'd reminded me—chided me like a brother—that the number can often point to serious illness. I know that, had he lived for me to share my illness with him, he would have given me good advice and calmed my fears when I didn't quite understand the Gleason Score used to rank prostate-cell mutation, or the differences between radiation oncology and hormone therapy, or the pluses and minuses of a radical prostatectomy. When the test results came back, I had a lower Gleason Score number than Barry had reported. His was 9+ on diagnosis; mine was 3+. But cancer is cancer. After considering all the options, the surgeon removed my prostate; the odds are good that the cancer will not return.

My slow pace hiking the Heritage Trail created a lonely but good space for reflecting. My mind kept flipping between thoughts of the incredible tourist wealth and privilege around us, and memories of Barry's friendship, his final illness, and his continued presence, especially while I passed through the heiau.

Relationships help map the retreating world of the past. Friendships, allegiances, partnerships, and alliances can act, through time, as coordinates that hold past experiences and ideas in a web of recollections and memory. Among non-writers, these relationships usually leave little paper trail. This aspect of relationships—as a repository of feeling and connection through time—has been little considered, as far as I know.

Among writers, at least up until the last decade or so, letters were one of the primary retrievable coordinates of these ties. But journals, diaries, and notebooks have also served a secondary function: to document the relationship of a writer's past self to present self, to map the contours. Read as missives from the past to the present, they are both map and instrument of the mapmaking itself, barometer and altimeter. They alert the mind to the old trails, still present but already walked.

Unlike traditional mapmaking, letters and journals do not bleed mystery from our lives. They layer it in, and they are never entirely scrutable. Neither the writer nor the reader can ever return to the point of origin of a letter or a journal entry and exactly recalculate their former position in time or space. Because they are a form of writing, letters and journals fall under the conventions of language. In the contemporary literary world, it's become a cliché; we accept that the map and the territory slide past and over each other, in the moment of mapping, and later even in the recall. The remembered world neither is nor was there in writing. We experienced it, and if we are writers, possibly recorded it, but the experience is never the recording or what is being recorded. Like beavers, we construct our structures against the flow of time. Letters and journals are two dams against forgetting. Relationships and affections are others.

I'm not writing here merely about the connections that come through interspecies affection. Place as well is a relationship, though one that grows more tenuous as what we call "human time" accrues. We, in the so-called developed world, are no longer mapped quite so bodily onto our physical environment. Our removal from it is both physical and intellectual—through our systems for living, like houses and buildings and streets, through our industrial food systems, and through the ideas we conceive about our environment. We are, as they say, what we eat, but what we eat is no longer so obvious. Even our intellectual apprehension of "out there" is muted by these systems. In my study, where I sit writing these words, I just opened the door because I wanted to hear the bird song "out there" more fully. I can hear Carolina wrens calling back and forth, but with this door open, I also hear the delivery truck on the next ridge.

In *Horizon,* Barry writes of Hawaii, "I also watch, with a mixture of curiosity and affection, the hotel's other guests, sunning on lounges around the pool or ambling past, completely at ease. The clement air and the benign nature of the light dispose me toward an accommodation with everything here different from myself."

My four-decade friendship with Barry helped me get a fix on who I am and how different and diverse individuals in a single species can be. There's no predicting how life will go, all of Barry's stories seem to say. One of my favorite Barry anecdotes is from *Of Wolves and Men,* in which the native hunters are watching wolves with spotting scopes and one comments, "I have never seen a wolf do that." Cancer came at us both like wolves out of nowhere. One day we were well and the next we weren't.

The last long letter I received from Barry was written in April of 2018. He talked of his struggles to finish *Horizon* in the face of his cancer and what gave him strength. "My inability to bring this book around has been a sort of joke I keep to myself," he wrote. "I am cautiously thinking I was doing alright, just hoping the cancer drugs will continue to do their work. . . . Every day as I stumble through this I am enlivened by the work and determination of my beloved friends."

In *Horizon,* Barry writes, "It's diversity that ensures perpetuity. The loss of diversity, on the other hand, threatens all life with extinction." Later in the book, he writes, "No matter our impressive history, every day we advance figuratively into evolutionary darkness. And because we are inescapably biological, we have no protection against extinction." Barry is likely referring to the extinctions of our own lives as well. He's gone, and since he passed, I've felt inescapably biological, especially since my own diagnosis.

On the way back to the Grand Hyatt, my wife and I received a blessing: a pair of native, threatened Hawaiian geese (*nene*) flew over just before we entered the heiau again. I thought of the "power of animals," that phrase used over forty years earlier to characterize the conference where I'd first met Barry. As he writes in his posthumous collection of essays, *Embrace Fiercely the Burning World,* "Each place is itself only, and nowhere repeated. Miss it and it's gone." I took healthy strides along the trail, attentive to the momentary swish of the nenes' passing wings.

ABSENCE, ANIMALS, AND OUTRAGE

LISA COUTURIER

8 August 2022

Dear Barry,

This letter to you began as a letter to Kurt. In it, I was going to tell him why I couldn't write an essay for an anthology he's editing—about you. First of all, I was going to tell him I'd left my "Barry Things"—our letters, my notes, and your books I'd notated over the years—spread across my desk in Manhattan. But now I was in Tampa *without* my Barry Things. Tampa, where the heat is excruciating and where I never expected I'd be this long. But here I still am—weeks later and for weeks still to come—camped out in a hotel near Tampa General Hospital where my brother is a patient in the cardiothoracic unit. He is an alone man, never married, no friends. Had he been born later in the twentieth century, he'd have been identified as "on the spectrum" and given direction, structure, help. But things weren't done that way then. He fell through the cracks, survived on odd jobs he often lost. Now here he is in a windowed room looking out over a bay, enduring Frankensteinian surgeries to reconstruct a body ravaged by the consequences of a torn esophagus: pleural empyema (a relentless and anti-biotic-resistant cave of pus in his chest), lung collapse, sepsis, and atrial fibrillation. Given these circumstances, I thought Kurt would understand why I didn't have the headspace, or the heart-space, for anything or anyone besides my brother. Even for Barry Lopez.

And so at dusk, another thunderstorm rolling in, I started my note to Kurt while waiting in the ICU for my brother to wake up after one of his lengthy operations. One of my favorite books of poetry, Donald Hall's *Without*, was in my lap. Monitors beeped. Tubes poked out from my brother's chest, pulsing with blood and infectious muck draining from his lung. Antibiotics and painkillers dripped through IVs into his arm. A small army of nurses came and went. Outside, lightning pierced through massive dark clouds. And then the deluge hit. Wind blew rain sideways over the Davis Islands. It was like being inside a washing machine. Somewhere in those minutes, when I thought about the possible loss of my brother, I remembered Donald Hall's advice to write to those no longer here with us, which was when I decided to write to you.

Whether we were at a writers' conference in Lubbock, Texas, or in Manhattan or D.C., the best way I found to break through what could turn into crippling shyness in your preternaturally calm presence was to sprinkle comments about your beautiful turquoise wrist cuff or your rockin' cowboy boots into our halting conversations about that which connected us most: a shared and visceral empathy for animals. At one of our Sowell Conferences, Kurt read passages from his arresting work "Death in Seville," about a bullfight. I don't recall the details of the scenes, just that I felt stabbed, myself. I started shifting in my chair, bowing my head into my hands. You were somewhere behind me. I felt a touch on my shoulder and turned to see your face, your white hair, your eyes inquisitive and alert.

"Are you okay?" you asked quietly. I thought then, and think still, that it takes one to know one. You must have felt stabbed, too.

"Yes," I said, but I was lying.

Most every time I left you and whatever crowd we happened to be in at whatever conference, I regretted not speaking up more and promised myself that, next time, I'd cobble together some relevant thoughts to contribute. But I never did. I just went home to my children and my horses and, grateful for your attention, wrote about what you said I was half-decent at writing about. Thank you for not counting me out when I felt like an outsider—a mostly urban woman who'd never extensively traveled the wild landscapes of the West.

When we first met in Manhattan, I was a five-months-pregnant East Coast mother writing about peregrine falcons nesting on New York City skyscrapers. I saw you again three months later when your play *Coyote* was in production at Arena Stage in Washington, D.C. I waddled down the aisle to say hello and reintroduce myself. You smiled, thanked me for coming, and introduced me to your wife, Debra, telling her, "This is one of my students." I left the theater wondering where the hell I'd gotten the audacity to impose on your private time with your wife. That you even remembered me was enough for me. A few years later, you invited a group of emerging writers to Junction, Texas, along the South Llano River, to immerse us in discussions of fate, community, and nature. One hot afternoon, outside in the wind, you pulled me aside with just a look and a turn of your head. You wanted to apologize.

"For what?" I asked.

"For introducing you to Debra as one of my students," you answered.

I probably over-responded and said something like, "No worries, that's okay, forget it, that's fine."

But if I could get a redo, I'd say this, instead: "I am one of your students. I'll always be one of your students. We are all your students."

And if I could get a second redo, it would be my turn to apologize to you—for the silence that sometimes fell between us. I wasn't trying to be aloof or disrespectful. Recently, in my attempts to reconcile this, I've started to think about silence in the way my horses have taught me, which is less about thinking and more about feeling. I keep six horses at my place in Maryland. They say a lot—in the way they breathe, in the way they move their eyes and ears and mouths and muscles—but they rarely utter a sound. I know you knew horses, too. Late the other night in Tampa, after I returned from the hospital, I found your 1975 essay "My Horse" online. It is, in part, about a quarter horse you rode named Coke High, and about whom you wrote: "When Coke High was 'with you,' he and I were the same animal. We could have cut a rooster out of a flock of chickens, we were so in tune. . . . There are other times when you are with each other but there's no connection at all. Coke got that way when he was bored and we'd fight each other about which way to go around a tree." As always, Barry, you were a good listener—with animals and with people. Maybe, during an impulse toward silence, when we couldn't cut words out of language, we spoke in ways more instinctual and emotional than intellectual, like the animals we already were, anyway.

Shortly after the gathering at Junction, on a late afternoon in June, you left a message on my landline: "Give me a call back, Lisa, I need to talk to you." I had just arrived home from Philadelphia, where I'd read from my collection that included the peregrine falcon piece you helped me with. So I called. Standing in swaths of golden-hour light and holding my old-fashioned phone, I felt somewhat absurdly like a groupie, thinking, I am on the phone with Barry f*&^ing Lopez. I was watching my little girls play in the backyard by the Potomac River, where we lived in a stone house.

We had just a few such calls, and each time you reminded me to be more of who I was, or who I wanted to be, instead of who I thought I had to be—for you or for "Nature" or for publishing. Though you were the inimitable writer of the natural world, you disliked being called a "Nature Writer." Nature is life; you were a Life Writer who told nuanced stories about all kinds of lives, human and nonhuman alike.

We met again eleven years later at a literary conference, at which I read an underdeveloped excerpt from a project I was working on about illness, birth, bullies, and little brown bats. Your mentorship had been the reason I was still hanging on to an obsession with the topic of childbirth: its landscapes, how it's tamed with meds and scheduled deliveries, the mystery and poetry of the pregnant body, the incomprehensible pain and grace of giving birth.

"This is good, good," you said to me after the reading. "How many pages do you have ready?"

"Not enough," I answered.

"Do you know the work of shamans?" you asked. "Read their wisdom about illness."

"I'll do that."

"Work on this. We need this," you said while you hugged me.

"Uh, thank you, alright, I will," I answered, as you slipped away. I'll tell you now what I didn't tell you then: I was stunned. I thought the excerpt was a mess and was almost embarrassed to have read it. That you, apparently, understood its intention and saw clarity and meaning in the fragments of work I'd shared energized my commitment to the crumpled stack of marked-up pages I'd stuffed in my backpack. But I remained confused, adrift. For two years—while also working on a manuscript about horses you'd encouraged me to finish—I traveled through various stages of "lost-ness." What I eventually started calling my "birth and bullies project" became not a book, but a longform essay published twice. It devastates me still to read it, and though the shamans couldn't help me, I shattered my own memories, which is to say I told some truths.

So, thank you—for leading me through being lost, and toward a stronger state of Being.

Before my brother was injured, I spent five months (on and off) two hours south of Tampa, staying in an impoverished town in the interior of the state so that I could help take care of my father, who has late-stage Parkinson's. My father's town is also in a Secondary Zone of panther habitat—a landscape, like the large tracts of forest around the Fort Myers Airport, that panthers may currently use or expand into from the Primary

Zone, which is land absolutely essential for panthers, like the Big Cypress National Preserve north of the Everglades. Down here, the panthers have long been in peril. In the 1980s and 1990s the big cats were hanging on by a thread, despite their listing on the Endangered Species Act, and things haven't really gotten much better.

My father sleeps a lot, and while he slept each morning, I walked for miles in the Secondary Zone along canals and scrubby forests of saw palmettos and pine flatwoods, hoping to glimpse a panther moving through heat to shade.

I thought of you on those long, quiet walks, as I have on so many other walks over the years. I thought of you when I saw crows mobbing a hawk—because when we worked on my peregrine piece you reminded me more than once to "look up, *show* that you looked up," which helped me cinch the ending. I thought of you when I heard something close scrabbling along the canal banks. Turtles! The world is more than what we see: we also need to listen. And of course I thought of your classic *Of Wolves and Men.* Because what we did to wolves we also did to panthers—we hunted them to the brink of extinction.

I never did glimpse a panther in the Secondary Zone, but I know they were near. Occasionally, local news stations sensationalize reports of panthers wandering into backyards on their way to more interesting places. Most often, though—just as you so heartwrenchingly described the deaths of wild animals in "Apologia"—panthers are hit by cars. In 2021, twenty-one Florida panthers were killed in vehicle collisions. Already in 2022, eighteen panthers, including numerous females of reproductive age—poised to render the miracle that is birth—have been struck by cars, mostly in Collier County where large swaths of critical panther habitat are being lost to continued development. It's the same story over and over again, isn't it? Why do we never seem to learn? What do we never seem to learn? What can be done? When it comes to panthers and wolves and birds and . . . and . . . and . . . and . . . and . . . and . . .

Do you remember Rilke's profoundly empathic poem, "The Panther," about a panther trapped behind bars in a Paris zoo in 1903? At roughly the same time Rilke wrote his poem, he advised a young writer in letters to "live the questions." The paradox, as I see it, is that while Rilke was living his questions, the panther was dying on display. In his poem, Rilke writes: "It seems to him there are / a thousand bars; and behind the bars, no world. . . . Only at times, the curtain of the pupils / lifts, quietly—. An image enters in, / rushes down through the tensed, arrested muscles, / plunges into the heart and is gone." How long did that panther wait—not to die, though that would end the suffering, but for something to change *while the panther was still alive?* Rilke's panther was just one of how many billions of animals all over the world, hurt in how many millions of ways over how many thousands of years? I remember your thoughts and what you wrote in *Arctic Dreams:* "There are simply no answers to some of the great pressing questions." But dammit, I'm impatient—for the animals' sake, for the sake of those Florida panthers. Yes, yes, lean into the light, make "life a worthy expression of a leaning into the light." But when little gets answered, when species keep falling away, and when the things of our despair plunge into our hearts and are gone, I'm unsure about the light anymore. Since you've been gone, it's only gotten darker. I feel darker, myself, as though I'm learning how to disappear in order to survive. Are we entering an entropic tipping point, a time when, in addition to everything else, even the questions are dying?

Dear Barry,

I had a dream about you last night and I understood that as a message—and that maybe I had something to say to you now.

In my dream, I, you and others who I guessed were your old friends were sitting on a grassy, windy hill looking out over a vast landscape of treeless earth. It wasn't exactly the desert, though it seemed that it once was. The ground was a soft, wavy, orange-yellow, almost like a blanket, and you commented that life once had been there, though it was not there now. Suddenly, children were running around us and rolling down the hill into the orange land that became an ocean flowing away from all of us, into the sky. The children disappeared. Horses cantered in front us, and I told you that those were my horses. They stood before us on what was now a fenceless field, staring our way, and then looking off, looking at us, and looking away, as horses do when they perceive what we cannot. You wanted to see what they saw, and suddenly you were with them. They began running toward the horizon, and I noticed that a gate had been left open—even though there was no fence—and the horses were heading for it. The last thing I remember about the dream was running down the hill and into the field, trying to get to the gate before the horses, so that I could lock it, and keep them close.

Sending this note to you with love and affection—

Your friend, however far in distance, and in whatever ways—

Big hugs—(*as you often closed your letters*)

Lisa

Well, I must sleep. Tomorrow will be another long day at the hospital, with my brother. I emailed you this letter, this dream, in December 2020, when your many friends were writing and calling to say goodbye. Over and again, I've thought about this dream, re-remembered it; and I want to say that I don't think I ever made it to the gate. And so, with the horses, you left us.

HOME GROUND AND HOMELESSNESS

SUSAN BRIND MORROW

Barry Lopez fought for preservation—the preservation of landscape and the preservation of the literature that describes it. He wrote about the Arctic and the desert; he created a literary dictionary of the American landscape and an archive of the papers of American writers who turned the specificity of nature into words. The close observation of nature is a keystone in the foundation of the American sensibility—a sensibility that pervades the work of American artists and writers down to the present day. It is a unique cultural manifestation of the empirical translation of the physical world, the translation of nature into art and memory.

One might look to another piece of writing that describes the phenomenon that Barry contributed to and understood: that writing is the true agent of preservation. An Egyptian New Kingdom poem on Chester Beatty Papyrus IV, miraculously preserved on the fragile medium of paper for over three thousand years, describes it well:

> If you learn this profession you will become a writer.
> Think of the writers of the past

Their names have become immortal
Even though they are dead, and their descendants are gone.
They didn't make themselves tombs out of copper
With tombstones of iron from heaven.
They didn't think about leaving heirs in order to perpetuate their names.
They made heirs out of books they had written themselves.
People they will never know are their children,
For a writer is a teacher to all.
Their houses are buried, their graves are forgotten,
Their children are gone,
But their names live on in the books
That they made while they were alive.
Be a writer, take this to heart,
And your name will be like theirs.
Writing is better than something made of stone,
Than a solid tomb, for it lives in the heart.
A man decays. His corpse is dust. His family dies,
But his books live on.

(Translated by Susan Brind Morrow)

Barry Lopez began the book project *Home Ground: A Guide to the American Landscape* in 2002. He gathered a group of writers and gave each one a list of recondite landscape terms to define for a new dictionary of the American landscape. It seemed at first a little like a parlor game, like Dictionary Game, I thought at the time, but it had a higher purpose: to bring back empirical science, to help people see the detailed world before their eyes.

I am from Upstate New York. I grew up in the Finger Lakes, the Great Lakes watershed that runs along the border region between New York and Canada. My mother was Canadian, and that freshwater-borderland sensibility permeated our lives. It was a love of the freshwater landscape—of fishing and canoeing and of particular shades of blue and gray, pine and birch woods and light through light-green maple leaves. When I was in my early twenties, I came home after my first months away in the Sahara where I was working as an archeologist. When I returned to that landscape of water, to a place dominated by deep blue lakes, I was amazed by it for the first time. This is the kind of heightened awareness that Barry sought. He wanted to bring language and definition to it, to help awaken a deeper sense of place in people so that they would really look at the physical world they were in—at the ground beneath their feet.

The art historian Barbara Novak's book *Nature and Culture* talks about the detailed scientific knowledge of weather, botany, and geology the Hudson River School painters brought to their aesthetic. These nineteenth-century artists knew in detail the world they were looking at. They knew that industry threatened the land. And they fought it with beauty and knowledge. They were fighting for preservation. This is what Barry was after as a writer a century and a half later with *Home Ground*, because all of the technology of our time has not helped in the development of the eye's native ability to see, to perceive. Quite the opposite. Computer and television screens have undeniably had the effect of flattening our perception of the world. Barry was heroic in his attempts to restore the earlier sensibility of the native perception of the world around us in all of its living detail. When he first called me to invite me to be part of *Home Ground*, this is what we talked about. I saw in the visual component of hieroglyphs not simply flat symbols but miniature animal studies that arose from a kind of delight in the close observation and knowledge of nature—where, for example, the small white egret becomes the verb to tremble, not because the egret itself trembles, but, in a much more subtle and knowing acuity of observation, because the long white feathers of this particular bird tremble in the wind. Barry brought this kind of detailed vision to the American landscape. If people knew in detail the place they were in, they would treasure it and they would want to preserve it.

The Greek word *nomos* means pasture. It is the greening up of a particular place after rain. A nomad is someone who knows a landscape in the home-ground sense, the dips and shadows in its topography that will make the green growth last. The traditional nomadic life is like a yearly pilgrimage of moving around from one known seasonal pasture to another. It is a life of privation and survival, but it is a life of pleasure too, because everything—time, soil, weather, light—means something. You have to know what you're doing, and to know what you're doing you have to know where you are.

In the 1970s *The New Yorker* ran an essay about what the author called *querencia*, the animal instinct of place—the patch of ground a bull retreats to in a bullfight or the patch of a living-room rug a dog will defend. Everyone has an innate sense of spatial orientation like a crab. This is a sense that has been damaged in modern life. We can see this damage all around us as we look at the homelessness crisis in American cities. I think of the *Home Ground* project and how the loss of that sense of place, of one's place in the world, is at the heart of this crisis. I lived as a homeless person for a while when I was young—drifting around, not knowing where I was going to be or sleep from one day to the next. It was one big adventure. What kept me from going off the deep end was the fact that my parents still lived in the house I grew up in. I wasn't going back, but I knew they were there—I had an anchor.

This querencia is precisely what must be restored as we address the homelessness crisis today. The new nomadism is a confused involuntary squalor, the result of neglect, hopelessness, and social collapse. People need more than shelter. They need a sense of what they are doing, of *who* they are and of *where* they are. They need food and water and shelter and community, and they need a sense of belonging. The remedy is to give people back a sense of place.

The creation of a new WPA or domestic Peace Corps has been discussed in Washington D.C., and it comes to mind as something that could work toward establishing sustainable communities for the people throughout our country who have been displaced in the modern world. Tracts of public land have been set aside for parks and other purposes: why not set aside tracts of public land to create small communities using converted shipping containers for homes? An American Peace Corps could staff clinics and schools—just as it does among people in foreign lands.

A community like this does not have to be a welfare state. It could be a place where people develop basic skills in things like agriculture and carpentry, where their lives and their work are of recognized value. This is the old American Utopian community ideal. It has been done before; why not give it another try? Something has to be done to help people now. The underlying principle is not socialism, but social concern and social responsibility. It is not about fostering dependency, but caring enough about people to help them recover the skills to care for themselves. President Franklin Roosevelt kept politics out of his social programs; he was only interested in what works. What works is giving people a sense of themselves within a larger community, a living arrangement that involves both privacy and positive engagement with others.

In *The Grapes of Wrath*, Steinbeck conveyed the tremendous relief that people who had been forced out of their homes felt when they came at last to a place like this, to a government-sponsored community where they were given their own simple homes and work and could finally find meaning and structure in their lives.

For this reason, I would take the *Home Ground* idea of Barry Lopez very seriously, and use it as a manual to help people recover that essential sense of place, of where they are and how they relate—first to the countryside, then to the country. Like Mole in *The Wind in the Willows*, the hope would be to awaken the memory of what it is to belong somewhere, the memory of the details, to awaken the animal awareness of the smells and the sights and the feeling—of light moving through the trees, across the desert hills, across the sky at dawn, and in the evening flights of birds, all the details the senses need to locate the human animal and allow one to be at home on this earth.

THE CHANTING GOSHAWK

JULIA MARTIN

It was 1987 and Barry Lopez was traveling through Namibia, in Southern Africa. Somewhere in the Kgalagadi Transfrontier Park, then called the Kalahari Gemsbok National Park, he noticed a pale chanting goshawk, a predator whose hunting depends on depth perception, in the top of a dead tree:

> The bird had its back to me as I approached. I imagined it gazing intensely at an expanse of savannah grass before it, searching for a creature upon which to swoop. As I drew closer, the bird rotated its head and stared down at me. Its right eye had been torn out of its socket. The hole was rimmed with blood-matted feathers.
>
> It turned back to its survey of the savannah, ignoring me.
>
> Often, when I want to give up, I think of that bird. How many other such severely wounded birds are there in the world, still hunting?

This description from *Horizon* is characteristic: fascination with the living world, and a precise and unsentimental attention to a specific animal or bird, a nonhuman person whose sentience is unquestioned. This being may be at once both real and metaphoric, and their behavior is likely to be instructive for our own.

The goshawk, who continues hunting even though the eye has been ripped out, comes to mind when Barry is camped in the Canadian High Arctic. He's joined an archaeological team on Skraeling Island, and they're investigating a site that was seasonally occupied by a small group of Paleo-Inuit people known today as the Thule. Eight hundred years later, much of their domestic stuff—bone implements, stone tools, wood carvings, harpoon tips, scraps of skin clothing—was still lying where they left it, frozen under the collapsed sod roofs of their winter houses. In *Horizon*, these remnants of the indomitable Thule who made a human life amidst unimaginable darkness and bitter cold remind Barry of the goshawk, and he finds courage in the memory of both.

Three decades in the making, Barry's manuscript for *Horizon* was a massive tome, a printout wrapped in a glossy beaver pelt. He showed it to me when I visited him and his wife, Debra, in 2018. Propped up beside the text was a cover design that Barry had imagined from the beginning, a rippling sea of blue that extends into a luminous blue sky. He began work on the book soon after publishing *Arctic Dreams*, and the travels and meditations that it brings together tracked alongside all his other writing ever since.

"But you see," he said to me that day, with a characteristically intent stare, "I couldn't have done this on my own. Whenever I simply couldn't go on, simply didn't know how to take it further, I would go down to the river. And every time I would find a beaver stick. *Every* time."

The sticks were different sizes, gathered in bundles or laid out on the writing table in what Barry called the "Horizon Room." Each one was the record of a moment when he thought he could go no further. When it seemed impossible. And each one was a witness to the urgent livingness of the world, and the possibility of continuing. Walk down to the river. Find a beaver stick. Bring it back. Keep on working.

It was that interstitial moment between the completion of a big project and its publication, a space of release and quietness before the babble of book tours and reviews. The manuscript lay in a room whose big windows let the forest in: deep ferns and deep moss, deep Douglas-firs clothed in old man's beard, deep silence. From 1970, this place was the home to which Barry would return from a lifetime of unassuageable wanderlust, a refuge of thirty-six acres of Oregon forest tracked through by elk and bear and fox and all the others, in which was planted a human house, a cottage for guests, a little outbuilding stacked with the notebooks and accumulated documents of his writing archive, and a lumber shed neatly packed with wood.

Once, years back, he drove me in his truck for hours on a small road through nearby old-growth forest, running the engine so slowly that we could notice and then get out to look at the leaves of a particular plant, the movement of an insect, the bark of four-hundred-year-old trees. Now walking had become difficult for him, the cancer having spread to his limbs, and when Debra and I took the elk path down to the river, a reach of the McKenzie below the house, he remained at home. It used to be his daily practice to contemplate the river—"It's a kind of animal, you know," he told me—but now his bench at the edge of the water was decaying back into the soil. It was early fall. The ground was splashed with bright leaves. In California, Oregon, and Washington, the world was on fire as never before. Just a few miles away, tens of thousands of acres of forest were alight, with hundreds of people working the firebreaks. At night, you could see the red flash of the fire trucks flying past. Climate fires.

The realization that one is living in a local-global emergency of apocalyptic scale pervades *Horizon*. It's a massive and capacious work in which the segue from the hunting goshawk to the Thule to the present moment of our early-twenty-first-century predicament is a typical gesture. The meandering effect of this way of writing makes it difficult to pin down exactly what the book is "about," except perhaps to say that its particular invitation to the reader is to enter a mind keenly attuned to a sense of how things connect, a mind which seems incapable of turning away. If one of the unreturnable gifts of the present moment—of the so-called Anthropocene—is an insight into interconnectedness, then the narrative is a fierce and unrelenting witness: the suffering and the beauty. All of it, inextricable.

The story of the expedition to Skraeling Island is one of a mesh of journey tales told with an acute awareness of the negative impacts of international travel, and a strong desire to bring something back of value to others. In Puerto Ayora in the Galápagos, Barry researches the horror of the conquistadores, is chased by feral dogs, and dives among brilliantly colored blue-eyed damsel fish. At Jackal Camp, in the East African region of the Great Rift Valley, he joins an archaeological dig searching for hominid fossils, ponders the origin of our species, and gets malaria. In Tasmania, he visits the nineteenth-century penal settlement at Port Arthur where boys as young as eight, brought in on the transportation ships and subsequently hounded, beaten, and sexually abused, jumped to their death off the cliffs, holding hands. In Antarctica, he joins a group of scientists looking for meteorites on the northern edge of the Polar Plateau.

I first read *Horizon* when it was published in 2019, and returned to it during the pandemic. Barry's steady attention to what is precious and pernicious in human culture, his enthralled witness to the resilience and wonder and fragility of the living planet, the sense the book gives of writing in response to a world on the brink, the intimate reach of its compassion, the hopefulness and curiosity and wonder—these all seemed apposite during that deeply strange time. But I think the main reason I came back to its interwoven stories was to do with craft: how to do this thing, to write an extended narrative essay about something you find extremely difficult, and to keep on doing it.

It was, I knew, a project that demanded everything of Barry. It had become a lifetime's habit to put himself physically "out there" in remote and very challenging parts of the planet. Now he was less mobile, but still working on a project that was right at the limit of what felt possible to him as a writer: a vast book of narrative essays about the state of the earth in prose that embodies a nonlinear sense of interconnectedness, completed while terminally ill and in pain, with a deep sense of his own inadequacy for the task.

This capacity for perseverance was and continues to be a strong example for my own writing. I felt it particularly during the lockdown when, as other distractions shut down, and I no longer had to commute to work, I began making a small space in the day to work on a new book manuscript. The practice was a consolation of sorts in that bewildering time, but I tended to work slowly and to feel that I'd taken on more than I could manage. In this context, Barry's approach was enormously encouraging, and I kept coming back to something he'd said to me several years earlier. We'd been talking about the craft of writing, and he described the terror of becoming lost in the midst of a writing project and being convinced that maybe this time he wouldn't find his way through. Crucially, though, wonderfully, he'd learnt that when he reached *that* point, he now knew that he was in the right place:

> I mean, you can look at my notebooks and see, "I have no idea what I'm doing." I write things like that to myself. "I'm in so far over my head . . . " And now at the age of sixty-five, I *know*, even though it's still very scary, that if I'm in over my head, that's where I'm supposed to be. And feeling lost and breaking down, actually breaking down in tears, because I'm feeling the depth of my own stupidity. Maybe it won't work this time . . . But, you know, I've gotten through it before, and you just have to keep going, push through the fear. (Lopez & Martin, *Syntax of the River*)

Not everyone needs to write like this—at the terrifying edge—but this was Barry's way, and I have found his view of it very comforting. It was his conviction that the vulnerability and the not-knowing, and the pain, and the determination to persevere, were in fact essential to the work: the work both of writing and of living a human life.

During that first year of the pandemic, we were in touch sporadically. Then in late August, just a few days before the fire that destroyed his forest, his lumber shed, his truck, and his archive, he wrote that he was at work on a new collection of essays and hoped to be finished within a few months. "My health is a bit shaky," he said, "but my attitude about it is the same as it's always been: onward."

His resonant voice comes back to me now from years ago when he was still well and fit, and I feel again the urgency of the vision he worked so hard to share, even when the courage it embodies seems impossible:

> I want to make a *pattern* in a story that allows a person to say, "I remember what I forgot about what I meant my life to be. And I'm going to go do that now." (*Syntax of the River*)

DARKNESS
AND LIGHT

SIERRA CRANE MURDOCH

Some days after Barry Lopez died, I pulled every book of his I owned from the shelves around my apartment and stacked them on a corner of my desk. Then I walked down the hill to the used bookshop in the small Oregon town where I live and found several books of his I did not yet own. For a year, I picked at the stack, revisiting passages I recalled vividly or had forgotten. My words would come when I was ready, I figured, so I scribbled sentences on scraps of paper, lost them, found them, rewrote them, in an ambulatory manner I thought might have pleased Barry. He was the only writer who made me feel virtuous for my slowness, which I once heard him call "patience," though I believe even Barry knew the fine line between virtuousness and slacking off. He had told me he sometimes admonished his students, "I cannot teach you discipline, and I cannot teach you hunger. You have to find those things inside yourself."

It was his request that I write this essay. Or maybe it was not a request, but a suggestion. He had asked it in a way so gentle, so lacking in urgency, that I would sometimes feel as if I'd dreamed it, but then I would relisten to a voicemail he'd left me, which I had saved, and there it was: "I've got a kind of favor to ask."

When I had returned Barry's call, he told me a man was writing a profile for the alumni magazine of the college Barry had attended. The man was interviewing some celebrated writers about Barry's legacy, but it had struck Barry that these writers were all of his own generation or one below him. Did he even *have* a legacy if few young people read his work, he wondered? Was there any space for his work in the collective consciousness, amid an economy of distraction and a literary world enamored with speed? This was two months before he died. I had known Barry only four months.

Barry asked me to "think about this," in case the man writing the profile gave me a call, and maybe also to write about his legacy myself if I felt compelled. This is how Barry was, his profound gestures composed of language so light it seemed to drift off.

I knew Barry Lopez's name from the spines of books on my parents' shelves, but the first works of his I read were essays and short stories in *Orion*, to which my parents subscribed when I was sixteen. By the time I became aware of his writing, Barry was already a bard among an international community of writers and artists defending the natural world against industrial exploitation. One of the short stories in *Orion* that glimmered out at me was about a man who comes across a sliver of obsidian while walking in the desert and considers pocketing the stone for his daughter, then decides against it. "He had come upon a time in his life when everything, even the things of God, needed protection," Barry wrote of the man's restraint. He implied that in being removed from the landscape, the stone became only an object, but if the man left the stone, he would "have to use his imagination" in telling his daughter about it, thus preserving its particular mystery.

I saw Barry speak at my college around the time I read the story. I recall, mainly, his bearing—turned-inward, serious, his words impeccably chosen.

After college, I moved West, and that year a friend sent me a link to an interview Barry had done with the journalist Bill Moyers. I watched the interview, rapt. Then I watched it twice more. Barry articulated beliefs I did not yet know I had, but in which I recognized myself clearly and immediately. "We have a way of talking about beauty as though beauty were only skin deep," he said. "But real beauty is so deep you have to move into darkness in order to understand what beauty is." He meant that to opt for beauty but not darkness was to cling to false hope—that *real* hope required an awareness of both darkness and beauty at once. To make space in one's own mind for both was to remain open to a "full expression" of life.

After I saw the interview, I began reading Barry's books, and I noticed how violence and beauty cohabitated in all his work. In *Of Wolves and Men*, he wrote of both the admiration and hatred humans have for wolves, the former rooted in a longing for intimacy with nature even as humans grow more distant from it; the latter, in a species of fear called *theriophobia*—"fear of the projected beast in oneself," or, as Barry saw it, fear of the darkness we all possess. In "Orchids on the Volcanoes," from his 1998 essay collection, *About This Life*, he observed a wreckage of dead birds in the Galápagos, "crumpled on the bare ground like abandoned clothing," and "the stark terror" of the place, where "innocent repose and violence are never far apart."

He often invoked the concurrence of light and dark by pressing life's fragility against the brutality of landscapes. *Arctic Dreams* was constructed almost entirely from this dichotomy, from the preface, where Barry wrote, "I had never known how benign sunlight could be . . . How run through with compassion in a land that bore so eloquently the evidence of centuries of winter," through to the end, where, after hundreds of pages of detailed observation, his point strikes the reader as startlingly succinct:

> If there is a stage at which an individual life becomes truly adult,
> it must be when one grasps the irony in its unfolding and accepts
> responsibility for a life lived in the midst of such paradox. One must
> live in the middle of contradiction because if all contradiction were

eliminated at once life would collapse. There are simply no answers to some of the great pressing questions. You continue to live them out, making your life a worthy expression of a leaning into the light.

I loved that line when I read it—"leaning into the light," a stalk tilting toward the sun—and I love it now, even after Barry's death when the passage containing it became one of the most quoted in his oeuvre.

In 2013, Barry published his famous essay "Sliver of Sky" in *Harper's* about being raped as a child. His rapist had been a doctor, a friend of his mother's, who feigned charity by offering to entertain her sons. In the years Barry suffered these serial assaults, he wrote, "the deepest and sometimes only relief I had was when I was confronted with the local, elementary forces of nature: hot Santa Ana winds blowing west into the San Fernando Valley . . . winter floods inundating our neighborhood when Caballero Creek breached its banks on its way to the Los Angeles River." Looking upward at a flock of birds filled him with "encouragement."

This nesting of natural beauty inside the horror of the essay's disclosures was perhaps a better explanation than any for why pairing dark with light felt necessary to Barry. He took from each of these observations of the world around him "a sense of what it might feel like to become fully alive," he wrote. But it was recently, in reading his posthumous essay collection, *Embrace Fearlessly the Burning World*, that this necessity struck me with a more devastating clarity. "The linchpin of my existence as a California boy was the ever-forgiving, ever-soothing light," he wrote in "Missing California," published for the first time in the collection:

> That, and for me the flocks of birds that pulled me into the sky, pulled me up and out of myself . . . Of course, it was the pedophile who gave me eight tumbler pigeons on my birthday, the pigeons that deliberately lose aerodynamic life and plummet to earth as though shot by a gun, only to pull out of it a few feet from the ground and soar stiff-winged toward the open sky.

The essay ends there, on the realization that the birds who relieved his suffering were a gift from the man who caused his suffering. He makes no attempt at explanation.

This is something else Barry wrote about often: the unfathomable. He wrote about unfathomable violence—his visits to Auschwitz, and the Washita River in Oklahoma, where, in 1868, the Seventh Cavalry massacred dozens of peaceful Cheyenne men, women, and children, then slit the throats of their horses.

He wrote about the unfathomable in a spiritual sense, too, for which he preferred the word *mystery*. In *Of Wolves and Men*, he advised his readers that he was incapable of answering all our questions, but we shouldn't worry, since "to allow mystery, which is to say to yourself, 'There could be more, there could be things we don't understand,' is not to damn knowledge. It is to take a wider view." He dealt similarly with a conflict he perceived between Indigenous knowledge gathered through generations of immersion in nature and knowledge derived from Western methods of scientific study. The former tended to allow some things to remain beyond human understanding, while the latter, he argued, too often discounted what couldn't be proven by science. "A solution to a mystery is perhaps not a sign of wisdom," he told Moyers. "I am perfectly comfortable being in a state of ignorance before something incomprehensible."

Among the many revelations that have come to me from reading Barry's work was one I found in his posthumous collection, in an essay titled "Madre de Dios." He described his Jesuit upbringing and how he found in Catholicism a "sphere of incomprehensible holiness which, in the Western imagination, stands beyond the reach of the rational mind." Then he recalled an encounter with the spirit of the Blessed Mother, when he was eight years old, trapped in the bed of his rapist. She hovered above the floor, hands reaching toward him, and said, "You will not die here."

The people I know who have endured unimaginable violence at the hands of others are also those who appear more open than most to spiritual or supernatural occurrences. This does not surprise me. To accept as real an act so evil, for which reason and motive could forever elude its victim, is also to accept that there are things we can't explain. This humility, Barry seemed to argue, is not just virtuous but essential to our survival, the antidote to unimaginable darkness being unimaginable light.

Still, spiritual belief is a hard thing to write about. Once, a writing professor told me that he avoided teaching Barry's work for fear his students might, in attempting to imitate him, "get a little mushy."

I admit I've found Barry's work dense and sprawling and difficult to read at times; if I don't quiet everything around me, my mind wanders. I've wondered if this was deliberate, if Barry was challenging readers to a meditation. "Pay attention," he wrote over and over in his books, as he did again in an essay titled "The Invitation" from his final collection: "Perhaps the first rule of everything we endeavor to do is to pay attention." And when I do pay attention, I am mesmerized: I see Barry's syntactical precision, the carpentry of his paragraphs, the framing built from the crossbeams of his experience. In fiction, especially, his philosophizing was tactile, as in a passage from *Resistance*, in which he made the case, yet again, for mystery:

> For me, the terrifying part was the ease with which you could lose your imagination . . . In every quarter of life, it seemed then, we were retreating into fundamentalism. The yes/no of belief, the in/out of fashion, the down/up of pharmaceuticals, the on/off of music, the hot/cold of commitment, the dead/live of electricity, the forward/backward of machinery, the give/take of a deal.

What I loved so much about this book of interconnected short stories, told from the perspectives of nine artists and academics who each receive a letter from their government declaring their work "unpatriotic" and thus a threat to national security, is that it precisely conveys the ideas integral to Barry's writing without straying into moralization or sentimentalism. Yet what made Barry's oeuvre radical, I now believe, was in fact his willingness to risk these qualities—to reject the common urge to construct from language a bulwark against emotion. "The things that make us uncomfortable in public are a person who wishes to speak of what is beautiful," he told Moyers. "That makes everybody a little bit nervous, because many of us keep this jaded, cynical separateness with the world."

I saw Barry speak once more, in the fall of 2019, at an event he facilitated for a friend. I watched, as rapt as I had been during the Moyers interview. When the event finished, I left without introducing myself. What do you say to a person whose work has influenced you so thoroughly that you feel their words and ideas as a substance coursing through your body? How do you convey to a person who has never read your work how much theirs has become a part of yours? You can't. It's desperate, and a little bit creepy.

So I left before I met Barry. I did not need to tell him that, in my own work, at his urging, I had gone into darkness to find beauty, and by beauty, I mean love.

And so the call came as a surprise. I was driving across Colorado one day in July of 2020 when a friend in New York forwarded me a voicemail he'd received from Barry. I pulled over, hit play. I recognized Barry's voice, serious but kind in its formality. He was explaining to my friend—whom I now realized was his friend, too—that he had finished reading the book I wrote. My friend had recommended it, and now Barry was asking my friend to pass along his number to me.

Barry and I spoke on the phone not long after that. For the same reason I fear meeting writers I admire, I now fear having to distill our first conversation onto the page. Can I just say it was one hour among the most essential of my life? He said kind things about my book. They seemed the kindest things anyone had ever said about my book, I believe because Barry was a writer whose perspective on the world I had long nurtured in myself, so the parts he chose to notice were parts meaningful to me already. Then he told me what he had been reading and writing and asked what I was writing, too. I explained my new book precisely as I could, adding, when I stumbled, that I had not yet decided how much I should write before I sent pages to a publisher. Barry replied that with every book he ever wrote he had, at some point, inevitably wondered, *Why wasn't this given to someone smarter than I am?* Then he advised me to never build an outline too soon because "the idea of writing is not to find what you're looking for." He added, "And you have to know what you stand for. You have to resist the temptation to do things for money or fame, because you'll wake up when you're forty and not know who you are."

I had turned thirty-three that week. I felt young all of a sudden, my life full of possibility. I felt a warmth toward Barry rising in my throat. He asked for my mailing address in case he came across an article or book he wished to send, and he suggested I visit him soon; we both lived in Oregon, a few hours' drive apart. It was the beginning of the pandemic, but I could stay in his guest cottage, we could eat outside, and his wife, the writer Debra Gwartney, could take me kayaking on the McKenzie River. In the meantime, Barry advised, I should call his landline whenever I wished. He would answer 90 percent of the time, and Debra the other 10.

"She's—" Barry began, pausing long enough for me to wonder what adjective he would choose. Then he said, "—first-rate."

We spoke a handful of times that summer and fall. We would talk about what he was working on and what I was working on, about books he recommended and ideas that had come to him lately, and then he would say, "Well, I shouldn't keep you from your writing." I could have talked to him forever, but I hung up because I didn't want him to think I was greedy, and of course it was not me who had limited time, but Barry. He only once mentioned his cancer. He was rationing his efforts, he said, finishing an essay collection and some short stories. He often referenced his most recent book, *Horizon*, which I sensed he was proud of. Later, Robin Desser, Barry's editor at Random House, and previously at Knopf, would tell me it had taken so long for Barry to write the book that she feared he might die before he finished it. He had signed the contract before Desser became his editor, and in her first years working with him, he wrote other books, until they agreed, in her words, "that it would be better to direct his energies to his major opus." Whenever Barry visited New York after that, he hand delivered a typewritten manuscript, requesting that Desser not read it but keep it on her desk so she knew he was writing. "Of course, I would sort of look at it," Desser said. "But I also thought, I'm preserving my own reaction to this, because I felt somewhat shamanistically that if I didn't read this version, maybe the final one would come sooner."

Horizon is indeed an opus—not a memoir, exactly, but a literary consummation of his wanderings. It revisits places that shaped his thinking, reinforces the stitching of his ideas across landscape and time. "A long life might be understood . . . as a kind of cataract of imperfectly recollected intentions," Barry writes:

> Some of one's early intentions fade. Others endure through the inevitable detours of amnesia, betrayal, and loss of belief . . . But, too, the unfathomable sublimity of a random moment, like the touch of a beloved's hand on one's burning face, might revive the determination to carry on, and, at least for a time, rid one of life's weight of self-doubt and regret. Or a moment of staggering beauty might reignite the intention one once had to lead a life of great meaning, to live up to one's own expectations.

The book rarely gets more personal than this, yet it strikes me as some of Barry's most intimate writing, deepening the idea fundamental to his work that what people most desire is "to love or be loved," and that all human pain, particularly loneliness, emerges when a person fails to feel either.

In the same way that he repeatedly invoked the coexistence of light and dark or insisted we pay attention, this idea is a refrain from much of his prior work. In *About This Life*, Barry wrote, "Although I'm wary of pancultural truths, I believe in all human societies there is a desire to love and be loved." Years later, in the interview with Moyers, he mused that everyone, at some time, "is driven to a point of despair. . . . I think they don't quit because there is a capacity for, a desire for reciprocated love that brings you back to life."

I asked Desser if she thought Barry repeated himself because he wasn't sure his readers heard him. She believed this was true, but added, "When someone writes music, you can tell that this is Beethoven, or this is John Coltrane. There's a theme that's recognizable. These are the things that matter to Barry, so they reoccur. . . . And this message about love, how many times can we hear that? Many times. We need to hear it many times."

She told me that by the time he wrote *Horizon*, and especially after he published the essay about his childhood abuse, she sensed that Barry felt relief in mostly having said what he wanted to say, and now his task was to unite all he ever said into a single work that refracted his ideas through the variable lenses of the far-flung places from which he had reported. The book, like his life's work, "contained multitudes," she said, in how it encompassed vast geographies and histories yet returned, always, to the same idea—to love.

The book wasn't everything, though. In its closing pages, Barry warns against taking it as his last word: "We assume sometimes that whatever the dying say at the end, or last write down, represents a conscious final thought, but I don't believe this is very often true. What is really going on at the end mostly goes unspoken and . . . remains unknown to the living."

Was Barry saying that death is a preservation of mystery? Those closer to him know better than I do how much of himself he left out of his books. My phone calls with Barry, like my experience reading his work, were intimate but never revealing. We said almost nothing about our personal lives. I never told him, for example, that his first call came the week I ended a decade-long partnership, that our conversations spanned the loneliest period of my life, that his voice brought me comfort, and that whenever I conjured an image of him in his home—in which he had lived for fifty years, in a forest he once described in an essay as the place a person knows so well they "sense that they *themselves* are becoming known . . . and this reciprocity, to know and be known, reinforces a sense that one is necessary in the world"—I felt relief from my own unmooring.

~~~

It has become a trope that writers whom publishers have long placed in the box called "nature writing" flinch at the term like it's an epithet. "'Nature writing' has become a cant phrase, branded and bandied out of any useful existence, and I would be glad to see its deletion from the current discourse," Robert Macfarlane has written. These writers' complaint is that the label consigns them to an obscure literary corner, whereas what they have chosen as their subject—most succinctly, survival—is as fundamental a story as it gets. "I'm not writing about nature. I'm writing about humanity," Barry told Moyers. "And if I have a subject, it is justice, and the rediscovery of the manifold ways in which our lives can be shaped by the recovery of a sense of reverence for life."

I agree with Barry. It was not his descriptions of the Arctic summer or of forests along the McKenzie River, beautiful as they may be, that drew me to his work; it was the way he made clear our predicament, which is that violence toward land begets violence toward people, and vice versa; that violence of any kind wounds both victim and perpetrator, heaving across space and time, marking land and bodies, drawing us all into a collective trauma that perpetuates by its own momentum.

Consider the way he describes the Spanish incursion into the New World in his most concise book, *The Rediscovery of North America:*

> It set a tone in the Americas. The quest for personal possessions was to be, from the outset, a series of raids, irresponsible and criminal, a spree, in which an end to it—the slaves, the timber, the pearls, the fur, the precious ores, and, later, arable land, coal, oil, and iron ore—was never visible, in which an end to it had no meaning.
>
> The assumption of an imperial right conferred by God, sanctioned by the state, and enforced by a militia; the assumption of unquestioned superiority over a resident people, based not on morality but on race and cultural comparison—or, let me say it plainly, on ignorance, on a fundamental illiteracy—the assumption that one is *due* wealth in North America, reverberates in the journals of people on the Oregon

Trail, in the public speeches of nineteenth-century industrialists, and in twentieth-century politics. You can hear it today in the rhetoric of timber barons in my home state of Oregon, standing before the last of the old-growth forest, irritated that anyone is saying *"enough . . . , it is enough."*

There are few writers who have made so clear that the exploitation of resources—as well as all the displacement, pollution, ecosystemic collapse, and climate havoc this exploitation engenders—is, as it has always been, a colonial project.

I am even less of a nature writer than Barry was, but this is where our work overlapped, in that we each spent much of our adulthood around Indigenous communities. Learning from Indigenous people had conferred on him a certain loneliness, in that he would never belong to nor attempt to belong to the communities he visited, and yet he more often identified with their perspectives and methods of existence than those of European American culture. "You end up on this odd ground where you don't have many people to talk to," he told me.

I wish I had asked him to elaborate. Had I never read his writing, I might have thought he was suggesting we shared some sort of romantic and voyeuristic curiosity about cultures unlike our own. But what I believe Barry meant is that being among people who have struggled and continue to struggle to maintain a relationship to their original home made obvious to him his position as a descendant of colonizers, illuminating the legacy he was part of. It helped him more precisely identify that which he now felt obligated to push back against.

He wasn't perfect on this front—nor is any White writer who has tried to find their place among Indigenous stories. If I have a criticism of Barry, it is that he too often wrote about Indigenous people in the past and not enough in the present. Perhaps he felt that history is a commons, while the ordinary, private lives of people today were verboten. Regardless, his work reads at times as a kind of salvage ethnography, edging dangerously close to reinforcing the falsehood that Indigenous cultures and people are dead, or that their value diminished as they were influenced by modernity. (In one short story, he implies the Mandan were "wiped out," which I imagine would offend the Mandan descendants I know.) Then there is a collection of coyote-trickster tales Barry published in 1978, which, though Barry carefully states his intentions at the start of the book, still strikes me as straight-up appropriative.

I will never know why he made these choices or how he felt about them later. What I do know is that in all his writing about the people he encountered in his lifetime, Barry was respectful, attentive, humble in his awareness of his own fallibility. Desser told me she saw him amend his approach to writing about Indigenous people over time, and his later work reflects this. What remained consistent was his message: that land and people are fundamentally linked, and that a disregard for both could ruin us all.

He called me a month after the Holiday Farm Fire, from a house in Eugene where he and Debra were living temporarily. He had finally gone back to the property, he said, and it looked "like a flayed human being." His voice broke when he said this, and it occurred to me that the fire erased for him the sense of knowing and being known. Then he brightened a little, explaining that a friend who accompanied him had found a bit of tree root, still alive. In the spring, they hoped to replant the forest.

Barry and I spoke only once more, a week later, when he asked me the favor about talking to the reporter from the alumni magazine, or perhaps writing something about Barry's legacy. Eight weeks after that, I learned of his death like most everyone else, from the news.

I never met him in person. I know he valued my work, but I also know he nurtured many similar, longer friendships, and ours was more significant to me than to him. I suspect Barry first called me to pass along a gift that he once received when he was young from an older, celebrated writer. The writer complimented him "in such a way that you felt you had to continue, and maybe do better just to live up to the implied expectation," Barry wrote of the encounter. "Here is this person whom I knew but slightly, who in our first meeting found a way to say, with such integrity, I love you."

I read of this encounter only recently, in *Embrace Fearlessly the Burning World*. Barry was working on the book when he died, assembling essays that had previously appeared in magazines, as well as several yet unpublished. Debra helped Desser finish the collection; Rebecca Solnit wrote the introduction. The essays span three decades, revisiting once again the places common throughout Barry's work—the Arctic and Antarctic; the California of his childhood—but lingering longer than his writing ever has in Finn Rock, Oregon, in the forests of the Cascades, his chosen home.

The title of the collection comes from an essay he published in *Orion* the month we first spoke, before the fires, in which Barry asks if it is "still possible to face the gathering darkness and say to the physical Earth, and to all its creatures, including ourselves, fiercely and without embarrassment, I love you, and to embrace fearlessly the burning world?"

If he had a last word, perhaps it would be this—a question calling from the dark, turning toward the light.

DRAGON FIRE AND SALMON FLIES

ROBERT MICHAEL PYLE

I will remember Barry Lopez by our encounters more than by his essays and stories, starting with the Red Lion Hotel on the banks of the Columbia River in North Portland in the spring of 1987. The occasion was a Pacific Northwest Booksellers Association (PNBA) trade show, where we were each given a PNBA book award—his for *Arctic Dreams*, mine for *Wintergreen*. After the ceremony, we repaired to the restaurant where we took to talking. We were still talking, working broad acres of common ground, till I a.m. I believe we would have gabbed right through to breakfast, had our patient wives not reminded us of our long drives home, in opposite directions.

Next came a dinner in Eugene, a couple of years later. I had just received a Guggenheim Fellowship for study, research, fieldwork, and the writing of *Where Bigfoot Walks: Crossing the Dark Divide*. Barry was a Guggenheim Fellow for *Arctic Dreams*. He was eager to share with me how the grant might best be employed not only for the project at hand, but also for simplifying life while one worked on it. So he invited me to dine with him when I was passing through Eugene for a reading, both to share his thoughts and to celebrate my good luck.

"This is the best opportunity you've ever had to say 'No,'" he told me over a beer. "When a request is too much, just say, 'I'm sorry, I'd love to help, but I am working on my Guggenheim and it must take precedence over everything else right now.' No one will persist after that." Boy, did he turn out to be right—that advice made a big difference to me in stretching the good fortune of that year! At one point during the dinner, Barry veered from the question of the grant's usefulness to the recipient, to what such benisons should mean in the broader social context: how we can best use them to do something worthwhile, and why we should care. "What are we doing here, after all?" he asked. "More, I hope, than simply gardening our reputations!"

Then I think of the last reading of 1993 at Seattle's storied Elliott Bay Book Company, then located in Pioneer Square. On that frosty December night, Barry was the featured writer, introducing his new book on Columbus, *The Rediscovery of North America*. His reading was powerful and shocking as it slid toward a crescendo of reckoning. But what I remember more is that Barry had chosen to begin the evening by first reading someone else.

Having recently discovered the work of the Texas and Colorado poet Pattiann Rogers, he was so taken with it (and with her) that he felt compelled to evangelize for her poems. Barry opened the event by reciting Pattiann's stunning "The Hummingbird: A Seduction." The effect on the audience was electric, and to use an adjective from *Arctic Dreams*, stilling. I wonder how many love affairs with Pattiann Barry kindled that night, besides my own. I was completely won over, never knowing then that Pattiann and I would become good friends and often read together, sometimes with Barry as well—all thanks to that one act of generosity on his part. As with so many of my other recollections about Barry, this one in the end came around to looking out for others.

I witnessed that impulse many times since, not least when we were both contributing features to a "Natural History"–themed issue of *Orion* magazine. Later, when my essay was selected for an anthology he was editing, Barry called me. One term stood out that he felt I might wish to reconsider. I had referred to the purge of the naturalists in the universities by writing that, while we'd gained "the young turks on the cutting edge," we'd lost "the old farts with all the facts." Barry explained that the common term "young turks" had its origins in the Armenian genocide committed by Turkey, which he had lately been looking into. In World War I, as Barry explained, Turkey's Young Turk government set out to exterminate every Armenian in the country. Hundreds of thousands were killed. Barry said, "Bob, I don't think this term will do you, or your piece, any good at all." I of course agreed, and Barry helped me to find an alternative wording. I was struck by his conscientiousness—a byword for Barry—taken to this level of detail: word for word, person by person.

With Barry, such devotion was likely to become ethics in action. An example I keenly recall took place one lunchtime at the National Conservation Training Center in Sheperdstown, West Virginia, at the Fire & Grit conference of place-based writers and activists convened by the Orion Society in 1999. The lunch was a command performance for Secretary of the Interior Bruce Babbitt, organized largely by Bill McKibben and Sue Halpern. Secretary Babbitt especially wanted to meet William Kittredge, so Kittredge was the bait to get him there. Our interest lay in discussing, and we hoped influencing, certain conservation issues. Among these was joint action between the United States, Mexico, and Canada toward saving the migratory monarch butterflies. Sue and I had each recently published books on monarchs, whose fate was becoming a big trinational issue thanks to illegal logging and GMO crops. We extracted some good promises that came to fruition some years later with the "Three Amigos" summit of presidents Obama and Nieto and Prime Minister Trudeau, furthering meaningful cooperation on behalf of monarchs and milkweed. We also discussed what the Clinton Administration intended to do for conservation in its closing acts.

For Barry's part, he was unwilling to let Secretary Babbitt get away with offering only generalities and bromides, latching on to the secretary like a terrier would a pants leg. As the lunch wound down, Lopez demanded of Babbitt: "What do you really want the legacy of this administration's record on protecting the public lands to be?" Babbitt could see he was stuck, with no way out other than a real answer, and that's when he made the first public announcement of the administration's intention to set aside a suite of new national monuments, never mind a contrarian Congress. After that, it had to be done—the Nature Writers had witnessed the pledge! And when Clinton left office, he indeed left behind a remarkable constellation of those very monuments. Did I say terrier? That day, we all saw Barry the Bulldog in action.

In 1998, Barry received the John Hay Medal at a gathering held at a resort along the McKenzie River. Barry read from "Effleurage," an essay he had written about the Anagama Dragon Kiln outside Astoria, Oregon. Here a community of potters creates extraordinary ceramics in long, arduous firings of the dragon-shaped furnace. Barry introduced the genius loci of West Coast Anagama, Richard Rowland, instructor of art at Clatsop Community College. One thing he and Barry spoke of was the constant hunger for good wood to feed the dragon's insatiable, fiery maw. That plea aroused an idea in me.

Not long thereafter, at Barry's home upstream in Finn Rock, we watched the big red salmon flies glittering over the McKenzie in the late-day sun. I mentioned to Barry that there were masses of fine, well-seasoned wood at my place—a great limb from the most massive red oak tree in Washington State, fallen under its own weight. It was bucked, but needed splitting, and Thea and I would love to contribute it to the ongoing Anagama project. I also happened to know that Barry loved splitting wood.

Next chapter: Some months later, two veteran pickups rolled up to Swede Park, our old farmstead in the Grays River Valley, across the Columbia from the Anagama Dragon Kiln. Out of one truck hopped master potter and dragon-master Richard Rowland, with his perpetual smile and his bright-blue incisor, and his assistant, Ben Thompson. Out of the other, which was towing a hydraulic log-splitter, emerged Barry and his tall stepdaughter, Amanda. Soon after greeting, we went to work, rolling the massive rounds of the tree-sized fallen branch down onto the level of our mail path, above the country road to the Grays River Covered Bridge. We settled into a rhythm, two of us handling the logs with peaveys, Barry expertly running his beloved splitter, the fourth and fifth hurling the splits into one or the other of the truck beds. The work was heavy, but it went fast with ten hands.

Meanwhile, Thea's good hands were making us a legendary lunch back up at the farmhouse. I would give a lot for one bottle of that lunch's distilled conversation, from logs to literature and back, via the vaguely Lincolnian connections of our great tree known locally as the Lincoln Oak, plus a tincture of the sweet tannin scent coming off its tawny grain as we sundered it. At day's end, the two old trucks, riding very much lower to the road, trundled off toward the Astoria-Megler Bridge and the great hungry dragon beyond.

Come the following New Year's Eve, Thea, her daughter, Dory, and I stood in the chill blue-green dusk to watch the magenta breath of the dragon issue from its blowhole. Richard's shop and precincts were a hive, with designated fire-feeders and others responsible for this and that during the long, intense firing. Everything—timing and temperatures and placating the creature's hunger according to a strict schedule—had to be done just right. Then the dragon would return an amazing bounty of hundreds of pieces of brilliant design, shape, glaze, and personality. We three got to take turns tossing chunks from our own Lincoln Oak into the flaming throat.

Thea was in her second year of a decade of ovarian cancer. A couple of months later, Ben showed up at our house bearing several beautiful and robust cream, brown, and oatmeal vessels from that very firing. He said Richard had sent them as healing bowls for Thea. How we were moved! And they worked, for several more years. All this was Barry's doing, making connections between other lives that mattered to him.

When Barry and Debra were editing their brainchild, *Home Ground: Language for an American Landscape*, that marvelous dictionary of geography written by creative writers, Thea was farther into her illness. Barry inquired as to whether I would be able to take part as an author, and I told him it was just what I needed, which I think he had guessed. As it turned out, learning about my great batch of assigned words in the old geography library was just the ticket during Thea's long days in the University of Washington hospital.

It would be wrong to suggest that Barry was perfect, and he above all would disapprove of such an impression. Happily, I can offer up one or two minor flaws of his. Even his writing wasn't perfect. When I was reviewing *Crossing Open Ground* for some newspaper, I was delighted to find one word that had irked me during my generally happy reading of the bound galley, so as not to be utterly without negative criticism. Even Barry, seldom guilty of cliché, could not resist using "scud" as the only verb authors seem willing to allow clouds to commit.

As for his spoken rhetoric, Barry was a superb speaker, never failing to arouse both the intellect and emotions of his listeners, as well as their full attention to whatever he chose to share, which usually had to do with his utter love for the land and its people. No one went away unchanged. But he could also go on a bit (it takes one to know one). I recall one particularly meaty and lengthy keynote that arrived at the perfect conclusion . . . three different times.

Only once did I witness a lapse in Barry's keen consideration for others. It was a big library launch for *Home Ground,* to which Barry, as speaker, had invited other contributing authors in the region. Several took him up on it, and came some distance to attend, expecting, perhaps, to take part in some way. The point came in the evening that would have been perfect for introducing his co-authors present, maybe asking them to read one of their definitions. But it didn't happen. They remained unacknowledged, just part of the audience. Maybe exhausted from the vigorous book tour, he let the moment go. It was a lost opportunity, and most un-Barry-like. I felt disappointed at the time. But now I see it as it is: a chance to realize anew that our heroes are seldom actually saints, and that Barry Lopez was, after all and first of all, a human being.

APPRECIATION FOR ALL THAT I HAD SEEN

ANNA BADKHEN

Dear Barry,

In the early summer of your last year here, we returned to the conversation we never seemed to finish, about what kind of a needful reassessment and goodness a writer must bring about, and how writers can counter despair. I am too solitary to make any kind of generalization about writers, but I imagine, or maybe hope, that these are the questions which all writers ask, or at least all writers worth their mettle.

You said that the role of a writer in America was to help readers be less afraid. But I am also afraid myself. I am afraid for the people in this country, forever confined by a war of occupation and resistance, afraid for the lives of my loved ones around the globe, afraid for the health and soul of the world. I regret that I never asked you if you weren't afraid also; I guess I was afraid to ask.

Dear Barry, for many years, when I worked as a war correspondent, I carried with me on my travels a paperback copy of *Arctic Dreams*. Many call that book your magnum opus, and it can be interpreted as a parable of the recent history and present of North America. But in my experience, it can, and must, be read more broadly. Part warning, part keening, part celebration, it anatomizes the myopic greed of the Global North and of the white supremacy that shapes our world entire, that dictates mass violence and crosshairs its victims. Most modern wars are both the result and the cause of climate disasters, most of which are conditioned by the abusive small-mindedness of extractive capitalism. There is no precedent in human history for the manmade geological changes that are destroying lives and livelihoods now, and for the yet worse catastrophes that climate scientists predict—new, unimaginable calamities that will extinguish more species, erase more habitats, kill and displace more people.

Violence bookends *Arctic Dreams*. You begin with a gory re-creation of an instance of whale slaughter by nineteenth-century Europeans, who, in unholy pursuit of blubber and baleen, left in their wake the carcasses of hundreds of flenched whales. You conclude with cruelty of a different kind, an insidious butchering of the soul that festers in the dismal man-camps of contemporary Arctic oil riggers, where "woman and machinery and the land are all spoken of in the same way—seduction, domestication, domination, control." The moral erosion you describe in this book is familiar to me from two decades of documenting the human condition in extremis, including in a dozen war zones on three continents. The backdrop changes, but the base in us, and the way we manifest it, varies little.

To guard against cynicism, you urge us to foster an "alertness for minutiae" and to "show an initial deference toward [the] mysteries" of a particular place and the human and nonhuman animals in it. You tell us to notice how water "whirled off in flat sheets and a halo of spray" from a polar bear shaking off after a dive; the way "the serene arctic light . . . came down over the land like a breath, like breathing;" the sound of several thousand lesser snow geese rising from the water at once—"like a storm squall arriving, a great racket of shaken sheets of corrugated tin." You are so open to astonishment that, in the tundra, you "bow slightly with [your] hands in [your] pockets, towards the birds and the evidence of life in their nests." The word "wonder" appears in the book thirty-two times.

To remain in awe; to linger; to reject "the kind of provincialism that vitiates the imagination," to reflect the world back at itself at unexpected angles and to invite us, the audience, to ponder and question while reminding us that we are not alone, that someone is as perplexed and bereft and amazed as we are: That is, I think, the obligation of a writer on our overwhelmingly volatile planet. It happens to be, too, an aspect of dreaming, which Merriam-Webster, in one definition, describes as "to pass time in reverie."

Among the other definitions of the word *dream* are "a visionary creation of imagination," "a state of mind marked by abstraction or release from reality," "a strongly desired goal or purpose." Many of your arctic dreamers are whalers, roughnecks, mariners, hunters, colonial polar explorers afflicted by the supremacy of either the white race or the human race or both—ambitious and often monomaniacal intruders who unpeople the landscapes of their imagining before they arrive in person to unpeople the physical landscapes, mutilating or erasing Indigenous cultures, human and animal and plant. That the book begins with what you call "the carnage of wealth" and ends with the degradation of the human spirit is no coincidence: one cannot exist without the other. The muffling of decency and self-respect both ensue from and facilitate the loss of respect for the world and the physical violence we commit.

Dear Barry,

I took a break from writing you this letter to go to a piano recital. Tianxu An was performing six pieces at the Curtis Institute of Music. The final in the line-up was Sergei Prokofiev's op. 82, the first of his *War Sonatas*, no. 6 in A major, the one with the creepy waltz in the third movement, which Prokofiev wrote in 1940 as Stalin and Hitler burned Europe. (Was

Prokofiev afraid when he was writing it?) After the recital, An took his bows and said: "It is an artist's responsibility to bring hope." I knew then what you meant by "teaching to be less afraid." Art does not alleviate my fear, but it does fill me with wonder. It reminds me that we have gotten here, somehow; that, somehow, we have remembered to keep going, somehow.

Dear Barry, the reason I carried my paperback copy of *Arctic Dreams* with me to wars was not to stave off fear, but because in times of depravity one must buoy oneself. One must reach for the decency that the world relentlessly kernels, against which to steady the soul. In the landmine-studded plains of Afghanistan; in the foothills of Chechnya, where fathers wept about sons abducted by government henchmen; in the dun Mesopotamian limestone, where men were killing one another with bombs and bullets, *Arctic Dreams* reminded me to do the reaching.

The last sentence of *Arctic Dreams* reads: "I was full of appreciation for all that I had seen." "All": the wingbeat of birds, the oil riggers' quarters "wretched with the hopes of cheap wealth," Yup'ik hunters cutting up a walrus they have killed, icebergs "so beautiful they also made you afraid." This sentence, as simple as it is magnanimous, suggests an emotional vocabulary for the way we live here, now, in many kinds of love and inadequate to the grief and suffering of the world. It invites an introspection: What can we hold onto and how, and how can we appreciate all that we witness, and how do we remind ourselves to pause before the ineffable, to quiver before a flock of geese lifting off the membrane of a lake?

Once, in Portland, Oregon, you and I spoke about the writer's role in public. I was watching all the people in the audience who had come to hear you, who later stood in line to have you sign their copies of *Horizon*. Every one of them had responded to your work's example (or challenge, or encouragement) to listen, to foster attention and astonishment and respect. I have no idea who any of those people are, or how they go about their daily lives; I do know that they look up to you, that you set an example, and in this way, through their attention to your encouragement, the world is changed, is changing.

Dear Barry,

On my desktop is a photograph my friend Thorne Anderson took in September 2003 from a fishing dock on the east bank of the Euphrates, in Fallujah, at sundown. It is a photograph of a boy jumping off the railing of the dock. The boy reminds me of Lazarus in the Caravaggio painting, the way he bridges the two chiaroscuro banks; he also makes me think of flight, his wings two-thirds of the way to an upstroke, tips pointed like an albatross's, as the sun skims a benedictory doubled flare off his shoulder blade. Directly beneath the boy the river ripples in two concentric circles that seem pursed in the middle to keep him in the air, to hold him aloft.

That evening in Fallujah, before Thorne and I met this boy on the fishing dock, I filed a newspaper story about how the US military had bombed a village and destroyed a farmhouse not far from the dock, and how that bombing had killed and wounded members of the family that had lived in it; two of the wounded were brothers, eleven and nine years old, Hussein and Tahseen. They were only slightly older than my own children back then. I will mourn them forever. And yet—and yet—that very same day, there was this bird boy, a fisherman's son, taking flight over the eternal river, glowing, pushing all shadow out of the frame. This is what a writer can teach readers to see, how we steady the heart and indeed how we soar, no matter the deepest shadow, and in such light.

DEATH MEMORY HEARTH

ANNICK SMITH

Death. December 2020 was a month of death. My longtime partner and husband, Bill Kittredge (eighty-eight years old), died of a massive stroke on December 4 in Missoula, Montana. Which made me take too little notice of the death, from longtime cancer, of our friend and compadre Barry Lopez (seventy-five years old) on December 25 in Eugene, Oregon. But I am paying attention now.

These two great Oregon writers and elders—Bill a native in self-exile, Barry a devoted immigrant—could not have been more different. Bill was oversized, rough, and hard drinking, with a booming voice and laugh. He was a disenchanted ranch guy from the high deserts of eastern Oregon— ironic, iconoclastic, and an atheist. Barry was diminutive, quiet-spoken, and deeply spiritual—a monk without robes. But he was also an outdoor adventurer, an explorer, and a devotee of remote spaces, harsh climates, and the Indigenous peoples and creatures who thrive there against all odds.

Barry's impeccable observations of Arctic life, the relationships of humans to the wild, and the mysteries of existence in extremis earned him a National Book Award and many other prizes. Bill's renderings of the authentic life and voices of working Westerners—the violence and the generosities—and his inspired teaching, earned him a circle of followers who called him the Dean of the American West.

Wide-open spaces. Peoples of the land. Violence and beauty. Barry searched out what Bill never escaped. But they shared an avid pursuit of knowledge. Both were compulsive readers, intellectuals, and storytellers to the core. They were masters of their craft—meticulous, specific, brilliant—and their hearts, minds, and prophetic voices delivered the same message: *We must change the old story of American conquest to a new story about living in harmony with nature, Earth, and each other. We must create a new myth.*

Now they are gone, and dearly missed, and we are waiting to discover who the new mythmakers might be.

Memory. As I approach ninety, my memory is not what it was. And though memory is part fiction, certain moments remain vivid and real. I don't remember the exact moment I met Barry, but I remember a time, an aura, a life-changing experience.

Bill and I had surely met Barry at literary events in the 1980s, but we really got to know him around 1992 as members of a group of writers participating in an environmental and social justice road show called the Forgotten Language Tour. The tour was sponsored by the Orion Society, and its concept was derived from a poem by W.S. Merwin called "Witness":

> I want to tell what the forests
> were like
> I will have to speak
> in a forgotten language

Traveling together in venues such as Klamath Falls, Oregon, and Ann Arbor, Michigan, with like-minded collaborators we did our best to retrieve the forgotten language of connection to the natural world.

Through readings, lectures, discussions, and excursions, we engaged in conversations with grassroots activists, local nature lovers, academics, students, and just interested folks. Who knows how well we succeeded in changing anyone's mind—let alone the language of connection—but one thing is sure: We bonded. We made lifelong friends. We celebrated together. We formed a community.

The effort later went national at Orion's big conferences: the Watershed event in Washington, D.C., (1996), organized by poet laureate Robert Hass; and Fire & Grit, a gathering of grassroots activists at the National Conservation Training Center in Shepherdstown, West Virginia (1999), where Bill and Barry were tandem speakers. "Get all of these people in the same town together," said Bill, and perhaps we can begin to "reimagine desire." Asked if writing books was futile, he said, "Everyone who writes a book may change the world a little bit," and hopefully those bits add up. "When dialogue dies," he predicted, "the result is doom."

Barry, in his turn, decried prophets, urging us instead to seek wisdom from elders, take care of our children, stay local, and have hope. "Genius," he reminded us, "is in the community." Then—as the preacher he could not help being—he admonished us to forgive, to have compassion, to make accommodation for "our riven souls." "The enemy," he concluded, "is no man or woman"; it is "Tyranny. Prejudice. Fundamentalism." And fundamentalism, he explained, is a lack of imagination. Although Barry was talking in 1999, his words could not be more relevant today.

Hearth. One snowy evening in 2014, as we warmed ourselves around her fireplace at the Valley of the Moon Ranch, in Montana, my friend and editing partner Susan O'Connor said, "Let's make a book about hearth." And so began a four-year adventure in compiling an anthology with contributors from around the world telling stories about the concept and realities of what we called Hearth—the home fires that have sustained human beings and communities from the Stone Age until now.

The person who supported us most during the long collaborative process was Barry Lopez. Susan was an intimate friend of Barry's and talked to him often. The two of them were spiritual questers far more intense than an earthbound skeptic like me. But I also conferred with Barry and sought his advice. Like pickle to hot dog, we complemented each other, and our core values were congruent.

Barry would become our consultant, advisor, and critic. He helped us find writers with enlightening stories and insights. He helped us find Helen Whybrow, a much-needed editor to work on a growing pile of manuscripts. And he agreed to write the introduction to what would become *Hearth: A Global Conversation on Community, Identity, and Place.*

Our starting recognition was the word itself: *hearth*, a word that encompasses *heart* and *earth* and *hear* and *art*. But the concept was larger than the word. Although the idea begins with fire, warmth, cooking, and a safe place where families or clans can gather, we realized that hearths might also be centers of community such as public squares, markets, dancing grounds, cathedrals, and mosques. Or, more abstractly, the origin stories or myths that define cultures; or a vital creative center; or the electronic web that binds vast numbers of people in purpose, understanding, and action.

In "Finding the Hearth," his introduction to the anthology, Barry opens with recollections of a long-ago journey to a small Nunamiut village in the Brooks Range of Alaska. He was studying wolves. Under the midnight sun—no night, no day—trudging the tundra with a fellow naturalist, he would stop whenever rest called, unfurl his sleeping bag, and make a small fire of dry willow twigs. "The geography that surrounded Bob and me on those July days," he writes, "was so immense we felt less than incidental when standing up in it. It was the fire each evening that gave us definition and meaning . . . Here was our reassurance . . . A tiny memorial, then, to our very old and particular hominid ways."

But in an era of climate change and natural disasters, of displacement of ravaged peoples on the ravaged earth, and the massive extinctions of animals and birds and sea creatures, Barry wonders if the fires that bind us are enough—if ancient values of home and community, of welcoming strangers and offering generosity, can survive. Today, as in past times, he writes, societies are indulging in the "divisive aspects of tribalism, its wariness of the outer world, its resentment or hostility toward other ways of knowing, its impulse to banish its own if they do not conform."

Acknowledging this quandary, Barry concludes, "What is the hearth of the Anthropocene? What, now, is the symbol of our allegiance and our concern for one another's fate? . . . We can lose the communal fire and survive, but survival without the values of the hearth . . . seems a brutish prospect, a retreat into intolerance."

"Finding the Hearth" ends where it begins, with memories of the Brooks Range—and Barry's enthusiasm for life, the pleasures of friendship, and a belief in the future. All of it made palpable "by the small fires of dry arctic willow twigs we constructed each day and lit."

Of course, when Barry wrote those words, he could not know that—perhaps ironically, perhaps prophetically, perhaps accidentally—while his long struggle with cancer was coming to an end, and his life was dimming, a wildfire would blaze through his beloved forest on the banks of the McKenzie River. He would lose the woods that had offered him refuge, and the shed that held his diaries and papers. "I felt like I'd been erased," he told a friend. But his smoke-damaged house would survive. His books and words would survive. His spirit survives.

Memory. Hearth. Death. This is Barry's message to me: *Build your small fires in the expanses of the unknown. Be warmed by them. Share the light you find with others. And hope the spark you set lives to fuel hearths of the future.*

Meanwhile, as Bill might say, don't fret. Have a drink. The forest will come back, as forests do, transformed but alive. Green shoots and blue lupine risen from ashes.

AT MORAL PEACE
WITH THE UNIVERSE

SCOTT RUSSELL SANDERS

I first heard Barry's compelling voice in the fall of 1978 when I read *Of Wolves and Men*, a few pages each night, during the serene hour after my wife and I had cajoled our two young children into sleep, and before I gave in to sleep myself. Those children now have offspring of their own, ranging in age from nine to nineteen, and all these years later I am still listening to Barry's passionate, probing, morally charged voice, most recently as it sounds through the pages of his last two books *Horizon* and *Embrace Fearlessly the Burning World*.

How Barry sounded in person I heard for the first time in 1989. He was teaching that fall semester at Notre Dame, his alma mater, in the honorary position of Welch Professor of American Studies. I had arranged for him to give a reading at Indiana University, and to stay with my wife, Ruth, and me during his visit to Bloomington.

On that September afternoon, he pulled up in front of our house in his road-beaten Toyota pickup, climbed out, and extended a hand. His grip and palm were those of a man who had done rougher work than grading papers and typing essays, and the same was true of my hands, because both of us cut and split wood for our stoves, hefted shovels and stones, and repaired our houses, as much for pleasure as for need. He was forty-four, stocky and vigorous, his trim beard and mane of hair still brown, and his eyes, also brown, alert and shining. I would turn forty-four the next month; my own beard and hair were the color of rusty steel wool. In the race toward baldness, I had a slight lead.

Barry followed me indoors, where he greeted Ruth. She is a quiet woman, who rarely initiates conversation with people she does not know well. As if sensing this, Barry drew her out by praising the purple asters and black-eyed Susans blooming in our front yard, and by asking about her research at the medical school. When our teenage daughter and adolescent son trooped in after school, he greeted them, as well, and followed up with questions that elicited more than the usual grudging, one-sentence replies they offered to grownups in those days.

I mention these courtesies toward my family because they show a cordial, unguarded side of Barry that would be less evident in our later meetings, which often took place in group settings. In 1989, he was already acclaimed—he had won the National Book Award for *Arctic Dreams*, the John Burroughs Medal for *Of Wolves and Men*, and numerous other honors—and he was much in demand as a speaker, though not yet wearied and weighed down by celebrity.

During that visit, we talked about writing as a vocation, a topic prompted by his noticing a volume of Thomas Merton's letters beside my reading chair. The two of us had been led to the works of this Trappist monk along different paths, Barry through his Jesuit schooling, I through my Quaker concerns for civil rights and peacemaking. We both admired Merton's effort to combine a contemplative life with care for the world, and his commitment to writing as a way of bearing witness, often in defiance of the censorship imposed on him by his religious order. There was more than a little of the rebellious, restless monk in Barry. He told me that when he'd enrolled as an undergraduate at Notre Dame, he carried two conflicting ambitions: to become either an aeronautical engineer or a priest. He was deflected from the first goal by higher-level courses in math, and from the second by reading Darwin. What he became instead, to our great benefit, was a writer informed by a deep respect for both scientific and spiritual inquiry.

On our walk to campus for his reading that evening, he asked me how I had kept teaching for so many years—eighteen, at that point—without burning out. After only a few weeks as a visiting professor at Notre Dame, he was losing patience with his students, who had read little, had rarely traveled far from home, and showed scant curiosity about anything beyond their private lives. It wasn't enough for them to be intelligent; he wanted them to hunger for knowledge, to buzz with questions, to ache over the world's miseries and rejoice in its beauties. I could have said the same about many—by no means all—of my own students. Yet I still loved teaching. He asked me why. So I explained that I saw each class as a potential community, and each student as a bearer of gifts, and I believed that all of those gifts, whether obvious or hidden, might be nurtured in our time together. And that prospect gave me joy. What Barry made of this, I can't say, but so far as I know, after his semester at Notre Dame he never again accepted a teaching position.

That evening, he read "The Stone Horse" from *Crossing Open Ground*, and "The American Geographies," which would appear that fall in *Orion*—the literary magazine with an emphasis on the natural world—and later be collected in *About This Life*. During the question period, he expressed his belief that writers are called not merely to make books but to help mend broken people and places. Writers are not entertainers, he said; they are seekers, trying to understand who we are, where we are, and how we ought to live. Speaking more generally of what it means to be human, he said, "Each of us must search for the divine and strive to serve it." The gravity of his speech and the dignity of his bearing, so different from his informal manner at our home, were aspects of a public persona I would observe in the following years every time I saw Barry before an audience.

The next morning, after Barry had left for South Bend, one of my graduate writing students told me she had been moved to tears by his reading. She and half a dozen other MFA students had gone to a local pub afterward to share their impressions. They had been enraptured, but also intimidated. After hearing Barry, their own writing seemed to them timid and narrow, and his standards for art seemed far beyond their reach. I told her I was glad she and the others had recognized the intellectual complexity of Barry's work, its geographical and historical range, its higher purpose. But I pointed out that he had achieved these qualities over the course of more than twenty years of writing, research, travels, field studies with scientists, and conversations with native people, environmentalists, musicians, photographers, painters, and countless other seekers. She had witnessed a talented, richly experienced artist in mid-career. She was also talented, I assured her, and she was young, about the age Barry had been when he set out on his writing path, and she would find a path of her own.

In April 2002, a group of writers affiliated with *Orion*, along with a dozen or so guests invited by Barry, met with him near his home along the McKenzie River. We had gathered to honor him as that year's winner of *Orion's* John Hay Award, and to spend the weekend discussing the theme he had chosen: "Literary and Artistic Responses to Terrorism." This was seven months after the 9/11 attacks. Since I would be facilitating the conversation, he had phoned me beforehand to explain that the terrorism he had in mind stemmed not only from Islamic fundamentalists but also from our own government, corporations, rightwing zealots, and the mass media. He was especially concerned about authoritarian trends in politics. "If we do not change the direction of American culture," he told me, "we will be obliterated."

At our opening session, I read a passage from *Arctic Dreams* in which Barry laments the "frailty of our wisdom," as demonstrated by the reckless industrial exploitation of the Far North, and then goes on to praise, by contrast, the robust wisdom of the region's Indigenous peoples, who have preserved the health of their lands and waters by maintaining "an intimacy with earth." For those of us caught up in the industrial order, I asked the group, where can we look for Earth-grounded wisdom?

The first person to respond was Lillian Pitt, a Pacific Northwest Native American artist, who told about once having arrived late at a salmon feast, during which she sat down in the sole vacant seat only to realize it was "a strong chair place," meant for an elder. By the way the others at the feast looked at her, she also realized that she had been meant to sit there, because it was her time to become an elder. Then she told Barry that it was now his time to serve as a bearer of wisdom, to provide guidance in a dangerous age. He demurred, quoting Wallace Stegner: "Don't heap honors on me. Instead, become the sort of person you think I am." But Lillian insisted: "It is not for you to decide. The people decide, and we recognize you as an elder. The old ones are dying off, and now it is your turn to sit in the empty chair."

In the ensuing silence, heads nodded, eyes glistened.

Barry knew well the sobering responsibilities borne by elders, whether or not they carry that title, for in all of his travels—to some eighty countries and every continent—he sought out people whose knowledge was crucial to the wellbeing, even the survival, of their communities. Many of those travels are reported in *Horizon*, the last book published before his death. In an essay called "Jackal Camp," he writes that in traditional villages, elders are "the people who carry the knowledge of what works, who have the ability to organize chaos into meaning, and who can point recovery in a good direction. Some anthropologists believe that the presence of elders is as important as any technological advancement or material advantage in ensuring that human life continues." The entire book is overshadowed by his awareness that the continuation of human life is by no means certain, nor is the survival of many of our fellow species.

Barry knew that his own death was imminent, as prostate cancer tightened its grip on his body. So there is an urgency in the prose of *Horizon*, a drive to record what he had learned from his travels, and to trace the shape of his life and assess its meaning. The same urgency is evident in the title and essays of the posthumous volume, *Embrace Fearlessly the Burning World*. Those two books total more than eight hundred pages. What kept him working through his final, difficult years? I believe it was the sense of vocation we had spoken of at our first meeting, which he might have understood back then as a religious calling, like that of his hero, Thomas Merton. By the end of Barry's life, however, it's likely he would have understood his calling in light of what he had learned about traditional elders, who "guide their people down the perilous roads all societies must travel," as he wrote in *Horizon*, and who "know that once they are chosen, they must never quit out of despair or fear. To do so would be an act of betrayal."

In an essay called "Love in a Time of Terror" from *Embrace Fearlessly the Burning World*, Barry recounts a 1979 sojourn in the Brooks Range of Alaska, where he enjoyed a spell of serene summer days in the company of a wolf biologist and other researchers, a peaceful, unhurried time of watching wild animals go about their lives "undisturbed by human interference." Here is how he sums up the impact of the trip: "The experience delivered me into the central project of my adult life as a writer, which is to know and love what we have been given, and to urge others to do the same." That life comes to us as a gift is a religious idea, but it is also the simple truth; that Earth provides us everything we need, an oasis of bounty in the void of space, is an even greater gift, unearned, amazing. Sheer gratitude should make us guardians of this bounty, and of the manifold lives it fosters.

Through his travels and writing, Barry sought to enlarge what, in his essay "The American Geographies," he called "our moral universe." He sought to expand the scope of our attention and compassion and care to embrace our fellow species, such as wolves and whales, as well as our fellow humans, especially those who have been colonized, enslaved, displaced, denigrated, or otherwise abused. This ethic is a secular version of what Jesus taught, according to the Gospels, and no doubt what Barry's Jesuit mentors also taught—a call to love our neighbors, with the enlarged understanding that our neighbors include not only every member of our own kind, but every earthly creature.

Near the end of the prologue to *Arctic Dreams*, Barry poses a series of questions about the meaning of wealth, and ends with a pair of questions that contain their own answers and point toward the heart of his work: "Is it to retain a capacity for awe and astonishment in our lives, to continue to hunger after what is genuine and worthy? Is it to live at moral peace with the universe?" What he meant by *moral*, a word he used with increasing frequency in his later books, might be understood in light of his reflections in *Horizon* on the Navajo Beautyway rites, wherein he suggests that beauty "refers to a high level of coherence existing everlastingly in the world." To live at moral peace with the universe is to recognize this coherence, this beautiful order, and to align one's life with it. This is what Barry sought to do, and what he urges us to do. Unlike a traditional elder, he served no tribe defined by shared geography, culture, or genetics. Through his books he offered guidance to people all around the world—the tribe of his readers—and he speaks to us still.

Listening

"The stories people tell have a way of taking care of them. If stories come to you, care for them. And learn to give them away where they are needed. Sometimes a person needs a story more than food to stay alive."

—Barry Lopez, *Crow and Weasel*

SIRI TELLS A JOKE

DEBRA GWARTNEY

One day when I was driving around, I asked Siri to tell me a joke. She gave me this: Three men are stranded on a desert island when one finds a bottle, and out of that bottle a genie emerges to grant each man a single wish. The first begs to go home and is dispatched. The second, too, wishes for home and disappears. The third hesitates for a moment then says, "I miss my friends. I wish they were here."

After my husband died on Christmas Day, I walked the streets near our rental house and wished him back. He needed to come back. I wanted him to return here, to the house where we'd set up camp after a forest fire rendered our own home uninhabitable. I missed his presence, his malty smell and whiskery face, his grouchy edge. His ability to recognize my edge. I walked up and down the rain-soaked hills looking for him, wherever he'd landed above the Oregon clouds that sagged like old pillows. I reminded him that I couldn't manage what he'd left for me. Didn't he know that? The glaring absence of the man I'd shared my life with. Our property largely done in by wildfire. Attorneys and adjusters and morticians asking mind-bending questions. Even this body of mine that seemed compelled to remain in motion, as if I'd been charged with wearing a hole in the neighborhood rug.

My agitation had to do with what felt unfinished. I still had things to work out with him: the last tensions between us, the ones that tend to collect and congregate in a long relationship like a few sour droplets clinging to a bowl. If he showed up again, we could find peace with each other—I was sure of it—and I might cook one more meal for him. We might make a last visit to the river, where he would point out the dorsal fin of a salmon just under the surface or spot a heron tucked into the brush. But mostly, on these post-death walks, I sent out the apologies that hadn't been issued before he was gone: my irritation over the cat-food cans he left in the sink. *I'm sorry.* The way I fidgeted in the passenger seat when he drove like an old man on the freeway. How I shut myself off after our arguments. *I'm sorry. I'm sorry.* It turned out the only person who could soothe me through the death of my husband was my husband, and if he'd only boomerang in again, I could show I was a kinder woman than the one he'd left. Look how nice I am now! The pettiness of my quotidian complaints fuzzed in me like rotting fruit.

Up the hills, down the hills, until I at last stepped into an overheated house that was not mine, not ours, to tuck myself into a bed that was bereft of him.

My husband had been sick long enough, a string of years, that I'd begun to think of his diagnosis as a rumor. He was interminably terminally ill. Until he wasn't. Until he was on a hospital bed with skin as pale as the sheets, except for a few age spots floating on the surface of his forehead like smooth boulders. His jaws unlocked to suck in air, and I stared into the cave of that mouth: the tinge of decomposition. The trembling tongue. The gone-black lingual frenulum, as if it were designated first to die.

I was with my husband, holding his hand, when he took his last breath. Two days later I stood by while the mortician nailed the lid onto his coffin and our daughters shoved it into the furnace. And yet I still managed to believe—for half a second—that he could return. I awoke on winter mornings and rolled to the right, away from his side, as is my habit. I didn't move—no shudder or flinch. I stared at the wall so I could let myself believe he was on the other side of me, his back to mine. If my faith was mighty enough, he would soon reach out to put his hand on my shoulder, pulling me toward him. A man made whole.

I once discovered a brochure from the 1840s that advertised lush agricultural land in Oregon's Willamette Valley, distributed free by the government, forty acres at a time. A bounty beyond imagination, the ad promised, while also claiming that a man who'd fallen dead in the dirt had stood up again in minutes, restored by the nutrients in the soil.

Shortly before his death, my husband knelt into a mound of ash at our property in the mountains above the Willamette Valley. He stood up again to rake through the devastation of the wildfire that had raged down the corridor where we lived together, where he'd lived for fifty years, a fire that miraculously had not reached our house and yet had burned nearly everything around it for miles. Our region's long drought had made perfect, crisp-dry conditions for fire. The smoke and flames had seemed to come out of nowhere, jarring us from bed in the middle of the night to run for our lives.

The day I'm remembering was weeks after that, when we were finally let back in to discover what was left and what was gone for good. The air was thick with smoke that lodged in my throat. Trees I had considered our sentries, well over a hundred years old, had been reduced to black pillars that would peel from the ground in the season's first windstorm, crashing into splinters. My husband's gloved hands were wrapped around the handle of a rake, his boots powdered gray, his pants, face, and hair spiky with particulates. He was sifting through the remains of the building where he'd stored five decades of his work, hunting for anything recognizable, a remnant of what had been decimated in a single night of howling wind and flame. I noticed his body jolt, a slight whip of the shoulders and a quiet gasp from his mouth. A few minutes later it happened again. That's when I realized the metal tool had hit a live wire snaking through the ash. "Put it down!" I said. He ignored me, as if I could not be trusted. Another jolt, and I stood up to take the rake. "Stop," I said. "That's enough."

I thought of those small shocks two months later as I rubbed ointment on his back, burned by defibrillator shocks administered in the ER. One dull and cold Sunday morning at the rental house, my husband's heart had decided not to beat on. An ambulance had transported him to a hospital, where doctors had startled his heart into continued service. I remember thinking of Mary Shelley's dead frog, its legs reanimated with pricks of electricity for purposes of entertainment and curiosity, not to give the frog a chance to jump, to safely land again. After a few days we returned to our temporary home, my reawakened husband and me. There, I spent the next few weeks watching the life drain out of him.

By the time Siri told me her joke, it was late spring, maybe summer, and my husband had been gone for half a year. Still, I hadn't given up. In my own interior, I conjured a genie's bottle made of the thinnest glass, which I rubbed once a day, twice if my mood was indulgent. I kept on making wishes for his return, imagining them swirling through the air like maple-tree samaras, landing on his shoulder or in the tangle of his hair. I waited for his response. A red-tailed hawk parked in the highest branches of a poplar tree. *Is that you?* The wad of twenty-dollar bills I found in the pocket of his jeans—a reassurance that I'd be okay? A wineglass that shattered in my hand. A folded note in his handwriting in the bottom of my purse. A sudden, familiar creak of his desk chair upstairs.

I might stand outside studying the hawk until the rain drove me in, or allow the blood to drip from my palm into the sink in the shape of a cuneiform inscription, but in the end I couldn't decipher these tidbits, these crumbs. *Genie, was my wish not clear?* I asked for the whole man to come home, as he was before, free of the illness that overtook him and the fire that crippled his spirit. A man, I hoped, who'd be glad to be reunited with me.

I guess we laugh at Siri's joke because the first two men have no choice: They're about to be snatched away from their dearest places and redeposited on the sand. They're helpless to do otherwise because another man has opted for himself. Does the third man believe the others will be the same people who left him? That's impossible. All three will be altered, whatever relationship they'd once had now in shambles.

I decided, a few weeks after hearing it, that Siri's joke was a retelling of the Lazarus story, in that the dead man from the Bible was returned to life because others willed it to happen. Lazarus had no say in the matter. I picture the stunned Lazarus, suddenly not dead, hobbling into his small house. Here the familiar sweat-soaked blankets on his bed, there the half-eaten broth congealing on the table, his spine tingling with confusion while new blood pushes out the dried-to-dust blood in his veins. The book of John describes the stink as Lazarus blinked his way out of the tomb four days after he'd been laid away, yanking off the strips of cloth he'd been wrapped in, onlookers folding into the shadows to avoid the stench of death.

I wondered how the sisters, Mary and Martha, had whipped up the temerity to ask Jesus to bring their brother back: a big request. But then a friend—a pastor, steeped in scripture—told me that Mary went out and met Jesus on the road not to ask for a miracle, but to complain. Jesus had failed to answer their urgent message of a day or two earlier, insisting that he rush to his old friend's side and save him before it was too late, and Mary meant to give him what-for about it. She might have wished, as I do, for her loved one to be alive again, but she wouldn't have asked Jesus for such a thing. Would she? At most, she might have raised her voice in a frustration: *Where were you?*

"Jesus wept." It's the celebrated shortest sentence in the Bible, and Jesus's reaction to the news of his friend's passing. He wept, and then he went to the sealed tomb and, surprising everyone, called to Lazarus to rise again, and Lazarus did.

The risen man has stuck like a burr in the human psyche, explored in songs and poems and films, a story of particular interest to those of us left behind when a loved one dies. What would it take, exactly, to get them back? Whatever it is, we'd like to be let in on the deal.

The sisters had to be overjoyed at their brother's return, if bewildered and somewhat undone. But what about Lazarus? What did he get out of it? He suddenly had time—thirty years, says the Bible—if time is what he longed for. Except that he had slipped inside the ultimate mystery, a gauntlet he must have pondered every day for three decades, aching for or else dreading its final tap.

Jesus returned to the village a few weeks after Lazarus's rebirth and sat with his friend for a meal. What passed between them? Did Lazarus thank Jesus for the gift of another shot at life, or did he lean in with a reproach? *How dare you—you who claim to love me—rob me of my peace?*

At least a year before my husband's death, before the fire, he flew to Alaska to attend a memorial service for a longtime friend, and he returned with a mug. It was a simple green mug with an image of a raven on one side. My husband had asked the dead friend's family if he could take it as a memento, a clean and unchipped remnant from a life that had become progressively more worrisome and disheveled.

When he went upstairs to take a nap, I set the mug in the sink along with a couple of bowls and various cutlery. I turned on the water, dribbled in soap, and was preparing to wash when I smacked the edge of a dish, and a perfect wedge popped clean from the mug. Just like that, the vessel my husband had carried home in his hands from Fairbanks to western Oregon was broken.

I didn't admit what I'd done right away. He found the cup and its wedge sitting by the sink. For a second I hoped he would decide a settling of the house or a gust of wind through the window had caused the break, but he knew it was me. He picked up the pieces and held them out. Not toward me, exactly, but toward any force that might staunch the confusion rising in his guts.

It sounds simple now (though for reasons I'm still sorting out, it was not simple then): I'd step up and apologize, steeling myself against his disappointment, and we'd soon put the episode to rest. But I didn't do that. I decided his disappointment was more than I could bear. I said instead that I'd make the cup right again. Good as new! I talked too much and too fast about how I'd find a person capable of fixing it. I didn't give my husband a chance to growl and spout, to eventually cool off, to reach the point where he could say, *It was just a cup,* and learn to live without it.

If he did say those words, I suppose I refused to hear him.

The ceramicist I found in Portland turned the mug over in his hands, then pointed out that it was likely a cheap souvenir from a gas station or café. If the mug was as important as I'd claimed, he suggested the Japanese technique of *kintsugi:* a delicate line of gold acting as seam between the broken pieces, riverine and subtle. "Embrace the flaw," this man told me. "Make it into art."

But when I returned to retrieve the cup, I found the opposite of art. It looked as if a child with a glitter glue gun had stuck the pieces back together with zero finesse. I paid the $150 and rushed outside, holding the mug and its bejeweled globs above the wet pavement, tempted to throw it down and smash it into shards that I could then cart home: *Here you go, husband— evidence of my folly.* But I put it in the passenger seat and drove the three hours to our house, disgusted by my habit of dragging things out. At home, my husband pressed the mug, remembrance of a beloved friend, into the far corner of a cupboard. We never spoke of it again.

The three-men-on-a-desert-island joke is the only one I've heard from Siri. My request that day was random, a whim. Still, I can't help but believe it was meant to be: that particular one laid on my doorstep as if it had been waiting to land there, a brown paper package that I have unwrapped and rewrapped, a gift that arrived overloaded with expectation. It's the joke that prompted me to read up on "Lady Lazarus," the Sylvia Plath poem ("Ash, ash— / You poke and stir."), and better yet, Anne Sexton's ("Lazarus was likely in heaven, / as dead as a pear / and the very same light green color.") The joke reignited the memory of the broken cup, unfinished business that rattles like a loose window in the middle of the night. All that reading and thinking over a period of months. I figure now that I was shaping one of those juicy life lessons about moving on, about release and liberation. Or maybe I was writing a fable for myself about cup shards spun into false gold, a story whose last line insisted that accepting brokenness is the only way to peace.

Except no wisdom of this sort emerged to serve me on the last day I spent on our property. I was alone that afternoon. The contractors who'd repaired the damaged house were finished, their trucks packed up and gone. A logger had carted off the charred and fallen trees, while the remaining forest detritus had been bulldozed into a massive pile to be dealt with later. It was early November, a year and two months after the fire and ten months since my husband's death. A time without time, though I recall details of that day: how I packed a final box, mopped the kitchen floor, inhaled the pungent air of our home (which had a smell like no other dwelling), locked the front door, and left the key for the new owners. I tied on my boots. I walked into our dark woods.

Once, when we were far into the Oregon wilderness, my husband taught me the word *preternatural*. That's what this final afternoon in the woods dished up: a preternatural ending. A preternatural quiet. The deeper I went—climbing over burned trunks and limbs until my shoes and pants and hands were covered in soot, stepping over tendrils of green ferns and tangled blackberry vines, taking care with this fresh growth—the more the quiet fell over me. Not even a soft breeze through the trees that had survived: the Douglas-fir, the cedar and hemlock, the alder and maple, missing their disappeared companions, trees that were part of the sky and the soil now.

The path was one I'd walked most days before the fire, when osprey had circled overhead and pileated woodpeckers had drummed on cedar trunks, but on this day all signs of the former trail were burned up, the old way hardly recognizable. No birds. No raptor calls or songs from a Swainson's thrush. No elk droppings or faint scent of cat musk. I made my way to the creek, which babbled at the lowest decibel, as if adhering to the day's code of silence. The log I sat on gave way under me, so that I was suddenly slung in a hammock of rotting wood. I stayed there for a good beat, waiting for what might unfold on this final afternoon at my home. The moment teetered on the verge of unbearable.

And though I knew better, though I was clear that it could not possibly happen, and clear on the disturbance it would cause if it did—that is, if I convinced Jesus or the universe or whoever was in charge to bend time and space—and though I'd read the part about how Lazarus never smiled again after this savior pulled him from the tomb, I couldn't help myself. I sent out yet another wish. This one as fervent as all the ones before, as if I'd learned nothing.

Husband, please return. Not for thirty years, not even for one year, but for this day. For this one hour. Land here beside me and give me a single, silent hour together in our woods. No one will see you, and I promise I will never tell.

This was my invocation, which sailed into the remaining canopy of our once lush forest, into the green and gold of autumn, into the hillsides slashed by fire, into the tumbling river that ran through the life we'd once made in this very place. *I miss my friend. I wish he would come back.*

BEGINNINGS

BATHSHEBA DEMUTH

One beginning: on a glacier in Alaska's Wrangell Mountains. Miles distant, the glacier appeared nearly vertical, filling a gap between the mountains with bus-sized blue seracs. But where I walked, low down near the glacier's terminus, the ice was close to horizontal. A landscape of slick, white hills at most twenty or thirty feet high, run through with sooty ribbons of ancient gravel and narrow cracks exposing deep blues. Everywhere the sound of melting. Water ran into miniature streams and oxbowed rivers and waterfalls, the erosive powers of geologic time rendered small and fast. In places, meltwater pooled, the color of a robin's egg refracted through a prism.

It was only possible to walk the glacier with crampons. At one point, the shank on my left crampon came loose and I fell, bare boot to sheer ice. It was not far or hard, but I slid twenty or so feet down a waterworn slope into bluish shade, stopping on my belly at the rim of a pool. Face to surface, gasping. At depth, all light vanished.

I scrambled back into the sun and paused to let my nerves settle. I thought: *I could start here, in this ancient frozen cave, looking into this water that begins so brightly but ends in profound black. I could start with Barry Lopez's writing about ice. Ice and light, that chapter in* Arctic Dreams *that is also about darkness. The chapter where he writes, "No summer is long enough to take away the winter. The winter always comes."*

Another beginning: late summer, Toolik Field Station, on the northern side of the Brooks Range, the tundra giving over from green to the mosaic of autumn. The station is temporary home to a shifting group of scientists, usually about a hundred at a time, most researching some aspect of how climate change is altering northern ecosystems. A typical conversation at Toolik begins in beauty—the colors, the light, "Did you see the musk ox?"—and ends in calamity. There are more shrubs here now. You heard how far north the fires came this year. Two degrees Celsius warmer. Four degrees. A community highly competent in the integers of dread.

One afternoon at Toolik, I walked several miles into the tundra with a hydrologist. She was studying where and at what speed surface water erodes permafrost. We set transects and measured the depth of active soil over frozen ground, numbers that across years would plot one small part of the warming land. Standing in a muddy gouge, fifteen feet high, where ice once held up the tundra, I watched her replant every cotton-grass root she had displaced while boring holes for subterranean thermometers. *A plant works so hard to live,* she said.

If I started here, I thought, I would turn to the essay "Apologia," in which Lopez writes about how the "forgiving embrace of the rational" exists in tension with the "wish to make amends." It is a short piece, only a few pages long, about the roadkill animals Lopez witnesses on the drive to a friend's home. A tiny microcosm of harms, and his own impulse to atone. As in much of Lopez's work, emotional states are material conditions, worth attending to alongside such things as the habits of caribou or the variability of light. He does not dismiss scientific knowledge, nor does he overstate its reach. Fear or joy or reverence are as fundamental to knowing the tundra or a raccoon corpse along a road as the physics of thaw or a list of species. There is a moral charge to this kind of emotional precision; essay by essay and book by book, it pushes us to see the act of re-rooting a plant—small and insufficient as it may be—as holding the beginning of a response to the world's dark hungers, the work of facing dread.

All these beginnings, a conversation in isolation. A small, intemperate, futile refusal to admit the end of a life.

I began writing this in the autumn, walking along the Koyukuk River in the Central Brooks Range. I had turned east up a wide gravel creek bed, trying to outpace a sheet of rain bearing toward me through a pass. Out of the bankside willows, gone saffron and bee-belly yellow, came a flicker of white.

It was a wolf, moving without hurry from the brushy shadow into the sun. A lone male. The wolf stilled and lowered his head. For a brief moment we stood, human eye to canine eye. Then he loped on, up the far bank, vanishing into a bright place of sunlight on the leaves.

The encounter was too fast to think much, the adrenal claxon of recognition—*wolf!*—interrupting the usual tide of analysis, in narrative, in my head. There was for a moment just the animal. Lanky but with the gloss of a good summer's eating, ninety pounds at least. He was the color the land would be in a few weeks, when winter took it—shades of white, blue-gray in the depths. The dark guard hairs in his ruff like blackened grass against snow.

The first thing I thought of, when the wolf was gone and my mind had returned to its usual relentless search for associations, was an essay called "The Invitation." In it, Lopez writes: "Perhaps the first rule of everything we endeavor to do is to pay attention." It is a call, among other things, to resist slipping into analyzed narration before experiencing something fully, somatically, as it evolves. It is an orientation he takes from watching how many of the Indigenous people he traveled with moved through their homelands. A moment like the wolf passing can be "a point of entry into a world most of us would have turned our backs on in an effort to go somewhere else."

If I began here, it would be to think about distance. Distance can be a physical thing—the wolf was only fifty feet from me—but it is also a habit of mind. The feelings I had in those moments with the wolf were of anything but, a not entirely comfortable thrum of having been recognized. The sensation of being reflected back to myself by the land and the wolf in it. Attention, Lopez reminds us, is a way to both know and be known. I knew the color of the wolf; he left knowing something of me. It is a call to see in the light or the wolf or the landscape a vibrancy that is more than a refraction of our human minds.

Attention is a way to shrink the distances thrown up by time, space, habit, and moral lethargy. So much of Lopez's writing worked to shift our habits of mind, particularly the habits formed in the society he and I share, to cultivate a kind of recuperative revolution through responsiveness. It is by collapsing the artificial distances many of us are taught to employ that a place can truly give shelter—that we can learn to know it through winter into summer, through dread into care.

In truth, the first beginning of this lone conversation was decades ago. I had just come back from two years of living in the Gwich'in village of Old Crow, in the western Canadian Arctic, where I was mostly on a dogsled or in a boat. Readjusting to life outside the Arctic was going badly. In my Iowa hometown, kind people asked about my time in the north. I sensed they wanted stories of a brash *I*, of adventuring. I did not know how to explain how years on that land and with its people had relieved me of the burden of existing in singular form, and that I had returned feeling that any sort of self was made in relationship to dogs or to a bear or to the land itself where the black spruce taiga dwindles into open tundra. This seemed barely thinkable, let alone something I could render in speech. So pat things came out of my mouth: *It is beautiful there. The winters are cold.*

Having language fail so utterly, being reduced to only an interior self, was isolation on the order of bodily pain. In the worst of it, driving to my job at a plant nursery, I would fantasize about crashing into the roadside ditches full of orange midsummer daylilies. Not out of a wish to die but a wish to escape the sense that there was no language for living.

There is a passage in *Arctic Dreams* in which Lopez wakes from a nap on the tundra and sees a ground squirrel nearby. The animal is tense:

> The feeling that it was waiting for something deadly to go away was even stronger. I thought: Well, there is a fox over there, or a wolverine. Maybe a bear. He'd better be careful.
>
> I continued to stare at him from the warm crevice in the earth that concealed me. If it is a bear, I thought, I should be careful too, not move from here until the ground squirrel loses that tension in its body.

I remember reading this, in that summer, when a copy of *Arctic Dreams* came to me via my parents' bookshelf. These and the proceeding pages were the first words that made sense to me after returning from the Arctic.

It was not just the descriptions of things familiar and missed: caribou moving over land, the sweet warmth of summer wind. It was more the way Lopez wrote himself into the narrative. He is not absent; but his presence is not falsely omniscient or heroic. The first person exists instead in a kind of exacting recession, refracting an *I* to us that is in constant relationship with place and the consciousnesses within—those of a ground squirrel, or long-dead diarists and painters, or the scientists and Indigenous hunters he shadowed.

And in relationship with land, which Lopez described as a partner in a dialogue, something "to have around you like clothing." *Arctic Dreams* offered a kind of permission to articulate—and the necessity to articulate, if only around a dinner table—the idea that things exist only when they are in association to others. Connection is what we pay attention to and atone for. In content and in form, my reading that summer broke through the dark singularity of the self.

To speak, but only after listening, and never claim to be the only voice: that is the quiet radicalism in much of Lopez's writing. It is a method, I think, not just of narration but of living.

On the glacier, if you keep walking toward the mountains, the ridges and crevasses grow larger. A deep crack opens in the ice, the terminus for three melt-streams. At the core of the fissure, far below, the water has worn a mouth shape, a glottis of blue ice in its center. The maw roars with water. Looking into it is vertiginous; a vast and diminishing field of ice, its ancient cold slipping away under the sun, suddenly unsteady.

"Most of us begin the day now uncertain of exactly where we are," Lopez writes in one of his final essays. To survive, "We will need to trust each other, because today, it's as if every safe place has melted into the sameness of water. We are searching for the boats we forgot to build."

To leave a legacy is to allow others to build. The tools Lopez left are those of beginning, and beginning again, over and over, the work of doing right by the world in all its transitory beauty and terrible change, full of darkness and light both.

I have no special claim to that legacy; I never knew Lopez, beyond the workings of his mind on paper, and was too certain of my own irrelevance to even write him a letter. Chances are you, like me, also know him at such a remove. We are thousands. A quiet, dispersed throng. We are the antithesis of an ending.

CARRY IT BEAUTIFULLY

KURT CASWELL

In the summer of 2021, I drove up the McKenzie River from Eugene, Oregon, to camp on a friend's land and then at a Forest Service campground called Paradise. I wanted, I think, to reacquaint myself with the place where I grew up and to see the devastation and rebuilding after the Holiday Farm Fire of the previous September. The fire had destroyed some seven hundred homes and businesses and burned 173,000 acres down the McKenzie River Valley toward Eugene. With the sun high and bright, I followed the road that followed the river through a corridor of black and burned Douglas-fir, cedars, and hemlocks, slash piles and stacks of salvaged logs, the ashy remains of people's homes, the understory cleared of vegetation and blanketed in hydromulch. I waited in stopped traffic where salvage and clean-up operations were ongoing ten months after the burn. I drove by Barry Lopez's house at Finn Rock where he lived and worked for fifty years. The timber here was once so dense and green you could hardly see the house from the road, but now the land was stripped and fire-shorn, exposing it like a bone bright inside a wound. There at the river's edge in front of Barry's house, I once stood with him as he pointed out the heavy stands of old-growth conifers across the river, Forest Service land that he said had never been logged. I now saw a barren slope interrupted by rock outcroppings and scattered with trees that looked like blackened matchsticks.

I live in Texas now, but I lived out my formative years here on the McKenzie where my dad was district ranger at Blue River with the US Forest Service. Barry lived just a few miles downriver from our house, and when I was in the seventh grade, my dad brought home a copy of Barry's book of short stories, *River Notes* (1979). He told me the author of the book lived here on the river, and that I should read it. I was just beginning to find my way as a reader, and as a fly fisherman and a river runner. I frequented the Blue River Library next to Mrs. O'Brien's house and I was learning to row drift boats and rafts, and paddle canoes on moving water. I thought of the McKenzie River as my river. Reading *River Notes* that first time was, for me, like dropping into a hydraulic in my boat and coming up upside down. To right myself, I had to acknowledge something that Barry's book had uncovered trembling beneath the surface. I had to acknowledge that whatever it was that was going on in that book, I wanted to be part of it. I wanted to write a book of my own. I wanted to be a writer.

At its heart, *River Notes* is a book about trespass, about beginning again, and about spiritual cleansing and renewal. The book begins with a narrator who is in a state of exhaustion and exasperation. The first sentence is "I am exhausted." Later narrators understand the river as a force in the landscape braiding together stories of people and animals. The narrator in "Hanner's Story" tells us that "when you feel the river shuddering against your legs, you are feeling the presence of all these agreements." And finally, the book rises to an apotheosis predicated on a narrator who learns how to die with grace and beauty. At the end of the last story, "Drought," the narrator tells us, "There was a power to dying, and it should be done with grace." And later, "Everyone has to learn how to die, that song, that dance, alone and in time."

Reading *River Notes* in those days opened me to a complexity and richness in the landscape that I could not yet have imagined on my own. In daily congress with the McKenzie, no longer could I gaze on a pool of slack water behind a rock as a surface on which to drop a fly, merely, or as an eddy into which to turn my boat and so assess the whitewater downstream. Now the river was alive to me, like an animal. Fishing the stretch between Blue River and Finn Rock with my dad in our drift boat, or standing knee-deep with my fly rod in that cold rush of water beneath Belknap Bridge, I wondered at the lives of blue heron, merganser, river otter, the rainbow trout I caught and killed. It struck me that to place my hands on the scaly bark of a Douglas-fir at the riverbank was to reach back into a long-ago time. I came to consider the waterline as a place where the terrestrial world I knew became a water world I wanted to explore. I did not know how to talk about any of this, these feelings that overwhelmed me, and so quietly and secretly, I began to write.

In 2005 I accepted a professorship in the Honors College at Texas Tech University, home to the Sowell Collection where Barry's literary papers are housed. Barry was serving as the university's first visiting distinguished scholar, and we worked together in the classroom and in the field until the time of his death in 2020. In the years I knew him, Barry told me many times that one of the differences between nonfiction and fiction is that when you finish writing a piece of nonfiction, your fingers are firmly planted on the keys of your typewriter (he wrote on a typewriter). When you finish writing a piece of fiction, however, your fingers are positioned just above the keys, suspended on air. Every time you begin work on a new piece, he said, you should be terrified—that's how you know you are working from a place of humility and respect for the story you are about to tell. The only way to write that story is to find a pattern in the language suitable for telling it, and each story is its own pattern. He told me that writing is a physical endeavor and when you are writing hard you finish your work physically exhausted. One of his early typewriters was in the Sowell Collection at Tech, and he said that if I looked closely at the keys, I'd see the wear marks from his finger pads and the scarring from his fingernails.

Perhaps like a lot of people, I first read *River Notes* as nonfiction. The voice I heard in that book is so intimate, so compelling, and so loving, and it expressed the way I had come to feel about the McKenzie River that I understood it as the author's voice. I understood Barry Lopez to be speaking to me, personally, and because he seemed to know me, I felt like I knew him. In fact, the copy my dad gave me is labeled "nonfiction" on the spine, and so is its earlier companion volume *Desert Notes* (1976)—a publisher's mistake, Barry once told me. And yet, in the earliest drafts of *Desert Notes* housed in the Sowell Collection, Barry clearly labels the manuscript as nonfiction: "Desert Notes: eleven essays in space." Other readers too note that these books read like nonfiction. For example, in a letter Barry received dated March 30, 1989, a reader writes, "When you go into a book believing the voice you are hearing is the author . . . you, as a reader, are making yourself quite vulnerable. . . . What a shock to learn that the book is classified as fiction."

I never asked Barry if when he was at work on *Desert Notes* and *River Notes*, he intended to write nonfiction, but then at some point realized that he was writing fiction. *Field Notes* (1994), the book that completes a kind of trilogy, is unquestionably fiction. I am not pointing out a deception here on Barry's part. My purpose is to illuminate what I think is one of his early innovations as a literary artist. During the time Barry was writing these books, academics were busy pushing the term "creative nonfiction," a new kind of nonfiction, they said, because it employs the tools of fiction, like character and plot development, and scene writing, especially scenes with compelling dialogue and engaging action. Creative nonfiction, these academics instructed, allowed a writer to suppose and wonder and wander into territory for which the imagination (as opposed to documentation) was at work. What Barry was doing in *River Notes* and its compan-ion volumes, it seems to me, was the opposite; he was using the tools of nonfiction to write fiction, namely historical and scientific information, analysis, and reportage. The effect is that most every narrator in Barry's fictional world feels like Barry himself. Barry's fiction stands apart from most other American writers of his time, and, it seems to me, it marked out new territory for new and established writers to explore.

Barry once told me that one of the reasons he accepted the invitation to work at Texas Tech was that it was time for him to give back. Others had helped him as a writer, and he felt it was his turn to help others. I admired his intentions here, but in practice, he protected himself and his work from outside distraction. He kept his work at TTU localized to his time on campus. He never accepted a formal teaching role, and on only a few occasions did he get involved directly with student work. When I first came to TTU, I invited Barry a number of times to join my class on weekend outings into the mountains of New Mexico, or on my annual ten-day intensive course on the lower Green River in southeast Utah. He told me he did not have time. He once asked a faculty member who was writing to him too often to stop because "when he was not at Tech, he was not at Tech." I did not fault him for so guarding his time, as I understood that he was daily fending off requests to write this and appear here and endorse that, and the only way he could get his own work done was say "no" to most of it.

When Barry was diagnosed with cancer, he told me that cancer was a teacher, and he had a lot to learn from it. He began to open himself to fac-ulty, and he became more invested in students' lives. He asked to join my classes in the field. He asked if he could be part of the planning process, and help imagine what students might learn from the places we traveled across the American West. We invited Juanita Pahdopony (Comanche, and a descendant of Quanah Parker) and her husband Harry Mithlo

(Apache/Comanche), and traveled with honors students to places like Medicine Mounds near Quanah, Texas; Palo Duro Canyon, where Charlie Goodnight first met Quanah Parker; Tule Canyon, where in 1874, the US Cavalry killed some 1,100 Southern Cheyenne, Kiowa, and Comanche horses; Adobe Walls, the site of two battles, one in which Quanah Parker led his Comanche warriors against a dug-in force of white buffalo hunters; and the Muleshoe National Wildlife Refuge to welcome home some 20,000 wintering sandhill cranes. Barry and I agreed that an essential part of teaching students to write effectively about place must include personal experiences in the places they are writing about.

Later, during the last few years of his life, Barry also talked about opening his home to a writer who might work alongside him. He said that he was not good at giving feedback to other writers on their work in progress, but there was a class of writer out there who didn't need his feedback, but who would benefit from being around him, from spending a few weeks, perhaps, in his guest cottage on the McKenzie to do their own work while he did his. He could then have meals with this writer, go for walks up in the woods, spend evening hours sitting on the front deck talking things over. This was the kind of mentorship he thought he would be good at. When I suggested that he give his plan a trial run with me—we knew each other, and I knew I wouldn't get in his way—he backed away sharply. "I'm just not ready to do that yet," he said. Some months later, he told me that if I happened to be in the neighborhood, I might consider stopping by for a visit. I did, and we walked in the woods together behind his house, talked over dinner, and leaned in over maps; he asked what was next for me as a writer, and how he might help.

Long before his illness, I came to understand that Barry had been quietly and even passively instructing and guiding me as a writer from the day I met him, and that he worked this way with other writers too. We talked a lot about writing over meals at my house and at his favorite Lubbock restaurants, on our way to movies, at small social gatherings, sleeping out under the stars, and in the classroom. I paid particular attention to what he said, especially when he said it more than once.

Always at the center of Barry's work is the reader. A writer's responsibility, Barry told me, is to come into a companionable relationship with the reader. The path to this relationship begins with trust, and trust leads to vulnerability, and vulnerability leads to intimacy. Once you establish intimacy with a reader, you can travel together to wherever the story needs to go. The problem with creative writing programs, as Barry understood them, is that they talk a lot about becoming a writer, but they don't talk about readers. Barry left the MFA program in creative writing at the University of Oregon in the late 1960s for this very reason. Far too many writers believe themselves to be an authority who has something valuable that a reader needs. But it's the reader who extends authority to the writer, if any is deserved. "It doesn't matter who wrote the book," he would say. "What matters is that the book was written."

In our conversations about the differences between fiction and nonfiction, Barry told me that he once thought the primary difference to be that nonfiction is braced by factual truth and fiction by emotional truth. Useful, but not conclusive. Once in a village in the Arctic, Barry asked a man he trusted what he thought the difference was between the two genres. The man said that he did not distinguish between fiction and nonfiction, but rather between authentic and inauthentic stories. An inauthentic story is about you, the storyteller or the writer. An authentic story is about all of us, which is to say, it's about the reader. In Jeremy Seifert's film *Horizons*, which is based on a series of interviews Fred Bahnson conducted at Barry's home not long before he died, Barry says: "It's not about you. You don't own the story. Carry it beautifully and give it to somebody else."

One afternoon at TTU when Barry was visiting my classroom, he asked me for a marker. It was the only time in fifteen years that he wrote on the board in my classroom, drawing a diagram of the way, to his mind, a writer works in the world. This is what he drew:

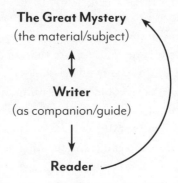

The Great Mystery
(the material/subject)

Writer
(as companion/guide)

Reader

In the diagram, the writer is in service to the material, or what Barry calls The Great Mystery, and if the writer is ready and open, The Great Mystery is in service to the writer (the arrow points both ways). The writer is also in service to the reader, but the reader is not in service to the writer (the arrow points from the writer to the reader only). And by agency of the writer's service, the reader can better access the material. So, the writer's responsibility is not to serve themselves, but to be in service to the reader and to The Great Mystery. This basic tenet governed everything Barry achieved as a writer.

Over the many years of hard travel to remote places, Barry felt a responsibility to bring back a story that might be helpful to the reader, that might be helpful to all of us. His technique for telling that story was not to be at the center of it. The only way to offer the reader access to The Great Mystery is to lead them into unfamiliar and sometimes uncomfortable territory, Barry said, while shielding and protecting them, and once there, to step aside, urge the reader forward and say: Look at this! Such an approach illustrates the difference between imposing and proposing. Imposing is a form of trespass, while proposing allows the reader enough space to see for themselves.

A writer must distinguish between a world of surfaces and a world of dimensions, Barry said. Computer and cellphone screens are part of the world of surfaces, while sandhill cranes rising off an alkaline lake at first light are part of the world of dimensions. We now live in a world of continual distractions, and most Americans (writers and editors included) are continually distracted. To go deep, a writer must pay attention. To go deep, a writer must be able to immerse themselves, entirely, in a world of dimensions. Camped on the Polar Plateau in Antarctica, Barry told me, he was pinned down by storms for days inside a small tent with his tentmate. While the experience was tedious and even monotonous, he said, there was nothing to do but be fully engaged with the place and the experience, and when you are so, something essential and special happens inside your mind.

When I first started working with Barry, he often said that his responsibility as a writer in the face of climate change and a host of other global injustices was to offer hope to the reader. In the last few years of his life, he told me that he had come to realize that all he could really do was offer comfort. We are not going to fix this, he once said. The world we so love is already gone. A writer can no longer ethically offer assurances and hope. All we can do is take care of each other. "For god's sake, take care of each other," he once told me. "I say that now everywhere I go."

In the spring of 2016, I gave a reading at the annual Sowell Conference at Texas Tech. After I finished, Barry wrapped his arms around me and held me for a long time. He said, "I don't know how much longer I'll be around, but it's okay because you're still here." Then he opened a space between us to look me in the eye. "Do you understand what I mean?" he asked. I told him that I did. And what I understand him to have meant is not about me, but about all of us. What I understand Barry to have meant is that after he is gone, it will be up to all of us to carry on, to carry the story beautifully and give it to somebody else.

Driving up the McKenzie that day, I knew that my boyhood town of Blue River had been completely destroyed by the fire, but to see it gave me a shattered feeling, like dropping a dish on the kitchen floor. The Forest Service house where we first lived was still there on the hill (now sold into private ownership), but the district office where my dad worked was completely gone, as were the stands of trees crowding the trail he walked to work. A little farther on, I crossed the Blue River Bridge and drove down the main street to find a few travel trailers set up as makeshift housing inside the ruins of what was once the town. The general store and post office, the White Water Café and gas station, the grocery store across the street, the Blue River Library—all of it was ash. I found heaps of twisted, tangled metal that had once been plumbing, melted plastics, spears of charred lumber, blackened concrete foundations, and other rubble, almost nothing recognizable as the thing it once was.

I drove on upriver, crossing the line where the fire had started. Winds had pushed the fire downriver, and so upriver from this place, things looked much like they always had. On Rainbow Drive—where my family had built a house on three acres—I stopped at the Upper McKenzie Community Center, where my older sister held her wedding reception some years ago. Here, volunteers had established a temporary home for a new Blue River Library. I introduced myself and told the volunteers that I had frequented the library as a boy when Mrs. O'Brien was still alive. They showed me the only two items from the library that had survived the fire: the steel placard that had been fixed to the front of the library—it reads "The O'Brien Memorial Library"—and a fire-scarred statuette of a seated girl in a blue dress reading a book. I asked if I could take a few photographs, and when I did, I discovered something the volunteers had not seen before. Printed on the surface of the open book in the girl's hands was the program from the dedication ceremony of the Blue River Library, dated September 7, 1975.

I think I know what Barry would have said had he stood with me in the interim library that day. I think he would have told me that while this kind of destruction is inevitable, and that we'll see a lot more of it in coming years, some things remain. I think he would have told me that while the town of Blue River is gone, the river is still here, coming down from the mountain snows and running out to the great Pacific. I think he would have told me that salmon are still coming up the river from the Pacific, as they have for some six million years. I think he would have told me that as a writer my responsibility is to pay attention, and to never look away, even when what I am looking at is the ruins of that which I love best. I think he would have said, speaking to all of us, that our responsibility now and forever is to take care of each other, and that's everything that any of us can do.

BARRY'S VOICE

DAVID QUAMMEN

What do we mean when we speak of a writer's voice? It's an ineffable literary dimension, harder to pin down than the dried corpse of a delicate butterfly—a zebra swallowtail, say, or a red-banded hairstreak—but it can be important. Not always. Some writing just rattles along, serviceable, informative, maybe even graceful, without much distinctive voice. But we know a good voice when we hear it. We give closer attention, slower consideration, and sometimes deeper respect to that writer whose voice somehow seems to command such regard. Barry Lopez had a voice—good lord, did he have a voice—that commanded regard. But he was the gentlest of commanders.

Scan the web for a definition of "voice" and you get a range of answers. "In literature, the voice expresses the narrator's or author's emotions, attitude, tone and point of view through artful, well-thought-out use of word choice and diction," says the website Literary Terms. Oxford Reference dismissively calls voice a "rather vague metaphorical term by which some critics refer to distinctive features of a written work in terms of spoken utterance." Such features might include "tone, style, or personality." A site called Literary Devices reduces it to "the form or format through which narrators tell their stories." These takes on the matter aren't wrong, but they sound a little arid. When asked to define voice myself, I've said that it's the deep character of the writer, reflected, for better or worse, in words on a page. It's not egotistical—or at least, it needn't be—but it's personal. One of the great talents Barry had was to offer that, to season his writings—about wolves or the Arctic or Captain James Cook or the Turkana people or whatever—with tincture of voice. And one of the reasons we loved Barry's voice, I think, is that it reflected such an estimable character. This was skill plus brave goodness.

It's there in *Arctic Dreams*. He is our guide, our storyteller, and his literary baritone is the soundtrack. It's there in *Winter Count*, one of my favorite Barry Lopez books, notably in the superb story "Winter Count 1973: Geese, They Flew Over in a Storm." It's there in *Of Wolves and Men*, of course, and in *Crossing Open Ground*:

> One summer evening in a remote village in the Brooks Range of Alaska, I sat among a group of men listening to hunting stories about the trapping and pursuit of animals. I was particularly interested in several incidents involving wolverine. . . . To hear about its life is to learn more about fierceness.

It's there in the fiction and the nonfiction, the anthropological and the confessional, the serious and the sly. It's certainly there in *Horizon*, his parting gift to us, a book for which I among others waited expectantly more than thirty years, to be not disappointed when it arrived.

My own first encounter with Barry's voice was in *River Notes*, his 1979 collection of short stories, subtitled *The Dance of Herons*. I had not yet heard of him (having missed *Of Wolves and Men* when it first appeared, a year earlier), but the music of the language and the narrator's quiet, somewhat mystic demeanor caught my attention. I didn't like every story in the book, to speak frankly, but it put this author on my radar screen. Back then he was publishing as Barry Holstun Lopez. He lived in Finn Rock, Oregon. Ed Abbey had praised him. That was about all I knew.

I still have my copy of *River Notes*, purchased forty years ago, and a glance at my minimal pencil notes reminds me which of those stories particularly engaged my attention. One is titled "The Log Jam" and begins with a confident, delicately spooky sentence:

> In September, when bearberry leaves were ready to pick, after the first storm had come upvalley like a drunken miner headed home, snapping limbs as thick as your arms off the maples, Olin Sanders caught a big tree barberchairing and was dead before they could get him out of the woods.

I didn't know the uses of bearberry leaves, and the term "barberchairing" was new to me then (though not to my friend Steve, who worked in the timber and advised me not to try that means of earning a living, notwithstanding that, like him, I was a starving young freelancer alert for a way to make some cash), but despite those points of opacity, I trusted this writer. I could sense that he would recount something worth reading about the people of that river valley, wherever it lay—or about people anywhere. I could tell by the sound of the writer's voice.

My next exposure to Barry's work came when the *New York Times Book Review* asked me to review his 1981 story collection, *Winter Count*. This book came as a revelation to me—the revelation of an exquisite and serious writer whose home terrain was the West, whose concerns and interests I shared, but whose sensibilities, I recognized, were so different from mine as to strike me as almost otherworldly. He was a pious man, this writer, though in no conventional religious sense. A fiction writer with the ears and the heart of a poet. I don't recall what-all I said in the review, and if I still have a copy, it's buried too deep in the basement for excavating, but I can recapture one phrase, because Barry's paperback publisher, some years later, saw fit to reprint it on the cover. I had called *Winter Count* "as painstakingly crafted and as resonant as a good classical guitar." This was carefully calibrated and not at all meant as tepid praise; I had great respect for the craft of building stringed instruments and for skilled guitarists like

Andrés Segovia. You could also consider Willie Nelson, Jorma Kaukonen, or B.B. King, and you would realize: a fine guitar, acoustic or electric, and even a seasoned old axe in the right hands, has its own voice. For instance, B.B. King's guitar Lucille.

Barry evidently understood the intended compliment, because our first direct personal contact, just a year or two later, was genial. One day he called me out of the blue (this was long before email), a friendly voice on the line, a mellow baritone, but a stranger. *Hello, is that David? This is Barry Lopez,* I suppose he said. He was treading carefully, politely, and offering an invitation. He asked if I might share teaching chores with him, for a multi-day class at an event called the Port Townsend Writers Conference. I'd never heard of it. A very nice thing in a nice place, he explained. It was put on by an organization called Centrum, in a converted army base—Fort Worden, Washington—way out on the Quimper Peninsula, at the mouth of Puget Sound. I was living in Tucson, while my wife of the time, Kris, worked on a biology degree at the University of Arizona. I didn't much care for conferences. I had zero desire to teach writing (or to try to) but, by that time, I had considerable interest in meeting this guy, Barry Lopez. So I agreed. He would handle the first half of the course (totaling a week, ten days? I don't remember) and I would relieve him midway through. He had to scram then for another commitment, and we would only overlap for one day. Someone arranged a Cessna to carry Kris and me out over the sound from Sea-Tac Airport to Port Townsend. It was a lark, that journey, kiting out over the waters beyond Seattle in our private air taxi. When we landed, Barry was there.

What I most warmly remember from that first encounter is a long walk on the kelp-littered beach, a couple hours of conversation and observation, the three of us, during which my friendship with Barry began.

And then for years there would be only the chance get-togethers at other conferences and events, the reading of each other's work, the mutual support, and the long phone calls. I'd pick up the receiver and hear him speaking two words, one a greeting, the second an entirely unnecessary self-identification: "David. Barry."

And we would talk—about the life of travel to remote places, about shared concerns for the world and especially (but not solely) the world of nonhuman living creatures, about other writers whom we admired, about history, about Catholic childhoods, about sports (little-known fact: Barry started his freelance career as a sportswriter), about basketball and baseball in particular and, lord help us, even about Pete Rose. We met often enough that he became a friend and enthusiast of my second (and final) wife, Betsy, as he had been of Kris.

Another little-known fact: Barry could be funny. He seldom showed that capacity in his written works, or in public appearances, but it flourished in private conversations, if my experience is any fair sample. We both knew that we were very different sorts of people, very different sorts of writers—I was an inveterate smart-ass and jokester, for one thing, and he not only indulged that but seemed to enjoy it. He was generally earnest in public communications, but in private he was well capable of irony, sarcasm, and laughter. Humor helped cement our friendship, and eventually I came to think of him as the older brother I never had.

On one of the early pages of *Horizon*, a book that draws on a lifetime of arduous travels, Barry left us a statement as candidly self-seeing as any I can recall from his work. "Initially I thought of myself on these journeys as a reporter, traveling outward from a more privileged world. I believed—as well as I could grasp the idea back then—that I had an ethical obligation as a writer, in addition to an aesthetic one." His duty as he saw it was to observe the world intensely, then do his best to put his observations into words. Others might see better but lacked his privilege to get around. Others, regarding what he reported, might draw conclusions different from his. So be it. "I saw myself, then, as a sort of courier, a kind of runner come home from another land after some exchange with it and its denizens," carrying fragmentary news of incomprehensible marvels. Now, writing his final book, he saw "that this ideal—to imagine myself in service to the reader—had me balanced on the edge of self-delusion." But that was how he worked, in those earlier times: "It didn't occur to me that taking life so seriously might cause a loss of perspective." Reading those sentences again now, three years after the book appeared, two years after his death, I want to argue gently against him.

I want to say: *Barry, you were never merely a runner. You were a singer, a shaman, an itinerant poet.* I want to say: *Yes, you took life and its glories and its wounds very seriously, because you knew it is only lived once by each of us, and everything is precious, everything counts.* I want to say: *We were all enriched by the things that you saw and reported, but what mattered was not just that, the observations, the tales, the facts. What made it all matter more was the voice you had found and earned—a voice so elegant and keen, so gentle and considering and companionable—and in which you delivered your news of the world.*

Here's the consolation, then: Barry is gone but his voice is not. It abides in the books. They remind us that the world is vast and wonderful, that the heart and the curiosity of one Barry Lopez were vast and wonderful too, and that his character was keen and strong and benevolent. That's the miracle of literature, I suppose. If there's an extraordinary voice, writing can be almost as good as a phone call.

THE UNSTONED RING

LAURA DASSOW WALLS

It's March 8, 2017, and we're having dinner, just the two of us, at a campus eatery on the evening of our first day together. What Barry Lopez says—"Notre Dame *made* me. It's *everywhere* in my work, and no one else sees that"—arrests my fork in midair. After six years teaching at the University of Notre Dame, immersed as an outsider in both the mystique and the vexing politics of this Catholic institution founded and led by the Congregation of Holy Cross (crucifixes overlook every classroom), I understand instantly; but the full truth of his words, which have haunted me ever since, is harder to get to. All the next day I will think about what Barry said, first as he spoke with my students, then as he gave a public lecture, "The Education of Barry Lopez," published in *Notre Dame Magazine*. One could ask it this way: By what alchemy did the seventeen-year-old Catholic altar boy who unpacked his suitcase in Cavanaugh Hall on a muggy September day in 1962 in South Bend, Indiana, certain he was destined for a monastery, become the self-possessed young writer who, almost exactly six years later, would load his car and set out for Oregon, where he would live for the rest of his life? The 1960s were an era in many ways like our own, beset by distant wars brought home by journalists and protests, a civic life splintered into violently hostile factions, a sense of utopian futures as the only way to survive an apocalyptic present. Paradoxically, Notre Dame would both exemplify all this yet resist it, in ways both inspiring and stultifying. It would leave him, Barry told me, like a ring without a stone—encircled, forever bound, but incomplete. He would spend the rest of his life searching for what was missing.

Given that, for a host of reasons, few American nature writers have emerged from a traditional Catholic background, Barry Lopez is an exception. His father, John Brennan, was Irish Catholic, so faithful that he refused to divorce his first wife before marrying Lopez's mother, Mary Holstun, in 1942—making him a bigamist and his two sons illegitimate. Six years later, when Barry was three and brother, Dennis, still a newborn, Brennan moved his family from Mamaroneck, New York, to the rural San Fernando Valley in Los Angeles, only to desert them in 1950. For the next five years Mary contrived to keep her family afloat by working as a seamstress and teacher, until she married Adrian Lopez, a single, wealthy, and childless New York magazine publisher originally from Spain, who moved them from California to his upscale Manhattan brownstone. Amidst all this turmoil there was one constant: although Mary had been raised a Southern Baptist, she insisted on baptizing both her children in the Catholic Church, and she sent them to Catholic schools, too, to get the best education possible. Adrian Lopez, also Catholic, felt the same. He enrolled his adopted sons first at Loyola School, a Jesuit prep school on the Upper East Side where Barry studied for six years, then insisted that both Barry and Dennis attend his own alma mater, Notre Dame (class of 1928). As an undergraduate Barry would take four years of philosophy and four years of theology, a rigorous program he would credit for giving him, not erudition (although it did, however lightly he wore it), but, as he said in his lecture, "instruction in how to navigate in the world."

Thus it was that a seventeen-year-old Barry Lopez, fresh from an eight-week summer school trip around the capitals and byways of Europe, found himself unpacking his suitcase in a single room with a private bath in Cavanaugh Hall (his stepfather had pulled some strings), and learning to follow the many rules: mandatory prayer at 6:30 a.m., Morning Mass, 10 p.m. room checks, lights out at 11 p.m. As David Schlaver, a fellow student, would later write, "obedience to rightful authority was the operative myth in Catholic society" as well as "the cornerstone of the old-time Catholic education." Absences from campus without permission were strictly forbidden, as were automobiles, drinking (priest-rectors searched students' rooms and patrolled the town bars), women, Communists, and *Playboy* magazines. The patriarchal hierarchy was absolute: faculty served the Holy Cross order, students obeyed it, and the university's president, the famous educator Father Theodore Hesburgh, was a pontiff, infallible.

Barry started off well, saying his prayers and attending daily mass and communion. The cult of athletics reigned at Notre Dame then as now, and so Barry, who at Loyola had lettered in at least two sports, signed up for a team—not Notre Dame football, which like his fellow students (and much of the nation) he followed keenly, but intramural soccer. The national panic over Sputnik, the satellite launched by the Soviet Union in 1957, challenged America's youth to enter the Cold War race for technological superiority, and so, given his childhood fascination with the mechanics of flight, it seemed logical to declare a major in aeronautical engineering. And given the looming war in Vietnam, logical as well to enroll in the Air Force ROTC. During his freshman year, young Barry Lopez must have looked like many another Notre Dame student: bright, willing, dutiful, patriotic—and safe.

It didn't last. He did play soccer for a couple more years before moving on to other things; as he commented, it helped keep him outdoors, and reminded him "to never lose sight of the importance of the body." As for ROTC, the fun went out of it during a freshman trip to nearby Bunker Hill Air Force Base: as he told William E. Tydeman in *Conversations with Barry Lopez,* "I got face to face with a B-58 Hustler, a fighter-bomber, and realized that I was preparing to actually kill people." Barry quit ROTC during his sophomore year. And as for engineering, his early grades were so average that several semesters of solid work couldn't lift his GPA above cum laude—a fact that stung all the more given that he'd graduated from Loyola at the top of his class.

Meanwhile, Lopez discovered that what possessed him was not the mechanics of flight but the poetry. During his freshman year, his close reading of D. H. Lawrence's poem "The Snake" earned him five points out of six from one Prof. Bennett, who wrote: "Mr. Lopez, this is excellent! Nature writing may be your *forté*." His new direction was affirmed on May 1, 1963, when the poet Robert Fitzgerald visited campus to read from his new translation of *The Odyssey*. As Lopez said in his public lecture, he almost didn't go. He wanted to, but that meant cutting his sociology class, which felt "disrespectful." Until, on his dutiful way there, an advertisement for Fitzgerald's reading caught his eye: "*My God*, I thought, *don't be a fool.*" What he saw "transfixed" him. Fitzgerald read beautifully, somehow disappearing into "Homer's mind, his meter and language," before an audience held rapt with attention, their faces "fulfilled." And he felt it, too: "It was, for me, an astonishing thing. We in the audience all felt, *Yes! That was us! Long ago.*" That summer Lopez dove in, making up courses in history and sociology at New York University before returning to Notre Dame for his sophomore year and a new major in communication arts: radio, TV, film, theater, creative writing.

Sitting that night in the auditorium with my students all around, listening to Lopez telling this story, I nodded. I, too, had entered college determined on a science major; I, too, had dived into mathematics and chemistry and biology; I, too, had been changed profoundly when I discovered in college that what moved me was something else, something in the power of language to lift and transport us, not away from our world but deeper into its mystery. As I listened, I began to think that here was someone whose life could help me comprehend my own, and whose history could help us all face our future with the courage born of greater understanding of how we got where we are today. Perhaps, I began to think, there was a future biography here, the story of a life that could help the people in this audience, help the students listening to Barry so avidly, in this auditorium so electric with attention. Was he doing for them what Fitzgerald had once done for him? *"Yes, that was us! Long ago."*

Sophomore year was the year he became Barry Lopez. He moved into Zahm Hall (named for Fr. John Augustine Zahm, the scientist who broke ranks to embrace Darwin's theory of evolution), and he and his new roommate, Pete Lewis, hung signs on their door: "If you can't identify fifteen species of rattlesnake, don't bother knocking!" and "If you don't know the difference between lesser and greater kudu, don't bother knocking!" Barry acquired a car, a pink-and-white two-door Chrysler which he hid off campus, and on weekends, while their classmates partied and drank, Barry and Pete took off to wherever they would reach in a day's drive: West Virginia, northern Minnesota, Mississippi, Louisiana, Missouri, even the north coast of Lake Superior, returning late Sunday nights after curfew full of travelers' tales that awed their classmates and would later become stories and essays. That spring of 1964, the pair captured a stray puppy up in southern Michigan, a "coy-dog" (half coyote), adopted her, and named her Lobo. Barry, who grew up with a dog always at his side, felt incomplete without one; he took care of Lobo for the rest of her long life. From then on she'd come along on all his car trips, making friends along the way. And all that spring, somehow their preceptor let it slide, benignly waving goodnight to the boys during nightly dorm room checks even as Lobo barked and scratched at the door. Dogs were, of course, strictly forbidden. The lesson Barry learned stayed with him: good grades and good behavior could buy freedom to stretch the rules, make it possible to live his own life rather than another's.

It was the perfect moment to be adopting such a lesson: the world in 1964 was starting to pivot, and fast. Barry's growing rebelliousness was both uniquely his and tightly aligned with the youth movement sweeping across America. Student activism reached Notre Dame on April 29, 1964, when the leaders of the class of '66—Barry's class—arranged to greet the presidential candidate Governor George Wallace of Alabama with seven hundred picketers protesting his racism. Ten minutes into Wallace's speech condemning the Civil Rights bill (which became law in July), five hundred students walked out singing "We Shall Overcome." Pandemonium erupted as Wallace supporters from the town responded with "Dixie" while more students chimed in with the protesters, each side trying to drown out the other. Weeks later, Notre Dame's President Hesburgh chimed in as well, linking arms with Martin Luther King Jr. at a Chicago rally to sing "We Shall Overcome" before the cameras. In July, Fr. Hesburgh was awarded the Presidential Medal of Freedom by President Johnson. Notre Dame was in the national spotlight.

Was Lopez there, jeering at Wallace? I'm sure he was. I wish I could have asked him, given what I've learned since: for instance, that his mother, who had grown up in Alabama, was just then teaching public school in East Harlem; that one of the few things Barry preserved from these years was a poster advertising Reverend King's visit to Notre Dame. Sitting in that auditorium, listening to the Alabama racist running for President, Lopez would have known exactly how much was at stake. And he was entering an era of private rebellion, too—although, characteristically, he went his own way. During the historic summer of 1964 that followed, when many Notre Dame students travelled south to register Black voters, Barry and his pal Lobo joined up with his brother Dennis to embark on an epic road trip straight out of Jack Kerouac: they drove west from New Jersey to California to the Canadian Rockies, hiking and camping all the way, while Barry snapped pictures with his first camera. When the trio stopped overnight in Wyoming on their way home, at a dude ranch near Jackson Hole owned by college friends, Barry refused to leave. For the next two weeks he fell in love, twice, and he wrangled horses and he packed mule trains, and he returned to New York in cowboy boots and a cowboy hat, resentful and rebellious, eager to imagine another life for himself.

Barry and Denny had driven through San Francisco just weeks before Mario Savio returned there from his own stint registering Black voters in the South, on his way to founding the nonviolent Free Speech Movement. Savio's famous speech of December 2, 1964, midway through Lopez's junior year, borrowed a line from Thoreau's "Civil Disobedience": when "the operation of the machine" makes you so "sick at heart" that you can't take part, it's time "to put your bodies upon the gears and upon the wheels . . . upon the levers, upon all the apparatus, and you've got to make it stop!" Around that same time, Lopez wrote a college essay praising "Civil Disobedience," and he stopped going to mass and taking communion. There was, he said in *Conversations with Barry Lopez*, "no dramatic incident, no pivotal moment." He simply "fell out of the habit" while turning to other things: traveling, theater, radio, all media that engaged an audience in the art of storytelling.

The summer of 1965, when many of his classmates were again travelling south to stand with Black protesters, Lopez again went west, returning to the same Wyoming ranch to work as a horse wrangler on pack trips into the Teton wilderness. He brought along a better camera, launching his career in photography, and a copy of Virgil's *Aeneid* to translate, exercising his extensive instruction in Latin toward the lyrical passion he'd witnessed in Fitzgerald. He was writing, too, transmuting his idyllic summers on the ranch into a series of short stories, culminating with "The Gift," in which Pedro, a wrangler at a guest ranch, lovingly tends a rare mariposa lily only to have a lovelorn woman present it to him, picked, as a gift. The editors of Notre Dame's student magazine, *The Juggler*, rejected Lopez's submissions with "nasty, condescending notes," but when his roommate showed "The Gift" to Jim Andrews, editor of the leftist Notre Dame–based journal *Ave Maria*, Andrews published it, in March 1966, in an issue featuring a grim cover photo from Vietnam and a banner essay on training Army chaplains. This was Lopez's first significant publication, and his first important professional contact: Jim Andrews went on to co-found Andrews McMeel Publishing and to publish Lopez's first two books, *Desert Notes* (1976) and *Giving Birth to Thunder* (1978).

Lopez's class of 1966 came into their senior year alienated and bent on revolution. They were a fiery, radiant, close-knit community, and Barry stayed lifelong friends with many of them. Their relations with faculty were sometimes tense: Lopez's favorite English professor at Notre Dame, the fiction writer Richard Sullivan, who, as Barry told me, "would give up his life for his students," was dismayed at the "young & ignorant rebels" suddenly populating his classes: "the new breed, rebellious, cocksure of new knowledge, never before glimpsed by man," as he scoffed in his journal. (Lopez was an exception: Sullivan's July 1981 review of *Winter Count* in *Notre Dame Magazine* is full of praise for his former student's "poised and evocative" writing and the "strange brooding compulsion" of his stories; "It is impossible not to follow each to its finish," he wrote, "and equally impossible not to be impressed in each by a kind of rightness which goes beyond logic to something like truth.") Sullivan also fretted about their drug experimentation (which Lopez shunned), their radical sexual freedom (one couple staged an erotic shower in a first-floor bathroom in front of an open window before "fascinated observers"), and their falling away from the Catholic faith into such troubling alternatives as "esthetic experiential pantheism." The phrase might have described the new territory Lopez himself was exploring, encouraged by his favorite theology professor, John S. Dunne, an iconoclast who, Barry told me, "radiated spiritual love and understanding without regard to narrow liturgies," and whose classes were so popular that most students had to wait until they were seniors to take them. It was Dunne who showed Lopez how to reimagine Catholic theology poetically and metaphorically, and to see God's liturgy written into the face of Earth itself.

The first big event of Lopez's senior year was October's International Day of Protest against the Vietnam War, which Notre Dame filled with a twelve-hour teach-in. It was the first time a Notre Dame professor articulated a radical Catholic critique of the war as unjust and immoral. This argument defied most of the students, who still supported the war, if passively; but Lopez, in his lecture, told how he stepped out as one of the anti-war dissidents, "recognizable by our Carnaby Street clothes and our long hair," becoming "the objects of ridicule and jeering—and worse—from other students." His own role during the teach-in was an attempt to inform the public by mediating between opposing views: by then Lopez was a well-known radio personality on the student-run station WSND-AM, and he organized and moderated a radio debate on anti-intellectualism at Notre Dame that was heard well beyond the campus community. By late November, student discontent was escalating. A small contingent traveled to Washington, D.C., for the March for Peace; back on campus, other students held a hunger strike to protest both the war and the lack of reform at Notre Dame. The strike, thanks to coverage on CBS, NBC, and a debate moderated by Walter Cronkite, brought Notre Dame national notoriety.

Lopez certainly would have sympathized with the hunger strikers, but he did not become one. His conscience was deeply troubled by the war, and the rampant injustices and systemic oppressions he witnessed on his travels had turned his thoughts to joining the Peace Corps—popular at Notre Dame, seen as part of President John F. Kennedy's Catholic legacy. But in the end, as Lopez said in his lecture, he withheld himself: "I came to understand that I was not a conscientious objector, that this ethical stance was true in my head—a reasonable conclusion—but not in my heart." So, one cold and snowy December morning, he showed up in Chicago to take his military physical. Volunteering meant you could choose your branch of the military and your form of service. Lopez chose the Army, and to be a medic. But he failed the physical due to some unhealed injuries, and he was never drafted. Nor did he join the Peace Corps, despite his strong attraction to it as a form of making amends—not, as he explained many years later, because he understood the risks of "institutionalized compassion," but more simply because of the tension he felt, and continued to feel all his life, between his head's call to act and his heart's call to write.

And after graduating in June 1966, writing was where Lopez finally turned—but not until he'd thrashed through four years of questing and floundering, of doors that closed and others that opened. That first summer he traveled again to Europe, this time with Dennis and their parents, a trip cut short by a ferocious family argument over bell bottoms and disrespect. Once home in New York, Lopez drove to Missoula, Montana, to act in summer stock theater with Sandra Jean Landers, a student at St. Mary's College near Notre Dame; they'd fallen in love while working together in St. Mary's theater program. Weeks later, Lopez was back in New

York to take a job as sales representative for the New American Library, driving across the Northeast to hawk college paperbacks to professors for classroom use. On the road that November he faced a fork in his path, quite literally: ever since childhood, he had felt destined for a monastic vocation. It was time to settle the matter. Lopez detoured to Gethsemani, the Trappist monastery in Kentucky, where one of his guiding spirits, the writer Thomas Merton, resided in solitude. For some days Lopez seriously considered the possibility of a life there. In the end he turned away, not because he didn't like it but because he *did*—liked it so much, thought it so perfect, so desirable, that he knew it couldn't be, for him, the right path. And so he drove on—not to his next college sale, but, remarkably, to St. Louis, Missouri, to affirm his marriage proposal to Sandra, who accepted. As Barry told me, the very week he was undertaking this rather stark choice—monastery, or marriage—Merton himself was in the throes of a similar struggle, asking in his journal, "If I cannot love this woman, how can I say that I love God?"

Back in New York by December, Lopez went to work for his stepfather, Adrian Lopez, as a staff member of his pulp publishing empire, including as associate editor of a soft-porn men's magazine named *Man to Man*—precisely the sort of risqué handbook to sexual freedom that Notre Dame had forbidden. Far from a stopgap, taking on this job meant immersion in the gritty, high-stakes world of New York publishing; Barry would continue to work for Adrian well into the 1970s, although he quit his full-time staff position around June 1967, when he and Sandra were married. They moved away together, back to South Bend, so she could finish her BA at St. Mary's while he, as he thought, would make a few dollars editing *Ave Maria* or working in TV or as a radio announcer at WSND. But right after the newlyweds had rented a house, those plans fell through. Desperate, Lopez applied to the local steel mill, but just before his job interview, a chance encounter led to the offer of a National Endowment for the Arts fellowship in Notre Dame's Graduate Department of Education. All he had to do was complete the requirements for a master's degree in teaching. Which is exactly what he did, while teaching at a local high school and making extra money recording radio advertisements for the local bank. A student later told Barry he was famous for tooling around town on his motorcycle in long hair and leather jacket like a character out of *Easy Rider*, Lobo sitting on the back seat with her paws on his shoulders.

That final year at Notre Dame saw a steady stream of publications, starting in December 1967 with "The Psychedelic Christ" in *Notre Dame Dialogue*, in which Lopez ventured that Jesus Christ was the first and the greatest "hippie" of all time, whose single command, "love," was more mind-expanding than LSD. Then came several publications through *Ave Maria*: passionate book reviews on Christian existentialism; a photo-essay with Justin Soleta—the first of a lifetime of collaborative efforts with visual artists—in which Soleta's photographs of a crucifix were accompanied by Lopez's narrative of the Passion of Christ; a travel sketch, "Odey's," on Odey Cassell, an eighty-nine-year-old West Virginia farmer with whom Lopez stayed in 1964 during one of his illicit off-campus adventures. He even started his own news magazine, *Focus Michiana*. Perhaps most remarkable of all was the unclassifiable story "Beneath," a prefiguration of *Desert Notes*, witnessing the rebirth of Christ from, and as, the body of Earth.

By the time he had his master's degree in hand, Lopez had learned from hard experience that his future did not lie in teaching. But he also had in hand a solid portfolio: philosophical essays, religious meditations, travel writing, journalism, collaborative work, experimental fiction—his six years at Notre Dame had flowered into the themes and genres of a potential career in writing. But to become a real writer, Lopez reasoned, required earning an MFA from a writing program. Iowa turned him down, but when Oregon accepted him, he jumped, eager to return to his western roots; and so, in summer of 1968, the young couple headed to Eugene. After just a single semester, Lopez dropped the MFA and switched to journalism, only to drop out entirely a year later, well short of a degree. He was impatient, he told me, felt he was spinning his wheels. After all, wasn't he already a seasoned author, editor, and publisher? What he really wanted to do, as he complained to his folklore professor Barre Toelken, was quit school and write. "Absolutely right!" replied Toelken. "I encourage you to leave this place, right now." And leave he did. In a frenetic burst of energy, Lopez leveraged his New York contacts into freelance journalism, located a stock agent to market his photographs, and worked his Notre Dame connections to become a stringer for both the *New York Times* and the *Washington Post* and publish his first two books. As soon as Sandra completed her master's degree, in June 1970, Barry and Sandra rented a house (which they would later buy) on thirty-six acres of land on the McKenzie River, forty miles from town, near the tiny settlement of Finn Rock—the home that Barry, no matter how far he travelled, would never leave.

So what did Barry mean that evening at Notre Dame, by saying that Notre Dame is "everywhere" in his work? Most obviously, his words offer a clue to the source and nature of the profound religiosity that permeates his writing, including the conflict he felt between sitting down at a typewriter and taking a stand at a protest: Which would best serve the world? While his fellow students were mounting protests and registering Black voters, his heart drew him in another direction, toward a quest for the divine and the language to convey it. But Lopez knew this was not the right choice for everyone. In his lecture he was more explicit: Notre Dame taught him "that you're responsible for your own education. If what you are looking for in your studies is not offered, it is your responsibility, not the faculty's, to find out what that missing piece is and to address it." In the lecture, he embodied this truth in his story of the "unstoned ring": during his senior year, playing a spring baseball game, an errant pitch hit his brand-new class ring and shattered the stone. Rather than get a new stone right away, he wore it empty, to remind himself of what his education, so insistently male, Catholic, middle-class, White, and European, had *missed*. Namely, most of the world—a world he would literally spend the rest of his life traversing, taking the exact measure, in his many books, stories, and essays, of everything that his inherited culture both granted, and lacked. Only years later, once he fully understood the empty ring's meaning, would he replace the old stone with a new one.

As I often told my own students, the root of "education" is "educe," to draw out what is latent or hidden. What I admire so deeply in Barry's work is his ability to educe both the beauty and the pain hidden by the coarseness of our conventional lives: to look into the eyes of a wolf and see both the history of human monstrosity and the human capacity for empathy, framed by the alterity of a being who walks the fringes of our consciousness; to see in a landscape of ice the gift of ineffable peace, yet also the indifferent cruelties of an America that lets a world melt away, with all its cultures and all its lives, for the most casual pleasures; to look for fifty years into the heart of a wild river and never exhaust its meaning. If Barry Lopez never resolved the tension that swung him from solitary creation to communal activism and back, first writing to illuminate then later acting to make amends—a tension scored into his conscience at Notre Dame in the 1960s—one can say this: in drawing on the fullness of his education to navigate this conflict, he learned to distinguish blind obedience from respectful cooperation, and to resist conformity by creating community. Two lessons that are, indeed, everywhere in his great work, and that all his writings seek to educe in all his readers.

CIRCLE, UNBROKEN

MARYBETH HOLLEMAN

A writing student once told me about encountering a polar bear. He was on a kayak trip along the Arctic coast, alone; he was asleep in his tent; he was awakened by a loud ripping sound, and opened his eyes to see dark sky and white fur, white face and dark snout, two dark eyes; he fumbled for his rifle as the white receded and only darkness remained. Why the polar bear didn't kill and eat him after ripping open his tent, why instead the bear ambled away while he reached for his rifle, which was, it turns out, jammed, he would never know. But he would spend the rest of his life grateful.

This wasn't the polar bear story I told at a gathering of writers at Texas Tech University in 2004. We were sitting, King Arthur–style, around a round table, all of us invited here by Barry Lopez, who sat just to the right of me and two other mothers, Lisa Couturier and Susan Cerulean. Barry had asked us three to speak about motherhood and nature, having heard us talk among ourselves about literature's outsized representation of men venturing solo into the wild. Women with children—now, that was a different kind of adventure.

And so, instead, I told of standing in line at the grocery store, a place mothers often find themselves. My son was pleading once more for a Hot Wheels, strategically placed at the checkout line, where parents, weary of the begging, might give in. I said no, again, and glanced up to see the cover of *Alaska Magazine*: a full-head image of a polar bear with the headline *Bound for Extinction?* I gasped, and turned to my husband, who told me, softly so my son couldn't hear, a story that struck like an arrow to my heart: A fellow marine biologist, while flying over the Arctic Ocean on a whale survey, had spotted four white forms floating in the sharp blue sea—four dead polar bears. It was just after a major storm, and with shrinking sea ice, storm waves are becoming stronger; polar bears, though excellent swimmers, can't endure the increasing distances and higher waves. As many as twenty bears, biologists estimated, had drowned in that Arctic storm. This mass drowning was the first ever recorded by scientists, but it would not be the last.

I set the story adrift in the soft, warm air of a fall evening in Texas. Polar bears, and climate chaos, and my son's move to adulthood in an uncertain future, all seemed far away. Even I, after fifteen years in Alaska, had yet to see a polar bear outside the zoo. Barry did not say anything after my story, nor after the stories of the other mothers; he just let our words resonate.

After college, I received a scholarship from my local North Carolina chapter of the National Audubon Society to attend the organization's camp in Maine. Most participants were teachers; only two were writers. Or, in my case, aspiring writer. This other writer told me we were of two kinds: those who write because they love it and will happily write about anything, "even," she said, "making bread;" and those who write because they have some question they are driven to explore.

The latter was me; she knew—and I knew—that this was me. My degree was in environmental studies, and my quest was to explore the relationship of humans to the rest of the living world, to comprehend why we imagine ourselves apart and why, in so doing, we act destructively toward our home planet. And to find the words—the words!—to bring us back into right relation.

A tall order. I had read, at an impressionable age, Edward Abbey's *The Monkey Wrench Gang*. I had rallied against the damming of wetlands in Piedmont North Carolina for a nuclear power plant. I'd gone with friends to sabotage the machinery of that destruction. I'd marched on Washington, D.C., in the No Nukes rally. I'd thought that, with more than 100,000 of us gathered at our nation's capital, we would effect change, lasting change. I was wrong.

I took a job at the North Carolina State Energy Office, working on alternative energy. I did my work, my homework, my due diligence. I got nowhere. The problem was not, as I'd thought, just a matter of conveying science to politicians, so that politicians would then make reasonable, life-sustaining decisions.

My father was an engineer who spent his free time working on old cars. My mother, a homemaker, worked in the family garden with the same intensity that her parents, both farmers, had worked theirs. We were a hands-on tribe. We believed in the power of our physical bodies to make immediate, visible change. None of these things happened in the political sphere, at least not in the rational way that I had, in my naiveté, expected.

So I returned to my roots. I saw how Abbey—and Annie Dillard, Rachel Carson, Henry David Thoreau—had infused my worldview. I realized the power of the written word to effect change. Visible change. Lasting change. And that became my sword and my shield, my wrench and my hoe and my watering can, as I stepped out into the world to be of use.

The first of Barry Lopez's books I read was *Of Wolves and Men*. I read it just before I moved from North Carolina to Alaska, from a state where the red wolf was being reintroduced into the wild to a state where the gray wolf was being slaughtered through barbaric state predator control. Even as the first red wolves, extinct in the wild since 1980, were being released from a captive breeding program into North Carolina's Alligator River National Wildlife Refuge, gray wolves in Alaska were still the targets of legal aerial hunting and were being poisoned in their dens.

The dissonance did not escape me. *Of Wolves and Men* deeply informed my understanding of the fraught relationship we had—and still have, decades later—with this animal we call wolf. I saw how wolves—rather, the human *idea* of wolves—never elicits ambivalence: we either love them or hate them. Wolves, of course, have no such issue—they don't live in that unnatural dichotomy. Barry Lopez knew that. He dedicated the book, "For Wolves. Not the book, for which you would have little use, but the effort at understanding. I enjoyed your company."

As I came into my new country, this wild northern landscape which both awed and excited me, Lopez's book became one of my tools. So, I could learn of the Anchorage dentist who boasted to friends on the VHF radio about getting so close to wolves running for their lives that one tried to bite the wing of his airplane. He thought it was funny; he laughed as he killed this wolf and a dozen others. Same-day airborne hunting was illegal, but otherwise this man was only acting within the culture's prescription. I could learn about this and feel the root causes, our cultural burdens, which elicit such ignorant actions, such tragic separation from the nonhuman world.

I came to Alaska for a summer job, but I wound up staying, curious about the long, dark winters, about snow that fell and stayed on the ground, several feet deep, all winter long, about the northern lights, about the sun circling the sky in summer, about all that this wild, wondrous land had to show me.

That first summer, I sold tickets on a train that connected Alaska's meager road system to the gloriousness that was Prince William Sound. It was the only way to get there, that train, so it was a melting pot. Blue-haired retirees just off the cruise ship sat next to disheveled commercial fishermen just returned from a twenty-four-hour opener, their fish-scent mingling with perfume, all of it inhaled by dogs who also rode in the train cars, sitting on seats beside their owners. I met an old Russian Orthodox fisherman who told me, "I could spend many lifetimes exploring Prince William Sound, and still not see it all." And a young cruise-ship bus driver who visited one new place in Alaska every year, compiling a list that was joyfully endless.

Then I read *Arctic Dreams*, and decided to dream, myself, of traveling to the Arctic, of witnessing polar bears and the great ice cap. Yes: Barry's books inspire people to go where he had gone. And yes: they inspire people to fight for these places, to revere and admire and respect these places and their inhabitants, whether four-footed, two-legged, winged, or flippered, and whether we ever see them for ourselves. Great writing like Barry's takes us places so completely that we don't need to physically go there in order to care about them.

When I first came to Alaska, to these raw, jagged mountains and roiling shorelines so different from the softly folded old mountains in which I grew up, I was nearly speechless. It was all I could do to keep my feet beneath me as I opened up to it. This was how Barry approached all his subjects, whether the Arctic or wolves or the forest near his home. "When we enter the landscape to learn something, we are obligated, I think, to pay attention rather than constantly to pose questions," he writes in *The Rediscovery of North America*. I knew that the answers we get depend on the questions we ask; that's how artists and scientists gain such different insights on the same subject matter. But what if we don't ask any questions? Then the land reveals itself, shows how it is far wider and deeper than we ever could have imagined.

I know Barry's wolf book echoes in my book *Among Wolves* as it likely did in the work of the book's wolf biologist Gordon Haber. I know his words have helped Alaska and Alaskans—our sense of, and responsibility toward, wolves and polar bears and this expansive northern landscape. But it's not just his words; it's his attitude: open to what is given, receptive to what the land has to offer and asks of us in return. "To approach the land," he writes in *Arctic Dreams*, "as we would a person." His writing helped me ground myself here, so that I could spread my arms wide and be more fully immersed, and so immersed, be embraced in an ever-widening circle.

Many years after moving to Alaska, I had the great gift of a correspondence with him. Just a handful of letters, all told, but it lifted me each time one arrived: a small envelope, a single typewritten page with words that hummed. I never asked for writing advice; we never discussed craft. Instead, what we discussed was the passion, the reason for it, the being-of-use that propelled us both. And the grief that whirled in the continual stormfront of loss: "[Loss] can push us through grief into a place of clarity about what needs to be done," he writes in one letter. "This is how we honor each other. . . ." He always shepherded things back to what matters. He reminded me, in another letter, of our need "to find our balance, to renew our effort to illuminate, to honor, to resacralize, and to protect the natural world."

When I finally met Barry, at a conference, I was like a groupie, all giddy and wordless, as I'd been when I met Edward Abbey and Wendell Berry and Annie Dillard. But it was brief. He was tired after giving a talk to six hundred people and tending the long line of admirers.

Fortunately, I would get another opportunity. A golden opportunity. An invitation from Barry to join a small group of writers in Texas, including those other mother-writers. We spent those fall days walking in woods and fields and along a stream, in conversation and connection. It was quite the group, including, among others, Bill McKibben, before he started 350.org. But our time together wasn't about hobnobbing. It was about creating and deepening friendships with people who share values and reasons for writing. Barry wanted to give us that which had nurtured his own writing life: connection to community. He knew that would help sustain us as we released our words out into a world of loss and grief. *"Un fuerte abrazo*"—"A big hug"—he signed many of his letters, including his last missive to me.

I sit now with Barry's letters and books on my desk. I pull out the thick hardcover of *Arctic Dreams*, flip it open to the chapter "Tôrnârssuk." Barry is telling me, again, about the polar bear's hollow hair. A fact I've remembered, and repeated, hundreds of times since. At the end of "Tôrnârssuk," Barry writes of the close-up view of a darted, unconscious female polar bear, a searing moment that conveys their supreme vulnerability. What prescience, to know, in 1986, that polar bears, these massive beings—legs sturdy as tree trunks, paws strong enough to swipe open my student's tent, minds wise enough to not eat him—would be among the first to fall before the greed and insanity of which our society appears to be mortally inflicted.

When I first read Barry's book, polar bears towered in mythic realms, far beyond my reach, still living, as John Muir writes, "as if the country had belonged to them always." Living in Alaska, I began to dream of seeing one in the wild, unmediated by even the most eloquent and sacred prose. Then I learned of the drownings, of the myriad ways climate chaos has unraveled their world, of their imminent demise. And then, one fall, I went to Kaktovik, where wild polar bears gather on a spit of land piled with the remains of the village's season of bowhead-whale kills. I watched those bears feasting, even as I knew they were leaving, heading for extinction. Not even their hollow hairs could save them.

I've come to realize that, as vital as it is to witness and write, to send my words out into the world and have them land where they might affect the minds and hearts of others, to be of use during my brief time on this stunning planet, what's also true is that, through this writing life, I've met people who I can honestly call my tribe. And Barry knew that. He knew the importance of sustaining one's relatively solitary writing life within a larger circle.

This is what remains with me now, this embrace of tribe. The embrace of people I've met through him, and those I've yet to meet, but with whom

I feel, all the same, kinship. The immersion within the widening circle of the lands and seas and all those with whom we share our home. I've been fortunate to meet some of my heroes, and I've learned that the hero is one who shines so brightly that their radiance penetrates our truest selves, lights us up, and lets us see our own shining light, our own heroism, which was there all along.

GEESE

ALAN WEISMAN

Among the greatest rewards for anyone who writes or teaches is hearing from readers or students that something we wrote, or said at some opportune moment, changed their lives.

For me, the opposite is also true. Somewhere out there is a former student I haven't seen for decades—we'll call him Greg—who changed mine. If by some chance he's reading this (an actual possibility, I realize, as it pertains to Barry Lopez) I am so grateful, because I lost track of him, his surname dissolved away by time. I never had a chance to thank him properly when I knew him briefly, because back then I had little inkling of how key his contribution would be.

At the time—this was 1982—I had just returned to my home, a cabin on an old gold claim in the mountains of central Arizona. For the past four years I'd been in and out of Mexico, trying to write a book. It wasn't going well, so to earn money I was again teaching a writers' workshop at Prescott College, a so-called alternative college founded in the 1960s. It specialized in field courses team-taught by faculty from different disciplines, their classrooms ranging from the depths of canyons to the tops of mountains, into the Sonoran Desert and down to the Sea of Cortez. Often, I'd tag along to write articles.

Greg, who had never before been to Arizona, had enrolled because he'd heard Prescott College let students design their own curricula. Some took more independent studies than actual classes—an option that appealed to him, I gathered, because of his violent stammer.

He appeared in my office doorway just before our first class: gangly, agonizingly apologetic. He'd signed up for my workshop, he torturously explained, because he so much wanted to be able to express himself. But he'd just learned that each week, every student had to read aloud work assigned the week before, which we'd then critique. "I . . . can't."

"No problem," I said. "I'll read yours."

Relieved, he relaxed. Then he grimaced again, struggling to form what turned out to be a strange question.

"Do . . . you . . . "—he turned scarlet; I waited—"know . . . where . . . to find . . . geese?"

Geese? I wanted to ask why, but I feared his reply would be excruciating, and class was starting. Maybe I'd get him to write about it. Central Arizona's conifer forests, I told him, were deceptively verdant. This was a high desert, with mostly intermittent rivers dependent on seasonal rains. Although I'd heard that snow geese sometimes wintered on some nearby dammed reservoirs, I'd never seen any myself.

I don't recall if he found them. I don't recall much else about him, because he didn't last long in my workshop, or at Prescott. I remember trying to convince him that since he also stammered on the page, he was in good company, as many writers, myself included, fight to squeeze out every sentence. "I can empathize with your emotional constipation," I told him. "That's why we rewrite."

What I do recall, though, is the last time he came to my office, his mouth contorted as usual, battling for words. Pulling a slim paperback from his pack, he thrust it at me. "THIS is what I want to say!" It was the only complete sentence I ever heard him utter straight through.

The book was a collection of short stories titled *Winter Count.*

I hadn't heard of its author, Barry Holstun Lopez. (A few years earlier, living in a tiny village in central Mexico, I'd entirely missed *Of Wolves and Men*.) Taking it home, I plopped in front of my wood stove and opened it. I presumed the title story, listed midway through the table of contents—"Winter Count 1973: Geese, They Flew Over in a Storm"—might shed light on Greg's enigmatic question. But first I glanced at the beginning—and for the next four hours, didn't move.

(The same thing has happened to me often over the years—yet again, as I prepared to write this remembrance. Like the Bach violin sonatas or recordings of Bill Evans that I return to continually, each time I open it, there's more.)

Winter Count wasn't a book: it was sorcery. It wasn't just that I didn't know words could do that. I hadn't even known *that* existed. To me, a truly great book is one that executes such an imaginative leap that I can't figure out how its author did it. *Winter Count* goes even further: I can't even fathom *why* it works. It just does. After reading it, I would never regard writing the same way again.

I'm sure many scholars have parsed *Winter Count*'s meaning and structure, but I don't want to know what they have to say. I just want to read, and keep rereading it. The book has become a touchstone to me. It doesn't matter that I don't know exactly what I'm touching.

I also don't know exactly what moved Greg about *Winter Count*—except for a snatch of their sound, geese never even appear. Possibly he longed for Lopez's ability to articulate the ineffable, to capture something beyond meaning, as in my favorite story, which precedes the title piece. I find "The Orrery" almost impossible to comprehend, but so powerful it's also impossible to forget. It's set in Arizona, in an imaginary valley so convincing that it was years before I checked a map and found that it only exists in this book. Like several other stories in the collection, it's written in the first person, so to the reader, the fictional narrator and the author are inseparable. At one point, watching windblown desert debris seem to levitate and coalesce into galaxies, even he says: "I can't believe this."

When, much later, I told Greg's story to Barry, he placed his hand over mine. "Thank you for telling me. That was the book when I suddenly felt my writing had reached a whole new level."

Maybe more than anything else he ever said to me, that comment lingers. He had already earned wide recognition—he told me how, upon entering an elevator at one of his first appearances at a writers' conference, he realized that the other occupant, a woman with a gray bowl of hair, was Ursula K. Le Guin. Speechless, he could only nod. Alighting at her floor, she glanced back at him and grinned. "You're one of us now, you know," she said as the doors closed.

He was, but there was still more. With *Winter Count*, he dared to take chances.

When he and I met, it was through our mutual good fortune of knowing the same right woman, one who boosted my career but transformed Barry's life.

After nearly four years in and out of Mexico, my attempt at a book had finally succeeded. From then on, I had steady magazine assignments, often in Latin America. In 1990, I was invited to work on a series for National Public Radio about how entire human cultures across the Americas were being uprooted in a frenzied rush for resources. I'd first crossed paths with its producer, the Tucson-based journalist Sandy Tolan, while I was writing my book *La Frontera* and he was producing a radio series on Sanctuary, an underground network of religious workers who smuggled Central American refugees into the United States (which ironically was financing the wars they were fleeing).

Our team for *Vanishing Homelands* included an immigration lawyer-turned-journalist, Nancy Postero, and an Argentine-American former NPR producer, Cecilia Vaisman. Sandy also recruited two highly recommended students from the University of Arizona's graduate journalism program to help research what we'd cover. Debra Gwartney and Mary Mandracchia proved indispensable during the two years we reported two dozen stories from fourteen countries, plus a trip I made to Antarctica to learn if the spreading ozone hole might threaten everyone's Earthly homeland. Whether they were tracking down key sources in Brazil, FedExing replacement microphone cables to Bolivia, or wiring us funds, we depended on those women—although after Mary was diagnosed with multiple sclerosis, increasingly it was Debra.

Mary's boyfriend, Ted Robbins, a reporter then for Tucson's PBS affiliate and later for NPR, responded by proposing to her. We considered him a hero. Surprisingly, Debra, mother to four daughters, abruptly ended her own marriage. By then we had returned to the United States with hundreds of hours of recordings. One night she and her adorable little girls came to our studio to say goodbye. They were heading, Debra said, to Oregon. Although she was already getting national bylines for her freelance stories, she needed a steady income to raise her daughters, and had accepted a university communications job in Eugene.

Why Debra felt compelled to leave their father, and the harrowing drama that ensued, is unforgettably recounted in her book *Live Through This*, a finalist for the 2009 National Book Critics Circle Award. Well before it appeared, however, she had connected with the man who became her second husband and her daughters' devoted stepfather, and grandfather to their children. Years earlier, Debra had interviewed Barry Lopez for the *Tucson Weekly*. When she attended a reading he gave in Eugene, he remembered her. Around then, his own first marriage was failing; after it ended, Barry and Debra's occasional lunches grew more frequent. Then he started turning up for dinners with her and her girls.

Not long after beginning her new job, Debra had called me. Some University of Oregon scientists, working with colleagues in Moscow and Kyiv, had devised a computer-based strategy to help people in regions surrounding Chernobyl deal with the aftermath of the reactor disaster. Was I interested in accompanying them there for a magazine article?

Portions of the cover story I wrote for *Harper's* about life in an irradiated landscape would figure prominently in my next two books. The first, *An Echo in My Blood,* resulted when a Chernobyl nuclear physicist helped me find the Ukrainian village where my father was born, where I unearthed a family secret. In 2004, I was researching the second, *The World Without Us,* when I was contacted by Texas Tech University.

It was where Pulitzer Prize–winning biologist E.O. Wilson, whom I'd recently interviewed, and Barry Lopez had helped found a program that blended the sciences and humanities. A retreat that fall would bring a dozen talented young nature writers to meet with Barry, Bill McKibben, Texas Tech professor and National Book Award finalist Dennis Covington, and editors from Pantheon and Milkweed. When Barry decided they also needed a journalist who could address international environmental issues, Debra suggested me.

That weekend, with our attention focused mainly on the young invitees, there wasn't much chance for extended conversation, but our invigorating exchanges promised more. A week later, I was in the herbarium of the New York Botanical Garden with its director, Barbara Thiers, when my cell phone rang. When I saw Barry's name on the caller ID, I excused myself for a moment. "I'm just calling to talk," he said.

As I was explaining why I couldn't right then, Thiers was opening a folio to show me. Inside was a shred of moss from Tierra del Fuego, with notes written in watery black ink and signed by its collector: *C. Darwin.*

"I hope you're on your knees," said Barry.

A year later, driving back together from an *Orion* magazine board retreat in upstate New York, we talked about Debra, my artist wife, Beckie Kravetz, and our respective paths to becoming writers. "I learned more about writing in the field with ecologists," I told him, "than from any composition or journalism class I ever took."

"Of course you did."

I described the first time I'd accompanied a Prescott College ornithologist into the forest. "Lock the van," he'd told the students, because we'd be gone most of the day. Three hours later, we hadn't traveled more than fifty feet, as he dashed from tree to bug to flower to lichen to scat pile, explaining the role they and every bird we could hear played in this niche, and how the system would weaken if any disappeared. I became fascinated by how ecologists could see that everything is connected; that nothing in nature, including human nature, can be understood in isolation. If I explained these connections to readers, I learned, they were fascinated, too.

"Exactly," said Barry. Our ancestors, living close to their sources of sustenance, had grasped these intricate webs. It was up to storytellers, he believed, to keep connecting the dots, lest we lose sight of all that holds us.

The following summer he came with Debra to hear me speak at the University of Oregon about a book I wrote in Colombia, *Gaviotas*. They came again when I was on tour for *The World Without Us*, to Powell's Books in Portland. During the Q&A, a woman from PETA, People for the Ethical Treatment of Animals, stood and challenged me to prove that I really cared about the environment, by pledging *right now, in front of everyone,* to never eat another animal.

"Sorry, you've got the wrong guy. I don't eat meat," I said. "Just fish."

Then I was a hypocrite, she declared, and no one should buy my book. As someone from Powell's ushered her out, I wondered what she'd make of the ardent carnivore seated just down the row from her, looking aghast, Barry Lopez.

He and Debra took me out to celebrate that book making the *New York Times* bestseller list. We'd connect at more Orion gatherings, including once in New Mexico when Barry pulled me into a blistering argument with an editor over literary standards, something he held sacred. Whenever he spoke in Massachusetts, where I now live, Barry and Debra came to see Beckie's latest sculptures and break bread.

His letters were always observant, and one from March 2014 proved prescient: "It's been a dry winter. Snowfall is down about 65% in the western Cascades and the ski resorts that never opened are now closed." They were typed on deckle edge stationery, until his first, sheepish email when a new assistant finally cajoled him into getting an iPhone. He got quite adept at it—complete sentences, real paragraphs—but he had no use for the alleged conveniences of the computer age when it came to his manuscripts.

"I hear," he once said to my colleague Sandy Tolan, when he came to record an interview with Barry, seated at his typewriter, "that word processing programs let you move a paragraph from one place and paste it somewhere else. Why would I ever want to do that?"

On that visit, Barry showed Sandy a room he said he was scared to enter, because it contained all the research for a book he didn't know if he'd ever work up the courage to write. Later, he worried he might not live long enough to write it. A first edition of *Horizon* on the shelf by my desk attests that he did.

Shortly after Barry's diagnosis, he called us to discuss his new dietary regimen. Recalling my own aversion to eating mammals, he was now meatless, too, he said, and not missing it. Europeans with their Mediterranean diets, he said, had long treated cancer as a condition to maintain, not to surrender to. Beckie sent him a vegetarian cookbook.

It may have helped, Debra told me later, because he lived long for a man with that much stage 4 cancer in him. More emails from him, exhumed from my inboxes, bring back those years of drugs and remission, of good scans followed by bad ones. The encouraging response to chemo of my *Vanishing Homelands* colleague Cecilia Vaisman's aggressive breast cancer heartened him and Debra—until it proved temporary, as would his own.

As if having a terminal illness weren't enough, then came something so unthinkable that it overwhelmed even his inexorably advancing metastasis: Winds, heedlessly fanned by our species' relentless cranking of the Earth's thermostat, blasted an unprecedented, colossal inferno down the western Cascades and through his beloved McKenzie River Valley. Our species, whose capacity for compassion and dignity—our *humanity*, derived from the word that defines us—that Barry exalted and honored with everything he wrote: our species had witlessly unmoored his world. Everyone's.

Smoke rising from that fire would darken all North America. Among everything that blew skyward was his decades-deep personal archive, destined no longer for the special-collections library at Texas Tech that preserves the rest of Barry's papers.

Three days later, gazing at the sinister currents swirling above New England, I wrote him and Debra:

> The sky here is colorless with ashes that once were your trees and books. Still readable, the message unavoidable.
> Love, which may be the last thing standing,
> A.

Back to dust, I put in the email's subject line.

In "The Orrery," the story in *Winter Count* whose meaning will always elude me—but no matter: Barry knew that some mysteries are meant to be embraced, not to be solved—in that gorgeously inscrutable story, the narrator finds a man who, confronted with the endless dust of a valley, takes a broom to it. The narrator asks him why he would bother trying to sweep the desert floor.

"He said it was an opportunity—an impossible task at which to work each day, as one might meditate or pray."

An opportunity, even though the imaginary valley was beset by winds powerful enough to lift rocks. We now know such winds: we've set them in motion. They reduced Barry's watershed and surrounding forest to cinders, surely hastening his death—and maybe ours, if we fail to act.

But act how, when even words as eloquent as his haven't yet been enough to stop our own kind from letting the winds and temperatures keep rising?

I return again to *Winter Count* and see Barry as a writer lost in wonder, delirious with possibilities. "If you are careful," says his man with the broom, "I think there is probably nothing that cannot be retrieved."

I contrast him with us now, confronting the loss of wonder as, plant by precious plant, endangered wolf by missing monarch, our reality is stripped bare. Yet even after the immolation of the woods and books that Barry loved most, he knew why not to quit. To the very end, he kept searching for, and finding, the right words.

"Everything is held together with stories," concludes a despairing Indigenous Plains historian in *Winter Count*'s title story, while he watches hurricane winds bend trees to the breaking point through a New Orleans hotel's lobby window. "That is all that is holding us together, stories and compassion."

Realizing that he can't hear the howling tempest through the thick plate glass, he goes to his room, throws open the window, feels the gale head on, and somehow, amid the roar, marks the distant barking of geese fleeing the storm.

THE COLOR OF THE RIVER IS LIGHT

TERRY TEMPEST WILLIAMS

Barry Lopez once showed me how to drive the back roads of Oregon near Finn Rock at night with no headlights. "Why?" I asked. "So you can learn to see in the dark like animals do and not be afraid." He was disarming. Playful. Beyond serious. Demanding. At times, exhausting. Always, illuminating. And like all writers, sometimes self-absorbed. I loved him. He taught me to not only see the world differently, but to feel it more fully. I cannot believe he is gone. Now where do I look?

Before he was a writer, he was a photographer. A good one. In fact, the cover image of *River Notes*, his collection of short fictions based on his own experience of living along the McKenzie River, was taken by him. It is a soft-focus rush of river met by a pair of moccasins placed on a rock facing the water. A credit is given inside the flap of the book: "Western Sioux moccasins courtesy of the Lane County Museum, Oregon." The composition is studied and deliberate, aesthetically pleasing and evocative like each of his stories.

On the back of *River Notes* is a horizontal strip of four black-and-white photographs of the author, reminiscent of the four flashes of pictures one would spontaneously pose for inside a photo booth with friends. The first shot is Barry looking down, with his index finger resting vertically on his upper lip, the tip of his finger just below his nose; he is deep in thought. The second frame shows him looking upward, his eyes glancing to the right. The third frame is a straightforward gaze, direct. In the last frame, he is looking down, slightly toward the left. Had there been a fifth frame, I imagine Barry's eyes would have been closed, his head in a slight bow with his two hands pressed together in prayer.

In our long, deep, and complicated friendship, I came to rely on his varied moods of mind and heart. I believe part of his genius as a writer was rooted in his access to the extremities between his vulnerability and strength; his knowing and unknowing—call it doubt; and the exquisite arc of revelations created from the depth of his searing intellect to what some critics saw as the naiveté of his beliefs in Nature. In truth, this is where the urgency and wisdom of Barry Lopez dwelled. His hunger to understand the roots of cruelty was located in his wounds. His longing to believe in our species was housed in his faith. When my grandmother died, I gave Barry her silver cross with a small circle of turquoise placed at its center. His own particular devotion to God and the power of our own creativity landed elegantly on each page he wrote, be it his fascination with travel and the intricacies of a ship or plane or an imagined community of resistance on behalf of peace with Earth where people took care of one another in the midst of darkness. Very little escaped his closely set eyes. You could say, with a smile, that Barry was the Michael Jordan of environmental writing, and when my father gave us his tickets to see the 1987 NBA championship game in Salt Lake City between the Chicago Bulls and Utah Jazz, Barry never spoke; he was transfixed on Jordan's every move, with his game stats squarely on his lap. We were rooting for different teams. When the Bulls won, he just looked at me and said, "It wasn't even a contest with Jordan in the game." Barry brought this same kind of dramatic intensity to every occasion. His fidelity was to his work where his devotion to language and landscape gave birth to stories—many beautiful stories.

Barry and I met in 1979 in Salt Lake City when he came to read at the University of Utah, paired with Edward Abbey for a special fundraiser for the Utah Wilderness Association. Two thousand people came to hear the rowdy irreverence of "Cactus Ed" court and cajole disruptive behavior. He did not disappoint. People howled like coyotes after Abbey finished reading. When the next speaker took the stage quietly, elegantly, with his head bowed, few had heard of Barry Lopez. But after he read from *River Notes*, with his deep, sonorous voice, a great and uncommon silence filled the ballroom. No one wanted to leave. A spell had been cast by a Storyteller. We left the reading altered, recognizing that we had not only heard a different voice, one of reverence and grace, but a voice that offered "a forgotten language" which brought us back into relationship with the sensual world of humans and animals living in concert.

In the story "Drought," from that collection, Barry Lopez shows us how one sincere act born out of love and a desire to help had the power to bring forth rain in times of drought if someone was "foolish" enough to dance. "I would exhort the river," his narrator says, and then a few paragraphs on, "With no more strength than there is in a bundle of sticks I tried to dance, to dance the dance of the long-legged birds who lived in the shallows. I danced it because I could not think of anything more beautiful." And, with a turn of the page, we learn, "A person cannot be afraid of being foolish. For everything, every gesture, is sacred."

The next day, I drove Barry back to the airport, located near Great Salt Lake. Curious, he asked me questions about the inland sea. I must have gotten lost in my enthusiasm about the lake, how it was our Serengeti of birds—with avocets and stilts, ruddy ducks and terns—how one could float on one's back and lose all track of time and space and emerge salt-crusted and pickled, and how the lake was a remnant puddle from the ancient Lake Bonneville whose liquid arm reached as far west as Oregon thirty thousand years ago. Before Barry boarded the plane, he turned to me and said, "I exhort you to write what you know as a young woman living on the edge of Great Salt Lake."

There was that word again, *exhort.* . . . I went home and looked it up in my dictionary: "to strongly encourage or admonish." It is a biblical word, "a fifteenth-century coinage derived from the Latin verb *hortari*, meaning 'to incite,' and it often implies the ardent urging or admonishing of an orator or preacher."

Barry Lopez had given me an assignment. I took his assignment seriously.

In 1983, I first visited Barry and Sandra, the artist he was married to for thirty years, at their enchanted home in Finn Rock. Sandra offered me my first cup of coffee ever, on their porch. Coming from the arid country of Utah, I had never seen such lushness—the softness of the air, the smell of water, and so many shades and textures of green, from the delicacy of ferns, yews, and the density of alders below to the Douglas-firs and red cedars that drew your eyes up toward a hidden sky. There was no horizon, but a vertical worshipping of trees. I recognized our differences: he was of the forest and I was of the desert. Our friendship grew from what was hidden and what was exposed. We pushed each other, trusted and challenged each other, and we relied on one another's perceptions.

Barry taught me early on that the color of the river is light. For him, the river was the McKenzie, which fed his life force for fifty years and where salmon spawned each year in the shallows just east of Eugene, Oregon. As an exercise, he would often put on his waders and walk across the river as the mergansers swam around him.

For more than forty years, I have known that wherever Barry Lopez was in the world— whether he was kneeling on the banks of the McKenzie in prayer awaiting the return of the salmon or watching polar bears standing upright on the edge of the Beaufort Sea in the Arctic or flying his red kite in Antarctica with unbridled joy—the world was being seen by someone who dared to love what could be lost, retrieve what could be found, and know he was listening to those whose voices were being silenced as he was finding an intimacy with, rather than a distance from, the ineffable. In those luminous moments, he would find the exact words to describe what we felt, but didn't know how to say. He exhorted his readers to pay attention through love.

After a pause in our friendship, we met in Jackson Hole, Wyoming. We held each other close for a long time—and then, for several days, our conversation continued where we had left off. We spoke of home, health, family, and shared stories. Always, the stories. And we laughed about all we had learned since we had become older. He had a cane due to a knee injury and he momentarily hung it in a tree. We stood on top of Signal Mountain facing the Teton Range. It began to snow with large goose-down flakes in full sunlight against a clear blue sky. He looked up and said, "Well, I've never seen this before."

Barry Lopez's very presence incited beauty. Even as his beloved trees in Finn Rock burned to ash in 2020, his eyes were focused on the ground in the name of the work that was now his—"the recovery and restoration of Finn Rock," the phrase he used in our last correspondence, even as Barry understood what was coming—his own death.

In one of his last essays, "Love in a Time of Terror," Barry wrote, "In this moment, is it still possible to face the gathering darkness and say to the physical Earth, and to all its creatures, including ourselves, fiercely and without embarrassment, I love you, and to embrace fearlessly the burning world?"

Grief is love. Barry's heartbreak, wisdom, and love in the world remain. At the end of the story "Drought," the narrator tells us, "Everyone has to learn how to die, that song, that dance, alone and in time. . . . To stick your hands into the river is to feel the cords that bind the earth together in one piece."

Peace, my dear Barry. The color of the river is light. You are now light. Hands pressed together in prayer. We bow.

WINGED RUNNERS

HANK LENTFER

Barry Lopez, like any great storyteller, was a great listener. He sought out the subtle and the seldom heard. He tuned his ear to stories buried beneath the din of modern life. He followed voices past society's edge, traveling through time, threading boundaries between cultures and creatures. Barry's curiosity lured him, repeatedly, to the Arctic, a landscape where he sensed "the oldest mysteries: the nature and extent of space, the fall of light from the heavens, the pooling of time in the present, as if it were water."

Vast distance invites close intimacy. Whereas strangers on a sidewalk may brush shoulders unacknowledged, someone silhouetted on a far, windswept ridge draws attention like an oasis in the desert. Arctic travelers may walk for miles to say hello and learn what the other has seen. Enduring friendships grow from the campfires and conversations that follow.

The cultural anthropologist and naturalist Richard Nelson was, like Barry, a keen listener drawn to Alaska's cultures and creatures. As fellow travelers through wide lands, Richard and Barry drew close. Early conversations swelled into future collaborations; initial kindness grew into an enduring kinship.

The summer of 1987 found them sitting shoulder to shoulder in a radio studio in Fairbanks, Alaska. For years, Richard had been working with village elders to produce *Make Prayers to the Raven*, a PBS documentary about Koyukon spiritual beliefs. Barry, as the film's narrator, was helping Richard with the final edits to the script. They worked long hours in the windowless studio, emerging into the welcome twilight of Arctic evenings to listen to ravens croak and caw on the edge of town.

In the decades that followed, Barry and Richard traveled to each other's home ground, one by a clear river, the other by the open sea. While camping with Barry on Alaska's Kruzof Island, Richard journaled: "Barry moves very slowly, absorbs everything he can, takes time for details, talks quietly. He seems to sense how special this place is, just as I do, and his voice glows with enthusiasm for it."

Barry and Richard collaborated on writing projects and shared stages speaking about place. They wrote letters, visited each other when they could. Even when apart, their lines of inquiry drew them together. Alone in the Arctic, Barry wrote: "I lay there knowing something eerie ties us to the world of animals. Sometimes the animals pull you backward into it. You share hunger and fear with them like salt in blood."

By himself on Kruzof, Richard wrote: "Closeness is the sacred power I seek. My amulet comes by moving within the touch of eyes, mingling scents, reaching out with my fingers toward feathers ruffled by the same wind gust that surrounds us both."

Both men were in their early forties when Barry asked if Richard would honor their friendship by sending him a few deer hides to drape over the back of his writing chair. Years later, reflecting on this request, Barry wrote, "I sensed that resting my back against a pair of cured black-tailed deer hides from Richard's hunts would put me in a more respectful frame of mind when I wrote, and that they might induce in me the proper perspectives about life. . . . I felt the hides might care for me as I stumbled my way through life, in the same way our friendship with each other would take care of both of us in the years ahead."

The letters and visits ebbed and flowed. In their seventies, both diagnosed with cancer, Barry and Richard reached for the phones more often. They spoke about projects they hoped to finish, about who in their orbits would carry on the work of blurring boundaries between people and the rest of creation.

In the summer of 2019, after months of radiation, Richard regained the strength to hike familiar trails on his beloved island and paddle a kayak through the lift and fall of ocean swells. He watched whales, listened to thrushes, and passed precious evenings with his tribe of Sitka friends. In early fall, when the cancer came roaring back, he traveled to San Francisco seeking help to beat it back once again.

I traveled south late that October to keep Richard company as he endured treatment. By the time I arrived, treatment was suspended and hospice had started. It was a twenty-minute walk from where I was staying to the hospital where Richard lay dying. Each morning, I'd buy a coffee and find a park bench and give Barry a call. Barry asked about the prognosis, the room's energy, the medical particulars about how his wild-country-loving friend ended up attached to tubes in a San Francisco ICU. Barry knew his friend was crossing terrain he would soon traverse. He wanted to be there in person, but his own health was too fragile for travel. Questions over the phone were the only way to cast a bit of light on this final, mysterious journey.

November 4, 2019, Richard's last day, I called Barry from the hospital room and held the phone to his dying friend's ear. I don't know what stories, wishes, or prayers Barry shared. I do know that when I held the phone to my own ear, Barry's voice was tender with the weight and levity of loss and love.

There were four of us, all from Alaska, in the room during Richard's final hours. Someone brought hemlock and cedar boughs, a frond of kelp—fragrances of home. From speakers came the voices of thrushes and warblers, crows and gulls, sparrows and flycatchers, a wren and nuthatch, kingfishers and woodpeckers, eagles and herons. And ravens. A sound-scape punctuated with the strident, complex dialogue of ravens. Richard himself had put the soundtrack together. He'd spent months combing through fifteen years of recordings, integrating his finest tracks into an intricate, ninety-minute acoustic tour through Alaska's coastal rainforest. We humans fell silent at the end. We let the birds call our friend home.

I last spoke to Barry precisely one year after Richard drew his last breath. We reminisced about our friend, tossing stories, funny and poignant, into the wide space of Richard's absence. Barry did not speak about the fire, no mention of the ashes of his writing life sifting into the scorched banks of his beloved river, no updates on the metastasizing cancer shifting through his bones like smoke between trees. One loss was enough for a single phone call. Before hanging up, Barry wondered about the next generation of "runners." Who were the storytellers traveling between worlds, carrying life-gifting messages across boundaries of knowing?

A few weeks later, when I learned of Barry's heart attack and ambulance ride and the transition to hospice, I sent him a copy of the rainforest-birds recording along with a note describing the comfort they gave Richard at the end.

Unable to get Barry back to his riverside home, his family brought in a truckload of cedar and fir boughs. They placed beaver sticks around the room, bathed Barry with vats of river water, and laid Richard's deer hide on his chest. Early afternoon on Christmas 2020, a chilly day thick with smoke, the family gathered around Barry's bed, certain his death was near. They played Arvo Pärt's haunting *Cantus in Memoriam Benjamin Britten*. Barry, beyond words, was visibly stirred by the music. Debra, Barry's wife, was astonished that he survived into evening. His daughters took turns drum-ming and reading poems sent by friends. Earlier in the day, there'd been music by Greg Brown, Mark Knopfler, Beethoven ("Ode to Joy"), and John Luther Adams (*Become River*). Come evening, the chorus of Richard's rainforest birds filled the room. "It felt only right," Debra recalls, "to have those birds at the end." The family gathered close, urging Barry to head toward the river as the ravens called.

Imagining Richard reaching back and offering Barry the gift of those wild voices evokes a shivering joy and reminds us that not all runners have legs. Some no longer have lungs. Others float and flitter on feathered wings and speak in languages we may only be able to fully comprehend after our last breath.

In the moments after Barry died, Debra stayed by his bedside. When the daughters stepped outside, a great horned owl flew overhead through the smoke and cold. Debra had not seen one there before and has not heard one since.

ACKNOWLEDGMENTS

Several of the essays in this book were first published elsewhere and have since been updated and revised: Fred Bahnson's "An Unbroken Grace" in *Notre Dame Magazine* (Spring 2021), and reprinted in *Emergence Magazine* (December 16, 2021); John Freeman's "Now That It's Come to This" online in *Orion* magazine (June 2021); Debra Gwartney's "Siri Tells a Joke" in *The Sun* (July 2022); Pico Iyer's "Elevation" and David Quammen's "Barry's Voice" online in *Orion* magazine (January 2021); Julia Martin's "The Chanting Goshawk" in *Daily Maverick* (May 4, 2021); Sierra Crane Murdoch's "Barry Lopez's Darkness and Light" in *The Paris Review* (May 31, 2022); Terry Tempest Williams's "The Color of the River Is Light" online at ASLE.org (January 10, 2021).

Going to See was a great collaborative project from the very beginning. Kurt Caswell had the original idea and asked Jim Warren to assist. Debra Gwartney was, from first to last, an inspiration and guide for the work we have done. She has been instrumental in finding the contributors and soliciting their support. Without her, this would be a smaller and much less important collection. Both of us feel enduring gratitude to her.

Derek Sheffield recommended the independent, nonprofit publisher Mountaineers Books to Kurt at an early stage, and Kate Rogers, editor in chief, responded enthusiastically to our proposal from the start. It has been a pleasure to work with the professional team in Seattle.

We have benefited greatly from the support of Joe Moll and the McKenzie River Trust.

We want to thank Diane Warner and Kristin Loyd at the Sowell Collection, Texas Tech University, for their generous expertise with questions about the Barry Lopez Papers and other sources. For access to finding aids in the Sowell Collection, see https://swco.ttu.edu/sowell/barrylopez.php.

We also thank Toby Jurovics at the Barry Lopez Foundation in Santa Fe, New Mexico, for his support of Barry Lopez's vision; see https://barrylopezfoundation.org.

SELECTED PUBLICATIONS BY BARRY LOPEZ

BOOKS

Nonfiction

Embrace Fearlessly the Burning World. Random House, 2022.

Horizon. Alfred A. Knopf, 2019.

About This Life: Journeys on the Threshold of Memory. Alfred A. Knopf, 1998.

Apologia, with woodcuts by Robin Eschner. University of Georgia Press, 1998.

The Rediscovery of North America. University Press of Kentucky, 1991.

Crossing Open Ground. Charles Scribner's Sons, 1988.

Arctic Dreams: Imagination and Desire in a Northern Landscape. Charles Scribner's Sons, 1986.

Of Wolves and Men. Charles Scribner's Sons, 1978.

Fiction

Outside, with engravings by Barry Moser. Trinity University Press, 2014.

Resistance, with monoprints by Alan Magee. Alfred A. Knopf, 2004.

Light Action in the Caribbean. Alfred A. Knopf, 2000.

Lessons from the Wolverine, with illustrations by Tom Pohrt. University of Georgia Press, 1997.

Field Notes: The Grace Note of the Canyon Wren. Alfred A. Knopf, 1994.

Crow and Weasel, with illustrations by Tom Pohrt. North Point Press, 1990.

Winter Count. Charles Scribner's Sons, 1981.

River Notes: The Dance of Herons. Andrews, McMeel and Parker, 1979.

Giving Birth to Thunder, Sleeping with His Daughter: Coyote Builds North America. Andrews, McMeel and Parker, 1978.

Desert Notes: Reflections in the Eye of a Raven. Andrews, McMeel and Parker, 1976.

EDITED BOOKS AND JOURNALS

Gates of Reconciliation: Literature and the Ethical Imagination, with Frank Stewart. University of Hawai'i Press, 2008.

Maps of Reconciliation: Literature and the Ethical Imagination, with Frank Stewart. University of Hawai'i Press, 2007.

The Future of Nature: Writing on a Human Ecology from Orion Magazine, selected and introduced by Barry Lopez. Milkweed Editions, 2007.

Home Ground: Language for an American Landscape, edited by Barry Lopez and Debra Gwartney. With an introduction by Barry Lopez and black-and-white illustrations by Molly O'Halloran. Trinity University Press, 2006.

FINE PRESS BOOKS

Outside. Santa Rosa, CA: Nawakum Press, 2013. Six stories, two each from *Desert Notes*, *River Notes*, and *Field Notes*, with 11 engravings by Barry Moser. Published in an edition of 50: 28 Roman-numeraled slipcased volumes; 12 lettered, deluxe boxed volumes; and 10 numbered volumes reserved for the press and participants. Each volume signed by the author and the artist. Designed by Barry Moser. Introduction by James Perrin Warren. Afterword by the author. Printed by Arthur Larson, Horton Tank Graphics, Hadley, MA. Binding, boxes, and slipcases by Craig Jensen, BookLab II, San Marcos, TX. Marbled paper by Pam Smith, Abiquiu, NM. Calligraphy by Judythe Seick, Santa Fe, NM. Published at Nawakum Press by David Pascoe.

¡Nunca Mas! Northfield, MN: Red Dragonfly Press, 2007. Published in an edition of 350 copies, 90 of which are numbered and signed by the author and artist. Wood engraving, "Gate of Death" [Birkenau], by Carol Inderieden. Designed, printed offset, and sewn by Scott King.

The Near Woods. San Francisco: Pacific Editions, 2006. Edition of 26 lettered copies. Using pages from the Tangram Press edition of 2005. Bound in boards by Charles Hobson with the assistance of Alice Shaw and covered with a reproduction of "Dosino del Rancho San Miguelito," ca. 1841, a drawing used to establish land grants in California. Includes a hand-colored digital pigment print by Charles Hobson as a back folder.

The Mappist. San Francisco: Pacific Editions, 2005. Published in an edition of 48, numbered and signed. Nine monotypes with pastel by Charles Hobson printed as digital pigment images, and three reproductions with commentary from "The Topographic Maps of the United States" by the director, United States Geological Survey, November 1937. Bound in boards wrapped with a reproduction of a 1911 map of Bogotá. Concertina binding uses original USGS maps. Letterpress printed in a Garamond Narrow typeface on BFK Rives paper by Les Ferriss. Interior slipcase and covers made by John DeMerritt, with Kris Langan. Designed by Charles Hobson, with Alice Shaw.

Barry Lopez. Eugene, OR: lone goose press, 2005. Published in an edition of 150 for attendees at a fundraising dinner for BRING, a recycling nonprofit organization in Eugene, March 31, 2005, at which Lopez spoke. Text is three paragraphs from "Apocalypse" in *Resistance*, pp. 17–18. Designed, printed, and bound by Sandy Tilcock.

Pulling Wire. Northfield, MN: Red Dragonfly Press, 2004. Published in an edition of 225. Title page woodcut by Gary Young. Designed and printed by Scott King.

Anotaciones. San Francisco: Pacific Editions, 2001. Published in an edition of 30. Story entitled "Ruben Mendoza Vega, Suzuki Professor of Early Caribbean History, University of Florida at Gainesville, Offers a History of the United States Based on Personal Experience" from *Light Action in the Caribbean.* Accordion-bound book with 16 footnotes printed on laser-cut puzzle pieces, all contained in an actual cigar box, enclosed with chemise. Assembling the puzzle organizes the footnotes. Book designed by Charles Hobson. Inkjet monotype, color photography, and offset lithography. Foldout reference sheet.

The Letters of Heaven. Eugene, OR: Knight Library Press, 2000. Published in an edition of 125 numbered copies, signed by the artist and author. Short story from *Light Action in the Caribbean*, with five hand-colored etchings by Robin Eschner. Calligraphic title, headings, and ornaments by Marilyn Reaves. Designed, printed, and bound by Sandy Tilcock.

Apologia. Eugene, OR: lone goose press, 1997. Published in an edition of 50 (16 copies reserved for the participants). With 23 woodcuts by Robin Eschner, designed to form a single continuous image. Designed by Charles Hobson. Edition printer, Nora Pauwels; letterpress printer, Susan Acker; binder, John DeMeritt. Boxed by Sandy Tilcock. Tire-tread print on Wyoming topographic map created by Barry Lopez and Sandy Tilcock and included in book pocket. Accordion bound.

Looking in a Deeper Lair. Eugene, OR: lone goose press, 1996. Published in an edition of 179 (150 numbered, signed, soft-cover copies and 29 deluxe, hardcover copies, signed and boxed; of the deluxe edition 26 are lettered A through Z and 3 are designated artist's copies). Eulogy for Wallace Stegner, with an intaglio print by Suellen Larkin. Designed, printed, and bound by Sandy Tilcock.

Children in the Woods. Eugene, OR: lone goose press, 1992. Published in an edition of 75, numbered and signed by the artist, Margaret Prentice, and Lopez. Essay from *Crossing Open Ground.* Woodcut illustrations, handmade abaca cover, and text papers by Margaret Prentice. Typeset and bound by Sandy Tilcock and Kathleen Wigley. Designed and boxed by Sandy Tilcock.

Coyote Love: Native American Folktales. Portland, ME: Coyote Love Press, 1989. Published in an edition of 99. Three Trickster stories, adapted by Lopez from *Giving Birth to Thunder*: "Coyote and Beaver Exchange Wives," "Coyote Marries His Daughter," and "Coyote Visits the Women." Illustrations by Gary Buch. Hand-illuminated by Allen Wong. Printed on Dresden Ingres paper, using Goudy Thirty, Kennerly, and Neuland types, and bound in Mexican bark covers, all by George Bennington.

Desert Reservation. Port Townsend, WA: Copper Canyon Press, 1980. Published in an edition of 300 in paper wraps, 26 of which are signed and lettered. Designed and printed by Tree Swenson and David Romtvedt.

BOOKS ABOUT BARRY LOPEZ

Syntax of the River: The Pattern Which Connects, Barry Lopez in Conversation with Julia Martin. Trinity University Press, 2023.

Other Country: Barry Lopez and the Community of Artists, by James Perrin Warren. The University of Arizona Press, 2015.

Conversations with Barry Lopez: Walking the Path of Imagination, by William E. Tydeman. University of Oklahoma Press, 2013.

No Bottom: In Conversation with Barry Lopez, by Mike Newell. XOXOX Press, 2008.

The Land's Wild Music: Encounters with Barry Lopez, Peter Matthiessen, Terry Tempest Williams, and James Galvin, by Mark Tredinnick. Trinity University Press, 2005.

ABOUT THE EDITORS

Kurt Caswell is a writer and professor of creative writing and literature in the Honors College at Texas Tech University, where he teaches intensive field courses in writing and leadership in Spain, and in the mountains and on rivers in the West. His books include *Iceland Summer: Travels Along the Ring Road, Laika's Window: The Legacy of a Soviet Space Dog,* and *In the Sun's House: My Year Teaching on the Navajo Reservation.* His collection of essays *An Inside Passage* won the River Teeth Literary Nonfiction Book Prize. His stories and essays have appeared in *American Literary Review, McSweeney's, Ninth Letter, Orion, River Teeth, Terrain.org,* and *The International Journal of Travel and Travel Writing.*

James Perrin Warren is S. Blount Mason, Jr. Professor of English emeritus at Washington and Lee University and the author of *Other Country: Barry Lopez and the Community of Artists.* He is the literary executor of Barry Lopez's estate.

ABOUT THE CONTRIBUTORS

Anna Badkhen is the author of seven books, most recently the essay collection *Bright Unbearable Reality*. Her awards include the Guggenheim Fellowship, the Barry Lopez Visiting Writer in Ethics and Community Fellowship, and the Joel R. Seldin Award from Psychologists for Social Responsibility, for writing about civilians in war zones. Badkhen was born in the Soviet Union and is a US citizen.

Fred Bahnson is the author of *Soil & Sacrament*. His essays have appeared in *Harper's*, *Emergence Magazine*, *Oxford American*, *Orion*, *Image*, *The Sun*, *Notre Dame Magazine*, *The Best American Spiritual Writing*, and *The Best American Travel Writing*. Collaborating with director Jeremy Seifert, Bahnson wrote and produced *Horizons*, a film based on a series of interviews he recorded with Barry Lopez in 2018. Commissioned by the Sun Valley Writers Conference, *Horizons* was published in *Emergence Magazine*. Bahnson is the recipient of a Pulitzer Center on Crisis Reporting grant, a W.K. Kellogg Food & Society Policy fellowship, and an artist fellowship in creative nonfiction from the

North Carolina Arts Council. He serves as the executive director at the National Center for Appropriate Technology, and lives with his wife and sons in southwest Montana.

Rick Bass is a wilderness advocate, activist, and author of more than thirty books. He is the recipient of numerous awards, including fellowships from the National Endowment for the Arts, the Guggenheim Foundation, the Lyndhurst Foundation, the Montana Arts Council, and others. His stories, articles, and essays have appeared in *The Paris Review, The New Yorker, The Atlantic, Narrative, Men's Journal, Esquire, GQ, Harper's, The New York Times Magazine, Los Angeles Times Magazine, The Boston Globe, The Washington Post, Tin House, Zoetrope, Orion,* and numerous other periodicals and book anthologies. His literary papers are housed in The Sowell Family Collection in Literature, Community, and the Natural World at Texas Tech University. He lives in western Montana.

Lisa Couturier was a finalist for the 2022 Annie Dillard Award in Nonfiction. She is author of the collection of literary essays *The Hopes of Snakes & Other Tales from the Urban Landscape.* Couturier is a Pushcart Prize winner for "Dark Horse"; a notable essayist in *The Best American Essays,* 2004, 2006, 2011; and winner of the 2015 Jean Pedrick Chapbook Prize from the New England Poetry Club for her collection *Animals / Bodies.* Her work has appeared in *Orion,* National Geographic Society publications, The New York Zoological Society's *Wildlife Conservation,* and the American Nature Writing series, among other publications and anthologies. Her literary papers are housed in The Sowell Family Collection in Literature, Community, and the Natural World at Texas Tech University. Couturier divides her time between a flat in Manhattan and a forest in Maryland, where she lives on an agricultural reserve with her husband, their dog, her horses, barn cats, a pair of black vultures, and a much beloved family of crows who bring her gifts.

Bathsheba Demuth is writer and environmental historian specializing in the lands and seas of the Russian and North American Arctic. From the archive to the dog sled, her research addresses how ecologies and people change each other. Her first book, *Floating Coast: An Environmental History of the Bering Strait*, won multiple awards and was named a best book by NPR, *Nature*, and other publications. Her writing has appeared in *The New Yorker*, *Granta*, *The Best American Science and Nature Writing*, and many others. When not in the north, she lives in Providence, Rhode Island, where she is the Dean's Associate Professor of History and Environment and Society at Brown University.

David James Duncan is a storyteller, essayist, memoirist, "hit and run teacher" and author of the novels *The River Why*, *The Brothers K*, and *Sun House*. He also continues to work in a way that suspiciously resembles play on a nonfunded study of languages spoken by Pacific-bound rivers. His literary papers are housed in The Sowell Family Collection in Literature, Community, and the Natural World at Texas Tech University.

Gretel Ehrlich is the author of fifteen books, including *The Solace of Open Spaces*, *Facing the Wave*, *A Match to the Heart*, *This Cold Heaven*, and *Unsolaced*. Her awards include a Guggenheim Fellowship, Whiting Award, two PEN awards, and the Harold Vursell Memorial Award from the American Academy of Arts and Letters. *Facing the Wave* was longlisted for a National Book Award. Her literary papers are housed in The Sowell Family Collection in Literature, Community, and the Natural World at Texas Tech University.

John Freeman is an executive editor at Alfred A. Knopf and the founder of *Freeman's*, a literary annual. He is the author and editor of a dozen books, most recently *Wind, Trees*, a collection of poems. He lives in New York.

Debra Gwartney is the author of two book-length memoirs, *Live Through This*, a finalist for the National Book Critics Circle Award, and *I Am a Stranger Here Myself*, winner of the River Teeth Literary Nonfiction Book Prize and the WILLA Award for Nonfiction, as well as many essays. She received Pushcart Prizes in 2021 and 2022, and her work was selected for *The Best American Essays* 2022. She is co-editor with her husband, Barry Lopez, of *Home Ground: Language for an American Landscape*.

Kate Harris lives off-grid with her wife and dog in a small cabin on Taku River Tlingit territory, in what has lately been called British Columbia. She is the author of *Lands of Lost Borders* and the forthcoming *Practical Experiments in Soaring*.

Marybeth Holleman's newest book is the poetry collection *tender gravity*. She's also author of nonfiction books including *The Heart of the Sound* and *Among Wolves*, and co-editor of *Crosscurrents North*. Raised in North Carolina's Smokies, she transplanted to Alaska's Chugach Mountains after falling head over heels for Prince William Sound two years before the *Exxon Valdez* oil spill.

Pico Iyer is the author of sixteen books translated into twenty-three languages on subjects that range from globalism to stillness, the Cuban revolution to Islamic mysticism, Graham Greene to the fourteenth Dalai Lama. His most recent work is *The Half Known Life: In Search of Paradise*.

Stephen Graham Jones is the *New York Times* best-selling author of some thirty novels, novellas, collections and comic books. His most recent novel is *The Angel of Indian Lake*. His literary papers are housed in The Sowell Family Collection in Literature, Community, and the Natural World at Texas Tech University. He lives in Boulder, Colorado.

John Lane is professor emeritus at Wofford College, where he taught creative writing, environmental studies, and directed the Goodall Environmental Studies Center. He is founder of the Hub City Writers Project, and has been inducted into the South Carolina Academy of Authors. His literary papers are housed in The Sowell Family Collection in Literature, Community, and the Natural World at Texas Tech University.

Among his many books of poetry, fiction, and nonfiction are *Abandoned Quarry: New and Selected Poems*, *Fate Moreland's Widow*, and *Neighborhood Hawks: A Year Following Wild Birds*. He lives in South Carolina.

J. Drew Lanham is the author of *The Home Place: Memoirs of a Colored Man's Love Affair with Nature*, which received the Reed Award from the Southern Environmental Law Center and the Southern Book Prize, and was a finalist for the John Burroughs Medal. Most recently, he is the author of *Sparrow Envy: Field Guide to Birds and Lesser Beasts*. He is a birder, naturalist, and hunter-conservationist who has published essays and poetry in publications including *Orion, Audubon, Flycatcher*, and *Wilderness*, and in several anthologies, including *The Colors of Nature, State of the Heart, Bartram's Living Legacy*, and *Carolina Writers at Home*. Lanham is a 2022 MacArthur Fellow, and an Alumni Distinguished Professor of Wildlife Ecology and Master Teacher at Clemson University. His literary papers are housed in The Sowell Family Collection in Literature, Community, and the Natural World at Texas Tech University. He and his family live in the Upstate of South Carolina, a soaring hawk's downhill glide from the southern Appalachian escarpment that the Cherokee once called the Blue Wall.

Hank Lentfer is a sound recordist and writer. His sound is featured in the film *The Singing Planet*. His most recent book is *Raven's Witness: The Alaska Life of Richard K. Nelson*. He lives by a creek flowing through Gustavus, Alaska.

Robert Macfarlane is the author of numerous books about place, people, and nature, including *Underland, Landmarks, The Old Ways* and *The Wild Places*. His work has been widely adapted for film, television, stage, and radio, and he has collaborated with musicians including Johnny Flynn, Cosmo Sheldrake, and Haushka. He is a professor of literature and the environmental humanities at the University of Cambridge.

Julia Martin teaches English and creative nonfiction writing at the University of the Western Cape and has published widely in the field of literature and ecology. Her publications include *Writing Home* a volume of narrative essays; *A Millimetre of Dust: Visiting Ancestral Sites*, a travel memoir about archaeological sites in the Northern Cape; and *The Blackridge House: A Memoir*, a story of her mother's quest for home. She collaborated with Gary Snyder on *Nobody Home: Writing, Buddhism, and Living in Places*, a collection of their conversations and letters over thirty years. *Syntax of the River: The Pattern Which Connects*, co-authored with Barry Lopez, is an extended conversation about the practice of writing in the face of the present environmental catastrophe.

Bill McKibben is an author, educator, and environmentalist who helped found 350.org, the first global grassroots climate campaign. He is also one of the founders of Third Act, which strives to build a progressive organizing movement for people over the age of sixty. Among his many acclaimed books are *The End of Nature*, *Eaarth: Making a Life on a Tough New Planet*, and *Falter: Has the Human Game Begun to Play Itself Out?* His literary papers are housed in The Sowell Family Collection in Literature, Community, and the Natural World at Texas Tech University.

Deborah A. Miranda is an enrolled member of the Ohlone-Costanoan Esselen Nation of the Greater Monterey Bay Area in California, with Santa Ynez Chumash ancestry. She is the author of *Bad Indians: A Tribal Memoir*, winner of the PEN Oakland Josephine Miles Literary Award, and four poetry collections: *Indian Cartography*, *The Zen of La Llorona*, *Raised by Humans*, and *Altar for Broken Things*. Her scholarship focuses on the lives and experiences of California Indians during and after Spanish, Mexican, and American colonization, particularly gender roles and survival strategies. Her current project is a collection of essays based on the stories of Isabel Meadows, born in 1846, who left behind extensive documentation of cultures and histories of Indigenous peoples in and around Mission Carmel.

Susan Brind Morrow is the recipient of the 2022 Award in Literature from the American Academy of Arts and Letters. She is the author of *The*

Names of Things, Wolves and Honey, and *The Dawning Moon of the Mind*. A former fellow of the Guggenheim Foundation, her literary papers are housed in The Sowell Family Collection in Literature, Community, and the Natural World at Texas Tech University.

Sierra Crane Murdoch is the author of *Yellow Bird: Oil, Murder, and a Woman's Search for Justice in Indian Country*, which was a finalist for the Pulitzer Prize, winner of the Oregon Book Award, and named a best book of 2020 by the *New York Times* and NPR. She has written for *Harper's, The Paris Review, This American Life, VQR, The New Yorker* online, *The Atlantic*, and *Orion*. Her work has been supported by a visiting fellowship in the investigative reporting program at the University of California, Berkeley, and a MacDowell Fellowship, among others. Her second book, *Imaginary Brightness: An Autobiography of American Guilt* is forthcoming from Random House.

Robert Michael Pyle writes essays, poetry, fiction, and natural history. His twenty-five books include *The Thunder Tree, Mariposa Road, Magdalena Mountain* (a novel), and a flight of butterfly books. *Wintergreen: Rambles in a Ravaged Land*, won the 1987 John Burroughs Medal; *Where Bigfoot Walks: Crossing the Dark Divide* earned a Guggenheim Fellowship, and *Nature Matrix: New and Selected Essays* was a finalist for the PEN America Award in the Art of the Essay. The latest of four collections of poetry, *The Tidewater Reach*, celebrates forty years as denizen of the Lower Columbia River watershed. A Yale-trained ecologist, Pyle founded the Xerces Society for Invertebrate Conservation in 1971. For his work with butterflies, he has been made Honorary Life Fellow of the American and Royal Entomological Societies. His literary papers are housed in The Sowell Family Collection in Literature, Community, and the Natural World at Texas Tech University.

David Quammen is a science journalist and the author of seventeen books, including *The Song of the Dodo, Spillover, The Tangled Tree*, and most recently *Breathless: The Scientific Race to Defeat a Deadly Virus*. His literary papers are housed in The Sowell Family Collection in Literature, Community, and the Natural World at Texas Tech University.

Scott Russell Sanders is the author of more than twenty books of fiction, essays, and personal narrative, including *Hunting for Hope, A Conservationist Manifesto, A Private History of Awe*, and *Earth Works: Selected Essays*. His most recent books are *The Way of Imagination*, a reflection on healing and renewal in a time of social and environmental upheaval, and *Small Marvels: A Novel-in-Stories*. He is a distinguished professor emeritus of English at Indiana University, and a fellow of the American Academy of Arts and Sciences. He and his wife, Ruth, a biochemist, have reared two children in their hometown of Bloomington, in the hardwood hill country of southern Indiana.

Annick Smith is a writer and filmmaker who lives on a homestead ranch in Montana's Blackfoot Valley. She is the author of the memoir, *Homestead*; the essay collection, *In This We Are Native*; and *Crossing the Plains with Bruno*, the story of a journey with her chocolate lab. She co-edited the anthologies *The Last Best Place* with William Kittredge, and *The Wide Open* and *Hearth: A Global Conversation on Community, Identity, and Place*, both with Susan O'Connor. She is a film producer of the homesteading drama *Heartland*, and co-producer of *A River Runs Through It*. Her literary papers are housed in The Sowell Family Collection in Literature, Community, and the Natural World at Texas Tech University.

Laura Dassow Walls is professor emerita at the University of Notre Dame, where she taught American literature and the history and theory of ecological thought. She has also taught at Lafayette College and the University of South Carolina. Her biography *Henry David Thoreau: A Life* received Phi Beta Kappa's Christian Gauss Award and the *Los Angeles Times* Book Prize for biography. Her other books include the award-winning *Passage to Cosmos: Alexander von Humboldt and the Shaping of America*; *Emerson's Life in Science*; and *Seeing New Worlds: Henry David Thoreau and Nineteenth-Century Natural Science*. She is currently working on a literary biography of Barry Lopez.

Alan Weisman has reported from more than sixty countries and all seven continents for *The New York Times Magazine, The Atlantic, Harper's, The New York Review of Books, Orion, Salon, Vanity Fair,* and NPR, among many others. His book, *Countdown: Our Last, Best Hope for a Future on Earth?* was awarded the *Los Angeles Times* Book Prize. His international bestseller *The World Without Us,* now in thirty-five languages, was named Best Nonfiction Book of 2007 by *Time Magazine* and *Entertainment Weekly,* was a finalist for the National Book Critics Circle Award, and was named one of the 50 Best Nonfiction Books of the Past 25 Years by *Slate* in 2019. His next book, *Hope Dies Last,* will be released in 2024. He lives in western Massachusetts.

Terry Tempest Williams is the author of over twenty books, including the environmental literature classic *Refuge: An Unnatural History of Family and Place,* as well as *Finding Beauty in a Broken World, When Women Were Birds, The Hour of Land,* and most recently, *Erosion—Essays of Undoing.* A recipient of a Lannan Literary Award and a John Simon Guggenheim Fellowship in creative nonfiction, Tempest Williams is writer-in-residence at the Harvard Divinity School. She is a member of the American Academy of Arts and Letters and divides her time between Castle Valley, Utah and Cambridge, Massachusetts.

PERMISSIONS

GIVING BACK

Mountaineers Books believes it is important to support organizations that share a love of the natural world while sustaining local communities. The McKenzie River Trust is working to support the restoration, stewardship, and community connections to lands near Barry Lopez's former home in Finn Rock, Oregon. Coeditors Kurt Caswell and James P. Warren are donating all royalties, and Mountaineers Books is directing 1% of all sales, of this book to help McKenzie River Trust in this effort.

McKenzie River Trust has been connecting people to the special lands and rivers in western Oregon for more than thirty years. In the years since the Holiday Farm fire burned more than 173,000 acres in the McKenzie River valley, restoration work has been underway to aid the recovery of the land in a post-wildfire landscape. From protecting important lands to working alongside partners to restore salmon-rearing habitat, McKenzie River Trust transforms community care into direct action on behalf of water, wildlife, and people. With your support, they can continue to work in partnership across the McKenzie basin to promote clean water, abundant fish and wild-life habitat, and thriving communities. To learn more about McKenzie River Trust and their work near Finn Rock, visit https://mckenzieriver.org.

MCKENZIE RIVER TRUST

MOUNTAINEERS BOOKS, including its two imprints, Skipstone and Braided River, is a leading publisher of quality outdoor recreation, sustainability, and conservation titles. As a 501(c)(3) nonprofit, we are committed to supporting the environmental and educational goals of our organization by providing expert information on human-powered adventure, sustainable practices at home and on the trail, and preservation of wilderness.

Our publications are made possible through the generosity of donors, and through sales of 700 titles on outdoor recreation, sustainable lifestyle, and conservation. To donate, purchase books, or learn more, visit us online:

MOUNTAINEERS BOOKS

1001 SW Klickitat Way, Suite 201 • Seattle, WA 98134
800-553-4453 • mbooks@mountaineersbooks.org • www.mountaineersbooks.org

An independent nonprofit publisher since 1960

ALSO AVAILABLE

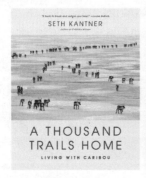

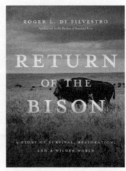